Women of

Consequence

Translated from the French by David Radzinowicz
Editorial direction: Catherine Laulhère-Vigneau
Design: Marie-Laure Miranda
Proofreading: Marc Feustel
Color Separation: Couleurs d'images

Simultaneously published in French as *Pionnières de 1900 à nos jours:
Elles ont changé le monde*
© Flammarion, S.A, Paris, 2010

English-language edition
© Flammarion, S.A., Paris, 2010

87, quai Panhard et Levassor
75647 Paris Cedex 13

editions.flammarion.com

10 11 12   3 2 1

ISBN: 978-2-08-030091-1
Dépôt légal: 09/2010

Printed in Singapore by Tien Wah Press

Xavière Gauthier

Women of Consequence

Heroines Who Shaped the World

Flammarion

Contents

Introduction

"Humanity owes woman not a single moral, political, or philosophical idea. Man invents, progresses, works and produces, he feeds her, yet she did not even invent her spindle and distaff."

Pierre-Joseph Proudhon (1809–1865)

A pioneer is originally someone who clears and settles uninhabited land, and then, as one dictionary puts it, "is the first to embark on an enterprise; one who blazes a trail." Broader than simply "being the first," this definition has more to do with building, creating, and fostering.

Admittedly, whenever a woman is first, chronologically speaking, to work in a particular profession, to obtain a particular degree, to lead a nation, to hold a sports record, etc., she too is, incontestably, a pioneer. Before her, in her country, in her chosen field, only men have been able to succeed as she now does; following in her footsteps, however, other women will now perhaps be able to do the same. In this sense, these pioneers, whether they want to or not, break new ground.

Exact criteria, however, are often more difficult to establish. How can a female writer, for instance, be called a pioneer? Did literature change after her work was published? And there are many cases where objective criteria do not exist, where one is forced to acknowledge a degree of subjectivity, of bias even. To keep this risk to a minimum, I have referred, as often as possible, to women recognized by some qualified authority, such as the Nobel Prize jury, for example. This is all the more telling since women winners remain extremely rare, men forming the crushing majority, even shamelessly crushing their female counterparts on occasion. A cursory examination of the attribution of the Nobel Prize reveals blatant injustices.

I began my research with boundless enthusiasm and no little naivety. Slowly, though, the titanic, even overwhelming nature of the task dawned on me. Many was the time I asked myself, how can I miss out such and such a pioneer from some far-flung place or another who has never been given her due? This book does not seek, then, to be exhaustive.

It obviously doesn't feature every woman pioneer in the period concerned. Some have been omitted, either because they were unknown to me or because I did not regard them as fitting the bill. Meticulously, methodically (never relying on a single verifiable source of information, but always at least two, wherever possible), I have combed a mine of information in a tireless effort to recapture the flavor, the color of the lives of these exceptional women.

Though I often thought I'd never reach the end of my allotted task, I never for a moment doubted its interest. Carried away by these pioneers, I was rewarded by discoveries of all kinds. There are many surprising facts here, as well as questions and even hints at answers. "Are there no heroic figures, no benefactors, no larger-than-life characters in the world of women?" asks Qiu Jin in *Stones of the Jingwei Bird*, written between 1904 and 1906.

There are indeed, and I have included several hundred here, some virtually unknown. I would like to think that this book will contribute to redressing various gender injustices of history, to raising the profile of women whom history has unaccountably passed over, and increasing our awareness of female creativity.

It is now apparent that, in spite of an incredible amount of misogyny, and the heartless "segregation" that has proved such an obstacle to the advancement of women, they too have played their part in building civilization—bringing, I believe, something new to the world. Even men are becoming aware of this.

One can gauge just how far we have come on listening to Ban Ki-moon, Secretary-General of the UN, on March 7, 2008, enthusiastically embracing the idea of working with women the world over, because, he says, "it is to them that we owe the gains of the past century, and it will again be they who, tomorrow, will be the champions of the cause". The cause: that of their emancipation, from which all society should benefit.

It's not over yet. The Millennium Summit held in New York in 2000 brought together 170 heads of state, of whom just six were women. Yet, if we want civilization to progress, one can only hope that, thanks to such pioneers, we are now on the path to a mixed world in which women will be as present as men.

X.G.

Activists

"Men do evil. You, women, be the remedy, and since on this earth there are fallen angels, be the good ones."

Victor Hugo (1802–1885)

Women have fought—and still fight—on every front. Just like men, we would like to say. Against poverty, against all forms of discrimination, against the ransacking of the planet, against colonization, and in favor of the people, of minorities, of democracy, of immigrants, of the socially exploited, and so on.

Some women have even combined these various struggles, like **Angela Davis**, who opposed class, sex, and race oppression; or **Eleanor Roosevelt**, who combated many types of inequality (for women, African-Americans, unemployed workers, the children of the poor) and who, in 1948, as president of the Commission of Human Rights, pushed through the signing of the Universal Declaration—a text which in theory precludes all these injustices.

They have fought and risked prison, their children have received death threats, they have been tortured and expelled. Just like men. But when a woman leaves her house, speaks in public, heads a street demonstration, or publishes an article in a newspaper, she is faced (even before the police and authorities become involved) with the anger of her

For years women have been demanding equal pay for equal work. Here a demonstration in Great Britain in the 1940s.

husband or her father, with the reprobation of family, with the scandal she brings to her village, to her caste, and to patriarchal society in general. She becomes a "public" woman—that is to say, to all intents and purposes, a prostitute.

Séverine, in despair at being excluded from acting against social injustice, one day fired a bullet in her chest, telling the men she was to have left behind: "I die of what makes you live: revolt and hatred. I die of having been just a woman, when burn within me virile and ardent thoughts. I die because I never backed down." Recovering from her wounds, Séverine became the first professional female journalist.

When starting off a woman is therefore more vulnerable; and yet when she succeeds, her impact is often less recognized. Thus in 1972, **Ela Bhatt**, the Indian lawyer, created SEWA (the Self-Employed Women's Association), an organization that has allowed many Indian women without access to a bank to obtain micro-credits and thereby set up small businesses or to carry out projects. Thus, assisted by vocational training courses, vaccination and literacy campaigns, such women are able to stabilize their often chaotic existence and develop their social roles. It was by creating a similar "bank for the poor," based on micro-lending, that the Bangladeshi Muhammad Yunus won the Nobel Peace Prize in 2006.

But if men and women may share a common cause, some struggles are more specifically female and some pioneers had first to fight in order to save their own skin. When Chinese women have their feet broken, **Qui Jin** protests against their suffering. When African girls have their clitorises mutilated, **Ayaan Hirsi Ali** denounces the procedure as barbaric. When Egyptian women are called upon to undergo hymen reconstruction, **Nawal el Saadawi**

Women's liberation movement, Washington, United States, in the 1960s.

condemns male chauvinism. When Indian girls hardly ten years old are handed over to be brutalized by their husbands, **Sampat Pal Devi** administers her own brand of justice. When Bengali women are forced to wear the veil, **Taslima Nasrin** contests the law. When American women are beset by repeat pregnancies, **Margaret Sanger** preaches birth control. When Nigerian victims are condemned to be whipped or stoned, **Hauwa Ibrahim** defends them. When Pakistani women are threatened with "honor killing" or are burned with acid, **Hina** and **Asma Jilani** set up safe houses for them. When Moldavian and Romanian girls are tricked into pros-titution, **Celhia de Lavarène** flushes out the culprits. When French women die during backstreet abortions, **Madeleine Peletier** employs her medical knowledge to help them. When Afar women are

violated on a massive scale, **Aicha Dabale** founds an association to protect them. And there are so many others, all over the world. Women are daring, for the first time, to rise up against their "destiny" of being nothing but mothers, incarcerated and submissive. Trailblazers everywhere are resisting all forms of mutilation and abuse inflicted on the female body.

As Simone de Beauvoir once said: "Freedom, for a woman, starts with the womb." Women have also had to fight against the incredible apartheid in which they have been immured: why did they not have the right to vote? At the very beginning of the twentieth century, suffragettes had to battle against a maelstrom of prejudices to earn a right which today seems no more than elementary justice. These militants, who often lived through two world wars, saw a correlation between the recognition of women

French women were not to earn the right to vote until 1945. Militants demonstrating in favor of suffrage by pretending to vote in 1935!

as citizens and the end of armed conflict. The argument ran that if women obtained voting rights, there would be no more war. Their cross-border solidarity, **Carrie Chapman Catt** believed, would act as a barrier against war. A splendid dream with which Dutchwoman **Aletta Jacobs** concurred, as did the American **Jane Addams** (who set up the Women's Peace Party), who declared that women could prove people were able to work together without aggressiveness, competition, and rivalry. **Hélène Brion** in France declared before a court martial: "I am an enemy of war because I am a feminist: war is the victory of brute force, while feminism can only triumph through moral fiber and intellectual worth. There is a yawning chasm between the two." After a meeting at The Hague, an International Committee of Women for Permanent Peace was set up; in 1919 this was to become the International Women's League for Peace and Freedom, chaired by **Emily Greene Balch** (Nobel Peace Prize). This was in turn the ancestor of the League of Nations.

Women are not necessarily angels, though. They are not good or nonviolent by nature, and it is not their destiny to save the world. Victor Hugo proclaimed: "Men do evil. You, women, be the remedy, and, since on this earth there are fallen angels, be the good ones." But, if the poet showered them with respect, he also added: "Since these men in their blindness have forgotten that they are brothers, be their sisters, go to their aid, make lint"— that is to say, tear up cotton into bandages! A subordinate role they have often accepted with glee, like

Florence Nightingale, who ennobled as well as professionalized nursing, or Clara Barton, the founder of the American Red Cross, known as "the angel of the battlefield."

Stark reality, however, has often dispelled these pious hopes. Suffragettes did obtain the vote but we all know that war has not ceased for all that. History has shown that nonviolence is no feminine virtue. Certain pioneers, such as **Emma Goldman**, **Voltairine de Cleyre**, and **Clara Zetkin** fought tooth and nail for revolution, others participated in wars, like **Dolores Ibarruri**, "La Pasionaria" of the Spanish Civil War, and **Nguyen Thi Dinh**, general of the "longhaired army" in Vietnam. Valérie André did her damnedest in two wars (Indo-China and Algeria), parachuting from helicopters and becoming the first female French general in 1976. Yet the revolutionary **Rosa Luxemburg** wrote: "A world has to be turned upside down, but each tear that flows that could have been wiped is an accusation." And another Vietcong combatant, **Nguyen Thi Binh**, launched an appeal to her "American sisters" fighting against Nixon's policy, because, "filled with an intense desire for peace," women are naturally empathetic. There is a recurring suspicion of an unspoken link between the feminine and pacifism.

In 1999 Swanee Hunt, United States ambassador to Austria in 1993, created the group "Women Waging Peace" to forge links between peace-loving women throughout the world. Its action now extends to forty countries, where it trains women to positions of responsibility and in conflict resolution. In 2005, Ruth-Gaby Vermot-Mangold, a member of the Swiss Parliament and the Council of Europe, led the "1,000 women for peace" event that she has nominated for the Nobel Prize. In 2000, the UN Security Council duly noted that women are often the first victims of armed conflict (their body is one of the spoils of war),

Demonstration by a women's movement, New York, 1970.

but they seldom play a part in brokering peace. In consequence, Resolution 1325 was adopted highlighting the importance of the contribution of women to the prevention and resolution of conflicts, as much on a local as on a global level. Without women, peacemaking tends to founder, UNESCO concluded as the resolution was ratified.

For the pioneers to come there are clearly plenty of struggles on the horizon.

Dolores Ibárruri Gomez on September 4, 1936 presiding over a huge public meeting at the Vélodrome d'Hiver in Paris in favor of the Spanish Republican government.

Dolores Ibárruri Gomez

1895–1989, Spain

Politician nicknamed "La Pasionaria." Married to a socialist militant, she settled in Madrid, where she entered the fledgling Communist Party. She made her name with articles in the working-class newspaper *El Mondo Obrero*, signed with her famous moniker that means "passion flower." As Franco's fascism was taking shape, she became a leading communist, and her fiery, vibrant, yet grave speeches attracted huge crowds. Her rallying-cry was *"¡No pasaràn!"*—"They shall not pass!"—spoken with a determination that earned her three stints in prison between 1932 and 1936.

On the victory of the left-wing Frente Popular in 1936, she became parliamentary member for the Asturias, before fighting intrepidly against fascism by the side of the International Brigades. As head of the Association of Antifascist Women, she organized their work so that the men could fight more effectively. In 1939, on the Caudillo's seizure of power, she went into exile in the USSR where she became secretary-general then president of the Spanish Communist Party. In 1977, she returned with some of the last exiles and was elected for the Asturias once again.

Hebe de Bonafini

born 1928, Argentina

Leader, with Morales de Cortiñas, of the mothers who stage protests in a public square in Buenos Aires, the so-called "Locas de la Plaza de Mayo." Since April 30, 1977, they have been walking round in front of the presidential palace, Casa Rosada, demanding to be informed of the fate of their children or grandchildren, who were abducted by the military junta headed by General Videla. At first they obtained only numbers: 30,000 had "disappeared." Then the government tried to buy off these troublesome females, offering them an indemnity of 100,000 dollars per family. An extraordinary sum, which they turned down. "Spilt blood will not be negotiated." At the beginning, each held up a photograph of her own son or daughter, but later they decided to exchange photographs. "We are mothers of all our children." In spite of the return to democracy, thirty years on they continue to take to the streets at the head of every movement for the defense of social justice.

Hebe de Bonafini in Buenos Aires in 1983.

Souhayr Belhassen

born 1943, Tunisia

First woman to be elected at the head of the International Federation of Human Rights Leagues (FIDH) on April 24, 2007. In 1978, her articles in *Jeune Afrique* were already warning against the rise of Islamism in her country. In 2000, Souhayr became vice president of the Tunisian League of Human Rights. In 2007, as president of the FIDH, she launched a multifaceted plan of action: an inquiry into Darfur; pressure on major companies accused of riding roughshod over universal rights in the name of profit; fighting against the violence meted out by certain states against their minorities, as well as that of extremist minorities against the people.

Eva Joly, 1994.

Eva Joly

born 1943, Norway

French jurist of Norwegian origin; adviser to the Norwegian and then Icelandic governments in the fight against international corruption and financial malfeasance. Coming to Paris aged twenty to pass the competitive magistracy exam, she found herself taking the place of the prosecutor at the Criminal Court in Orléans, before joining chambers at Évry. In 1989, she was appointed to the highly prestigious CIRI, a financial organization in charge of industrial reconstruction. In 1990, named examining magistrate to the financial arm of the High Court in Paris, she became known to the general public during a probe into the Elf affair. This marked the first time that a woman was seen attacking—with exemplary courage, fearlessness, and tenacity—major acts of financial double-dealing, which were being protected by political interests. She dared to hand down a sentence to a business leader, Loïk Floch-Prigent, and even indicted the president of the French Constitutional Council, the "untouchable" Roland Dumas. During the seven years of the Elf case, she was constantly intimidated—she even received death threats, but she never flinched. She was also the initiator of the Paris Declaration that denounced the devastating effects of large-scale corruption. "All the firms quoted on the CAC-40 possess subsidiary companies in tax havens used to facilitate inside dealing," she has affirmed. She raised fundamental questions concerning the rightful operation of any democracy: should there be individuals above the law able, in complete impunity, to siphon off vast sums? Does democracy stop where financial business begins? Should one just stand by and despair in the face of the huge reach of global corruption? She joined the political fray on the side of the Greens in the 2009 European Elections, and has been elected to the European Parliament, continuing to fight for "supranational justice."

Aung San Suu Kyi

born 1945, Burma

Winner of the Sakharov Prize for Freedom of Thought and of the Nobel Peace Prize, in 1991. Her father, Aung San, the man who liberated Burma, was assassinated when she was only two years old. Her mother was a secretary at the Foreign Ministry in 1948 and ambassadress to New Delhi in the 1960s. Aung San Suu Kyi studied in India and then at Oxford. In New York, she became secretary to the committee on administrative and budgetary matters in the United Nations. When she returned to Rangoon to look after her dying mother in 1988, a popular uprising against the regime broke out. As daughter of a Burmese national hero, she found herself caught up in the struggle. With other opponents, she founded the National League for Democracy, winning the 1990 election, but the result was dismissed by the governing junta.

Aung San Suu Kyi was placed under house arrest in complete isolation. In September 2007, a hundred thousand people took to the streets shouting "democracy!" and offering her their support, only to be crushed by the military. She was imprisoned once again in June 2009.

Anna Politkovskaya

1958–2006, Russia

Russian journalist committed to denouncing the war in Chechnya; international reporter for the twice-weekly *Novaya Gazeta*. She traveled to Chechnya forty times, endangering life and limb. Her work has been recognized by several prizes; she published *A Small Corner of Hell, Dispatches from Chechnya*, an impressive book in which she offers proof of exactions and ethnic cleansing, torture and cruelty, rape and evisceration, as well as murder. Having been poisoned so seriously that she fell into a coma and abducted by special forces in 2001, she was assassinated on October 7, 2006. In late 2007, another Russian woman (Natalia Petrova, author of several film-reports on Chechnya, Abkhazia, and Nagorno-Karabakh) was set upon in front of her daughters by three policemen in plain clothes, who stamped on her hands, screaming at her: "Now you won't be able to write anymore!"

Cynthia Maung

born 1959, Burma

Burmese doctor who fights against dictatorship in her country. She campaigns especially for the Karen, an ethnic minority of some four million that has suffered discrimination. Like so many Burmese, Cynthia has taken refuge in Thailand to tend her patients: suffering from malaria, malnutrition, and often maimed by mines laid by the Burmese army. They receive free care in the Mae Tao clinic, which has only 120 beds with a staff of laboratory assistants, orderlies, and nurses. Hastily thrown-together outbuildings also offer a safe haven as a maternity unit, in particular for Karen women raped by Burmese soldiers. She has compiled a report on the health and human rights of the Karen ethnic group in the hope that international opinion will further "political change in Burma."

Clara Zetkin, in 1925, flanked by two militants.

Clara Zetkin

1857–1933, Germany

German militant revolutionary and feminist. Born Eissner, Zetkin was the name of the father of her children (her husband was called Zundel). She fought for divorce rights and free love.

From 1892 to 1917 she edited the newspaper for German Socialist women, *Die Gleichheit* (Equality), her strong personality imprinting the international movement of socialist women devoted to the cause of the working class. In 1907, she became president of the International Secretariat of Socialist Women. It was Clara who, with Rosa Luxemburg, launched "International Women's Day" in 1910 on the occasion of a conference in Copenhagen "in order to campaign for voting rights, equality between the sexes, and socialism." The first Women's Day took place in March of the following year in Germany, Austria, Denmark, and Switzerland, mobilizing one million women. (In 1921, Lenin fixed the day at March 8.)

As war raged, in March 1915, Zetkin summoned to Bern some seventy women from eight European countries (including the Frenchwoman, Louise Saumoneau), pushing through a resolution condemning the war and demanding a halt to the engagements, not through idealist pacifism, but because the war was a capitalist conflict in which the people—and especially women—had nothing to gain. Moreover, she pointed out that women could on no account be held responsible for the conflict since they possessed no power. She was imprisoned from July to October 1915, before helping to set up the German Communist Party with Rosa Luxemburg in 1919. Elected to the Reichstag, she had a seat there from 1920 to 1933. Her attacks against Hitler became increasingly virulent, until she was harassed into exile in Russia. There, she was elected president of the Women's International. The post led to serious disagreements with Lenin on the gender question, which, according to the leader, should be entirely subordinated to social struggle.

Her tomb now stands in the Kremlin, while her face once appeared on a ten-Mark bill in the GDR.

Emma Goldman

1869–1940, Russia/United States

Anarchist and feminist and "one of the most dangerous women in America," in the opinion of the police. From childhood she was a fighter: born in a Jewish ghetto in Russia, by the age of thirteen she was working in a factory. She emigrated to the United States and became an anarchist, living, unwed, with Alexander Berkman, who was to be condemned for the attempted murder of an industrialist. She too was thrown into prison for her views and the fiery rhetoric of her many speeches. Her positions on the social changes required and on the transformation of humanity were extremely radical: she saw that women, being subordinate to men, were frightened of asserting themselves and of "throwing themselves into life." If only they could become more self-serving, they would discover that they already have the tools for their liberation in their hands. She also realized that the principal weapon in the struggle is control over their fecundity. Like the French neo-Malthusians, Goldman distributed information on contraception, and, like them, was jailed for her propagandizing.

At first delighted by the Russian Revolution of 1917, she soon saw that the Bolsheviks were far from concurring with an anarchist concept of freedom, and she became disillusioned. Expelled from the United States, she traipsed about various European countries and supported the Mujeres Libres at the time of the Popular Front in 1936; like her, these Spanish militants demanded female contraception.

Rosa Luxemburg

1871–1919, Poland/Germany

German Jew of Polish origin, revolutionary, internationalist, and socialist. The only woman among the leaders of the socialist parties that gathered at the Congress of the Second International in 1904. Founder, together with Clara Zetkin, of the Socialist Women's International in 1907. Brought up in Warsaw, she suffered from a debilitating hip problem which kept her bedridden for a year and left her with a permanent limp, for which she was mocked by her many enemies. Fleeing from Poland when eighteen, and already under surveillance for her activism, she took refuge in Zurich, studying for a doctorate in economics and political science. It was there that Rosa met Leo Jogiches, a companion in her struggle and her lover for many years. Genuine socialism, she affirmed, is a combination of the most resolute revolutionary energy and the most generous humanity.

Rosa the Red, as she was called, was a passionate militant, hurling herself body and soul into the revolutionary cause. A motivational speaker, she chose as her adopted homeland the cradle of Marxism: Germany. Though she protested fiercely against the conflict, her party, the Social Democratic Party (SPD), "in chauvinist intoxication," voted in favor of a war chest. The authorities tried to silence her by keeping her in jail throughout most of the war, but she never ceased expressing her indignation: "The world war today is demonstrably not only murder on a grand scale; it is also suicide of the working classes of Europe."

Categorically rejecting reformism and the "fusion of the left," from which, she protested, there could only arise a "formless pap," she felt that personal happiness and enjoyment of life were a luxury she could ill afford. From her cell she hailed the October Revolution: "The splendid events in Russia have the effect on me of an elixir of life. It's our cause that is winning over there," even if she went on to criticize Lenin for narrow-mindedness.

In 1918, with Karl Liebknecht, she founded and headed the Spartacus League (in reference to the

Rosa Luxemburg at the International Socialist Congress, Stuttgart, in August 1907.

revolt of the Roman slaves led by Spartacus) and its journal, *The Red Flag*. Dauntlessly, she refused to hide, even when a price was put on her head. "I hope I die at my post, in a street battle or in prison," she declared. In fact, she was set upon by right-wing Freikorps, who beat her with sticks and shot her in the head, throwing her body into a canal.

Leonard Comber, whose name (as Elisabeth Comber) she used in everyday life. She subsequently wed a British army colonel, Vincent Ruthnaswany, adopting two girls. Working as a midwife in Henan province and as a doctor in Hong Kong, she headed private clinics in Malaysia and Singapore, and was a part-time lecturer in Asian literature at the University of Nanyang; she lived between Nepal and Switzerland. A rich and busy life, then, but her over-riding concern was with China, whose revolution she defended (her view of Mao Zedong was ideal-ized) in countless lectures, especially in the United States, and in books in Chinese, English, and French, whose readers run into the millions.

She denounces the extreme misery of peasants before Mao's arrival in *Destination Chungking* (1941), and provides insights into Nepal in *The Mountain Is Young*, and into Cambodia in *Four Faces* (1963). In 1985 in China, she set up a foundation that sends scientific experts for training in Europe and the United States.

Han Suyin

1917–2009, China

Anglo-Chinese novelist and militant in Mao's China. She published some ten books, including five volumes of autobiography. With her "little voice" (the translation of her penname, Han Suyin), and more woman of action than literary lady, she protested loudly against injustice.

Born in China to a Chinese father and a Flemish mother who seems to have had little time for her, she was certainly multicultural. A student of medicine in Beijing and Brussels, then in London, she married Tang Paohuang, a staff officer of Chang Kai-shek's. She had a passionate affair with the English jour-nalist Ian Morrison, before becoming the wife of

Nguyen Thi Dinh listening to a soldier telling her how he brought down an enemy plane, on February 17, 1966.

Nguyen Thi Dinh

1920–1992, Vietnam

Known as the general of the "long-haired army," assistant commander in chief of the National Liberation Front (Vietcong). She joined the Resistance in 1937, aged seventeen, her comrades-in-arms teaching her how to read and write.

Her husband was arrested three days after the birth of their son, dying under torture. She too was arrested by the French in 1940, tortured, and spent three years in prison. Released, she managed to rush a French naval blockade (1946) and transport a vast quantity of weapons to South Vietnam. In 1960, she incited a revolt numbering thousands in Ben Tre, heading an insurrection that liberated the whole province and drove out Diem's force of thirteen thousand soldiers. This victory sparked a general uprising in the South. Mrs. Dinh—elected director of the Committee of the National Liberation Front at Ben Tre—was appointed general. In 1965, she was elected president of the South Vietnamese Women's Liberation Association, and then president of the Union of Vietnamese Women.

Nguyen Thi Binh

born 1927, Vietnam

Vietnamese revolutionary. "I am foreign minister and chief of the GRP Delegation to the Paris Conference. But I'm also vice president of the Union of the Women for the Liberation of South Vietnam, and for me it is that post that is the most important of all." These are the words of Nguyen Thi Binh, speaking to actress Jane Fonda. Disgusted by French colonialism, she joined the rebellion, taking part in a massive demonstration against the American fleet in 1950 and engaging in the Patriotic Women's Movement. The French authorities imprisoned her for four years. On her release, she married (having two children), and she and her husband separately joined the resistance against the French. Binh was one of the leaders of the women's battalions known as the "long-haired army." Principal negotiator at the Paris talks with Ho Chi Minh, she is a member of the presidium of the International Afro-Asian People's Solidarity Committee, and represents the provisional Revolutionary Government of the Republic of South Vietnam in Cuba and many countries in Africa and Asia. In 2009, she was made a member of the Patron's Committee for the Russell Tribunal on Palestine.

Nguyen Thi Binh at the signature of the Paris Accords that brought the Vietnam War to an end on January 27, 1973.

Vilma Espin (right) welcoming Rigoberta Menchú of Guatemala on a visit to Cuba.

Vilma Espin

1930–2007, Cuba

Cuban revolutionary. She finished her studies in chemical engineering at the Massachusetts Institute of Technology, being one of the first women to obtain a diploma in that subject. Joining the struggle against Batista, she was charged with the arduous mission of transmitting messages to Fidel Castro in Mexico. She took part in the armed uprising headed by Frank Païs in Santiago de Cuba (her native town), where her home was turned into the rebel headquarters. She was well known to the city's inhabitants and they saved her life on several occasions. Threatened with death by Batista's police, she headed for the Sierra, joining the armed guerrillas there under the orders of Raul Castro, whom she was to marry in 1959 (they had four children). She set up the powerful Federation of Cuban Women, whose

purpose is to integrate women into social life and help children in need. From 1992, she started publicly denouncing the repression of homosexuals. She has been awarded many titles and decorations.

Irene Fernandez

born 1946, Malaysia

Malaysian, prizewinner of the Right Livelihood Award (an alternative Nobel Prize) in 2005 for her actions against the negative effects of globalization. Initially a teacher, in 1970 she founded the first textile workers' union in her homeland and fought for the right of women to occupy top posts in trade unions. In 1980, she launched several campaigns against violence towards women, setting up an association that soon became extremely powerful: the All Women's Action Society, thanks to which laws dealing with domestic violence and rape have been voted on or updated. In 1990, she chaired the Pesticide Action Network, which promotes sustainable agriculture, without pesticides or genetically modified crops, and publicizes the often-neglected importance of the contribution of women in the countryside. She is the founder, in 1991, of the NGO Tenaganita ("Strength of Women"), which demands justice for pariahs such as enslaved migrants and prostitutes suffering from AIDS and their children. When, in 1996, she dared denounce the terrible living conditions in detention camps, she was arrested by the Malaysian government on the pretext that she was spreading "false information with malicious intent." Her cause was taken up by Amnesty International, she was released and immediately took up campaigning once more.

Harriet Tubman

c. 1820–1913, United States

Having long suffered ill treatment on her plantation in Maryland the slave born Araminta Ross was on the point of being sold. Plucking up her courage, she ran away and, with the help of white abolitionist Quakers, managed to make her way to Philadelphia. Nonetheless, rather than settle in the haven of Pennsylvania, she returned to the hell of slavery to rescue several members of her family, and then dozens of other slaves.

As the leader of the Underground Railroad network and undertaking many such expeditions, the fearless and resourceful Tubman soon had a price on her head. During the American Civil War, Harriet acted as a valuable auxiliary to Colonel Montgomery, to the point that the famous John Brown dubbed her "General Tubman." Opening a home for elderly and impoverished Blacks, the woman they called "Moses" defended the African-American cause throughout her life.

Ida Wells

1862–1931, United States

African-American and, in 1900, the first president of the Negro Fellowship League, which worked for equal civil rights. Born into a slave family, orphaned in adolescence, she had to bring up five brothers and sisters. Earning a living as a teacher, she fought with fortitude and intelligence to set up her own newspaper in Memphis, Tennessee. She directly challenged President McKinley on a lynching in South Carolina, thereby earning herself many dangerous enemies. Even her white Suffragette friends did not always want to become compromised with the struggle for black equality. Ida was a victim of racist attacks and her offices were destroyed. Indomitably, however, she persisted in making speeches and holding meetings against lynching throughout the United States and even in Europe. Shortly before her death, she marched at the head of a group demonstrating against the segregationist rules operating in a deluxe hotel in Chicago.

Ella Reeve Bloor

1862–1951, United States

Known as "Mother Bloor." Leader of a labor organization, and campaigner for the rights of women and African-Americans, for peace and for socialism. Member of the Socialist Party from its foundation, she rose through its ranks. An excellent speaker, she supported the tram drivers during their strike in Philadelphia, as well as other workers. She headed the American delegation to the International Women's Conference in Paris in 1934 and was a staunch supporter of the struggle for African-American freedom.

Ella Reeve Bloor.

Anita Whitney

1867–1955, United States

Pioneer in the fight against racism. White and of middle-class origins, Anita started out in charitable organizations, campaigning for women's suffrage and adhering to the League for Equality, whose president she became. In 1914, she joined the Socialist Party and, in 1919, the Workers' Communist Party, getting caught up in the "witch hunt." On November 28, 1919, she spoke courageously at a prohibited rally in Oakland against the lynching of black men accused of rape. Arrested, she was indicted for "criminal trade unionism." In 1936, she became secretary-general of the Communist Party of the State of California and then a member of the central committee.

Eleanor Roosevelt at a youth employment center in New York, May 28, 1940.

Mary McLeod Bethune

1878–1955, United States

African-American community activist. Born to enslaved parents, she was lucky enough to study and graduate from the Moody Bible Institute of Chicago in 1895, and was of the opinion that only a similar education for her brothers and sisters could enable them to evolve in a positive direction. With this in mind, in 1904 she opened an institute for girls at Dayton. Such was their thirst for knowledge—since many schools were reserved for whites alone—the school was besieged by hundreds of candidates. In 1923, the successful establishment became mixed. She was called upon to administrate youth policy, and participated in the creation of the National Council of Negro Women in 1937, becoming its president. With her softly-softly approach, she considerably improved the social status of African Americans and their image in the eyes of the white population.

Eleanor Roosevelt

1884–1962, United States

American delegate to the United Nations (UN) in 1945. She was the wife of Franklin D. Roosevelt, president of the United States, and was first and foremost committed to her husband's career and to the education of her five children. But, after 1929, she took an independent role in the feminist struggle, with the League of Women Voters of the United States and the Women's Trade Union League. She was against racism and unemployment, committed to the civil rights movement, working for deprived children, and striving for peace. She was remarkable for her dynamism and ability to mobilize the media. In 1941, during the Second World War, she co-chaired a national committee on civil defense. She subsequently played a crucial role in the creation of the UN: in Paris in 1948 she signed the Universal Declaration that stipulates that no discrimination should exist on grounds of gender or race, for "all human beings are born free and equal in dignity and rights."

Rosa Parks

1913–2005, United States

Born McCauley, African-American secretary of the NAACP (National Association for the Advancement of Colored People) and "mother of the civil rights movement." On December 1, 1955, in Montgomery, Alabama, this dressmaker refused to give up her place on a bus to a white passenger, as the law required. Arrested by the police, she was fined ten dollars, but a massive protest campaign was mobilized by Martin Luther King. The day before the young woman's trial, 35,000 leaflets were distributed, appealing to black people to boycott the bus routes. For 381 days, they took no buses: they either walked, or occasionally taxis picked them up for the same price as a bus ticket. An international scandal around the cash-strapped bus network then ensued. The Supreme Court finally quashed segregationist laws for bus transport, declaring them anticonstitutional.

Dulcie September

1935–1988, South Africa

South African and representative of the African National Congress (ANC). Of mixed race, in her native Cape Town she was forced to live in a district reserved for nonwhites. Her father was a teacher. Having worked in a factory, she followed the same path. But everything was turned upside-down in 1960 when she learnt of the notorious massacre at Sharpeville, at which sixty-nine unarmed black men, women, and children were killed by the police. She took the decision to join the fight for civil rights, devoting her life to the cause. With other militants, she founded the NLF (National Liberation Front), which took up the armed struggle to destroy

Rosa Parks with the American actor Morgan Freeman.

apartheid. She was condemned to five years in prison, then, until 1973, five years of house arrest. Exiled for a time to London and then to Lusaka in Zambia, she joined the ranks of the ANC, a party headed by Nelson Mandela, who named her his representative to France, Switzerland, and Luxembourg. Sensitive and courageous, Dulcie condemned the full horror of apartheid, convincing many of the justice and urgency of the fight against it. In 1988, she was assassinated in Paris in front of her office in the 10th *arrondissement*. A police investigation revealed little, though a French mercenary seems to have been implicated in the arms trade between Paris and Pretoria and she found herself in the way. Thousands of people followed her funeral cortege. A Paris street now bears her name.

Angela Davis

born 1943, United States

African-American feminist, campaigner for the Black Panthers, and symbol of the anti-racist and anti-capitalist struggle. Originally from Birmingham, Alabama, a segregationist state, she listened to the tales told by her grandmother whose parents had been slaves on a southern plantation. In the United States, young black people were opting to go beyond the pacifist stance adopted by the generation of Martin Luther King. Angela Davis joined Black Power, submitted her thesis and joined the Communist Party in 1968, something Ronald Reagan used as a pretext to dismiss her from her professor's chair at the University of California.

By 1970, she was supporting the Black Panthers, even though she did not agree with their violent actions. Creating a support committee for the "Brothers of Soledad," she soon found herself at the head of a mass movement. When one young African-American in despair botched a hostage-taking operation that ended in death, she was promptly accused of complicity. Hunted down as "one of the FBI's ten most wanted fugitives," for "murder, kidnapping and conspiracy," she risked the death penalty. Arrested, she was initially jailed in a psychiatric unit and then shuttled between prisons. By then a widely known

figure, she received international backing. Her face and Afro hairstyle started appearing on billboards in major cities. After an intelligent defense, during which she stigmatized the discriminatory system of America, she was finally discharged in June 1972 by a white-only jury. A figurehead in the fight against the Vietnam War, in 1981 she published *Women, Race, and Class*. In 1980 and 1984, she was a candidate for the vice presidency of the United States. A member of the Central Committee of the Communist Party, she was sidelined in 1991 for opposing the Stalinism prevalent among the upper echelons. Married, and now retired professor of the history of consciousness at the University of California, she has never ceased voicing her position, continuing to publish books inciting readers to resist racism, sexism, and capitalism.

Angela Davis giving a press conference at her trial in San Jose, California, on April 12, 1972. She was accused of having participated actively in the fight for the liberation of the Jackson brothers, but was acquitted in June that year.

Hilaria Supa Huaman

born 1958, Peru

Peruvian Quechua, head of the "Anta Sterilized Women's Committee." Since 1997, Hilaria, a peasant leader in the Cuzco region, has been protesting against the enforced sterilizations she and others suffered. Between 1995 and 2000, 331,000 Peruvian women (Amerindians for the most part), underwent tubal ligature operations. Some did not understand the effects, some were promised money, while others were simply tied down and anaesthetized. This policy originates with the government, under pressure from the USA. It gradually began to dawn on the Amerindians that they would have no more children; they have endured pain that hinders them in their work, while their husbands started treating them as worse than useless.

In 2001, Hilaria succeeded in gathering together a dozen peasant women, convincing them to start a lawsuit, organizing, in spite of pressure and death threats, a march on Lima. They demanded official condemnation of the state, health care (which they are too poor to afford), and compensation for having been treated "like animals." The association mushroomed and Hilaria Supa Huaman, now a member of the Peruvian Parliament, is determined to take the cause of her Peruvian sisters to international courts.

Juana Rosa Calfunao Paillalef

born 1958, Chile

Mapuche leader. The Mapuches, Chilean aborigines, are threatened by extinction: from a population of 1,800,000 in 1870, twenty years later it had slumped to 360,000. Juana is Lonko (traditional chief) of one of the Mapuche communities and fights with her companions against discrimination, deforestation, and the fly-tipping that contaminates land on the miserable reserves on which they eke out a living. Her reward has been a prison sentence for destroying court files.

Rigoberta Menchú Tum

born 1960, Guatemala

Winner of the Nobel Peace Prize in 1992. Born into a woefully impoverished community, she reportedly began working when only five. In 1967, and many times since, soldiers invaded her village, raping, killing, and driving from their homes the indigenous people, who organized resistance against the heavily

Rigoberta Menchú and the Dalai Lama, Vienna, 1993.

armed soldiers with the weapons that were at hand: "machetes, sticks, pickaxes, rocks." As a young girl, Menchú witnessed the full horror of their actions: her father was burnt alive, while her sixteen-year-old brother was dragged before the villagers (after the soles of his feet, fingers, testicles, and cheeks had been ripped off) and doused with gasoline. Her mother was raped and hacked to pieces, taking days to die, her wounds seething with worms.

Of uncommon fortitude and intelligence, Menchú understood that the once divided twenty-two ethnic groups had to join forces. A fine orator, she organized resistance and became a true national leader of the CUC (Committee for Peasant Unity). She was the driving force behind the 1980 strike of 80,000 peasants, who learnt how to make Molotov cocktails out of lemonade bottles; the army responded by bombing entire villages. She fights by the side of the Revolutionary Christians, an organization that took the name of her father, Vicente Menchú. For this organization, the Bible is "an essential weapon," which validates the idea of "justified violence." Declaring that machismo is a "common disease" that one can hardly hope to cure, she dedicated her Nobel Prize "to the indigenous women of the world," adding, "The Nobel Prize belongs to the Guatemalan people, to victims of unpunished repression. It belongs to all women without a voice." Thanks to the Prize, she created the Indigenous Initiative for Peace Foundation that demands "global ethics." She has also established a chain of "Farmacias Similares," a hundred or so chemist's that dispense generic drugs essential to impoverished patients. Another of her demands is that the authors of crimes perpetrated during the civil war (more than 200,000 died and "disappeared") be judged by a penal court. Menchú was a candidate for the 2007 presidential election, her platform centering on the fight against the "chronic lack of nutrition among seventy-nine percent of indigenous children," but she failed to get through to the second round.

In Slirt in Turkey on June 2004, a crowd gathers around Leyla Zana to acclaim her return.

Leyla Zana

born 1961, Kurdistan

Winner of the Sakharov Prize for Freedom of Thought, in 1995. When her husband was condemned to a prison term of thirty-five years, she founded an association for the women, mothers, and wives of political prisoners. Tortured in detention, the illiterate young woman studied and wrote articles in the press, even founding a (banned) newspaper in which she dared expose the torture and rape to which Kurdish women are subjected, particularly in prison.

In 1991, she became the first Kurdish woman to be elected to the Turkish Parliament. Taking the oath, she spoke first in Turkish but then in Kurdish: "I will fight so that the Kurdish and Turkish peoples can live together peacefully in a democracy." She was condemned to fifteen years in prison. The strength of her convictions and extraordinary courage have won her immense popularity and international support. In 2001, the European Court of Human Rights condemned Turkey for a trial that had been a travesty of justice. An embarrassment for the national government, it tried to release her on health grounds, but she refused to leave without her comrades. After ten years in jail, she was finally released in June 2004. She has been nominated for the Nobel Peace Prize, for peace, humanitarian causes, and the planet.

Édith Cavell

1865–1915, Belgium

Founder of a nursing school in Brussels in 1907. Of English origin, Cavell's methods followed those of Florence Nightingale. In 1914, when the German army invaded Belgium, her nursing school was converted into a Red Cross hospital. Cavell refused to hand over young men to be mobilized by the Germans, allowing them to escape; she also smuggled more than one hundred and twenty soldiers over the Franco-Belgian border towards Holland. Arrested in August 1915, for these acts of immense courage she was killed by a firing squad.

Berty Albrecht

1893–1943, Switzerland/France

Co-head of a Resistance network from 1941 to 1943, and feminist. A nurse in the Red Cross in the First World War, she attended the World League of Sexual Reform, whose policy was "to free the human spirit and body from the prejudices that oppress them." She grew close to the Communist Party and worked with the League of Human Rights. As an overseer in a factory, she set up an office to defend factory workers' rights. From June 1940, she organized a network assisting escaped prisoners, helping them across into the Free Zone. With her companion Henri Fresnay, she created the movement Combat, editing the clandestine journal of the same name. She gleaned a great deal of information concerning German armaments. Arrested, and fearing she might give away her fellow fighters, she hanged herself in her cell in the prison at Fresnes. She is one of only six female Companions of the Liberation (alongside 1,024 men).

Danielle Casanova

1909–1943, France

Born Vincentella Périni, communist Resistant and feminist. In 1928, she joined the Communist Youth and in 1936 founded the Girls' Union of France in 1936, which had a feminist agenda. She collaborated on clandestine newspapers and founded *La Voix des femmes* (The voice of women). Heading the women's popular committees of the Resistance, she was seized in February 1942 and deported to Auschwitz on January 24, 1943. A dentist, Casanova treated deportees, taking advantage of her position to conceal drugs and woolens that she handed out to the women to give them solace. She even managed the extraordinary feat of smuggling out a document describing the horrors of the camp that reached the BBC and Radio Moscow. One-time honorary president of the Union of French Women, many streets and schools bear her name.

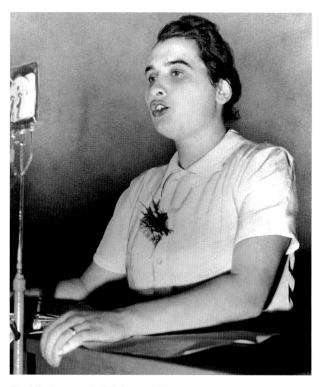

Danielle Casanova in full flow, c. 1933.

Lucie Aubrac speaking to school students in 1997.

Lucie Aubrac

1912–2007, France

One of the few women in the French Resistance to have fought machine-gun in hand. Born Lucie Bernard, Aubrac was the nom de guerre of her husband, Raymond Samuel. When he was taken prisoner in Lyon, she headed a detachment of irregular forces and attacked the van carrying twelve partisans, including Raymond, setting them all free. Five months pregnant, she gave birth just four days after her arrival in London. Lucie Aubrac performed administrative duties in the Liberation network and, after the war, tirelessly continued the fight against injustice as a campaigner for human rights, peace, and freedom, expressing the belief that "today's foe does not wear a uniform, it's the financial corporations."

Geneviève de Gaulle-Anthonioz

1920–2002, France

Member of the Resistance and leader of the "fourth world" movement, ATD Quart-Monde (meaning "assistance to all distress"). She was the first woman to receive the Grand Croix of the Legion of Honor in 1998. She joined the Resistance even before her uncle, General de Gaulle, launched his famous appeal on June 18, 1940 and was part of both the "Defense of France" and "Musée de l'Homme" networks. Arrested in 1943, she was deported to Ravensbrück. President of the Association for Deportees and the Interned of the Resistance, she testified concerning the camps at the Nuremberg Trials and at the trial of Klaus Barbie. She published a short but devastating book, *La traversée de la nuit* (Crossing the night), in which she described how she opposed the murderous hatred of the SS with absolute Christian charity. In 1958, she joined the founder of ATD Quart-Monde, Father Wrezinski, later taking his place at the head of the movement. The organization's goal is to demand that every human being be allowed to live with dignity.

Sophie Scholl

1921–1943, Germany

Anti-Nazi militant, decapitated at the age of twenty-two. In 1942, together with a few comrades, Sophie and her brother posted a hundred or so letters signed the "White Rose," urging passive resistance against the regime. They mailed five tracts of this kind, printing several thousand copies, some already denouncing the massacres of the Jews in Poland. They then placed leaflets in a Munich railroad station and at the university where they were philosophy students, but they were given away by the caretaker. Arrested by the Gestapo, they were promptly condemned to death for "high treason, subversive propaganda, complicity with the enemy, and demoralization of the army," and executed. In recognition of her role, a bust of her stands in the University of Munich and a stamp in her honor has been issued.

Florence Nightingale

1820–1910, Great Britain

A world pioneer in nursing, and a recognized statistician. The first woman to receive the Order of Merit in 1907. Her announcement that she wanted to become a nurse was received with horror by her well-connected and well-heeled family. She was of the firm conviction that a woman who gives herself a humanitarian mission must give up all hope of marrying. In 1854, she distinguished herself in the Crimean War, looking after the casualties with devotion, determining the causes of the high mortality rates (appalling sanitary conditions) and, using her knowledge of mathematics and statistics to present her findings persuasively in the form of pie charts. She was the first woman to be elected (in 1858) member of the Royal Statistical Society; in 1860, at St. Thomas's Hospital, London, she opened the first training institution for women wishing to embark on a health career. Nightingale thereby turned the "female vocation" of nursing into a fully fledged profession.

A century later, before the General Assembly of the United Nations, NIGH (the Nightingale Initiative for Global Health) tabled two resolutions: one instituting International Nurses' Day (on the anniversary of Nightingale's birthday, May 12) and another planning a decade's effort promoting health worldwide. In Canada, National Health Day is also fixed on her birthday. The following all bear her name: a London museum, a university department in England, three hospitals in Istanbul, an American medical evacuation fleet, a plane belonging to the carrier KLM, and even a geological feature on the planet Venus.

Bertha von Suttner

1843–1914, Austria

First woman to be awarded the Nobel Peace Prize, in 1905. Her father died before she was born and her mother was in fact a commoner. Hence a rather chaotic life with highs—high society—and lows (her attempts to marry a rich elderly man to escape her life), as well as outlandish episodes such as her secret wedding to the young son of a lord for whom she worked as a companion to his daughters, becoming Baroness von Suttner. She was also a writer and journalist, and secretary to Alfred Nobel. She published a pacifist tale entitled *Die Waffen nieder* (Lay down your arms), a late–nineteenth-century bestseller. In Vienna she founded an inter-parliamentary Union, a peace group, and an association to combat anti-Semitism. On every front she urged "brotherhood between peoples" and advocated social democracy. By the time she received the Nobel Prize, she was living poor and alone. War was fast approaching, but she was still writing articles on the "The barbarization of the air." She viewed the conflict started in 1914 as the "summit of lunacy!"

Jeannette Rankin at the women's march to Washington in 1968.

Jeannette Rankin

1880–1973, United States

From Montana (a state where women obtained their civil rights in 1914), Rankin was the first woman elected to the Chamber of Representatives, in 1916. A pacifist, she set up the "Jeannette Rankin Brigade" to protest against war, voting against the United States' entry into both the First and Second World Wars, and still protesting against the Vietnam conflict when aged eighty-seven.

Betty Williams

born 1943, Ireland

Máiread Corrigan

born 1944, Ireland

Irishwomen who won the Nobel Peace Prize in 1976. On August 10, 1976, two young children and a newborn baby were killed and their mother seriously wounded by an IRA car pursued by the British army. In what was a miracle in the midst of a civil war that had already cost 1,600 lives, Betty Williams, who was quickly joined by Máiread Corrigan, the aunt of the dead children, organized a peace walk with some twenty thousand demonstrators, Catholics and Protestants both. Ninety-five percent of the demonstrators were women. "Let women everywhere," Williams exhorted during the award ceremony for the Nobel Prize, "from this day on encourage men to have the courage not to turn up for war, not to work for a militarized world but a world of peace, a non-violent world."

For some, these pious wishes, without political or feminist foundations, proved to be whistling in the dark. Very quickly, the heads of the Peace People movement slipped out of the grasp of the women and lined up behind a media-savvy journalist. Corrigan and Williams were reduced to flying around the world and accepting invitations by the media, becoming the targets of all kinds of criticism in their country, on the receiving end of humiliations, pelted with stones, and threatened with letters signed in blood. The Northern Ireland Committee was of the opinion that the women's movement for peace was a deception since it did not demand the withdrawal of British troops and was predicated on a phony, dewy-eyed image of the Irish woman as a mother, as a protective and apolitical being. Unable to see eye to eye, the two women each kept their own share of the Nobel Prize money instead of joining forces.

Máiread Corrigan.

Michelle Montas

born 1947, Haiti

First female to be spokesperson of the UN. Named in January 2007 by the new secretary general, Ban Ki-moon, she was one-time director of the French-speaking unit of UN radio.

Jody Williams

born 1950, United States

Nobel Peace Prize winner in 1997. There are an estimated one hundred million landmines held in the arsenals of more than one hundred countries (especially by the United States, China, India, Pakistan, and Egypt), three to five million delivered every year, and one hundred and ten million already laid and remaining active for ten years. Williams, a terrier-like campaigner has, since 1991, devoted her life to trying to rid the world of these weapons.

The forces involved are so far from being equal that the fight against mines seemed lost in advance. Nonetheless, on December 3, 1997, in Ottawa, 122 states signed a treaty prohibiting landmines, covering the production, storage, import and export, and deployment of this type of weapon. A few days later, Williams, as coordinator of the worldwide campaign for the prohibition of antipersonnel landmines, received the Nobel Prize.

As director of humanitarian organizations in El Salvador, Honduras, and Nicaragua, she alerted her fellow citizens to the huge damage caused by American policy on the matter. Children, maimed, mutilated, or with their limbs amputated after mistaking a mine for a plaything, women blasted with shrapnel and dying of blood loss—she has seen it all. This combative woman led an international campaign involving 1,300 NGOs from 75 countries against this scourge. She had made the struggle political. "The main obstacle to the treaty is President Clinton," she protested, but fifteen American generals, including the commander-in-chief of Operation Desert Storm, affirm that such mines have negligible military usefulness. The Ottawa Treaty took effect in 1999, but antipersonnel mines continue to take their toll. And even if every country was determined to no longer lay these mines, it would still take decades and thirty-three billion dollars to remove them from the planet. In 2008, Williams also spoke out against the use of rape as a weapon of war, in particular in ethnic conflicts in Darfur and Burma.

Luz Mendez

born 1954, Guatemala

President of the Advisory Board of the National Union of Women of Guatemala. For thirty-five years, Guatemala was rocked by a civil war between pro-Castro militants and extreme right-wing paramilitaries: in 1991, she was the only woman among peace negotiators who helped put an end to the conflict. A feminist and a pacifist, she succeeded in making women's rights a key part of the peace agreement. Since 1996, Luz Mendez has once again been active in the union that had been sidelined during the war. Violence inflicted on women is a neglected topic in Guatemala. Since 2001, more than two thousand women and girls have been abducted, tortured, raped, and killed: a femicide—like the one waged with such impunity in Mexico (and against which Luz Estela Castro campaigns). Moreover, Luz Mendez has also made a stand, together with the Global Fund for Women, in the ongoing peace processes in Burundi, Iraq, Colombia, Israel, and the Palestinian territories.

Sister Emmanuelle in the 1990s.

Sister Emmanuelle

1908–2008, Belgium/Egypt

Belgian-born Egyptian nun (Marie-Madeleine Cinquin), renowned for her devotion. When just six, she watched on helplessly as her father drowned. Seized by the "burning desire to save people," she started studying philosophical and religious science, pronouncing her vows before the Congregation of Notre-Dame-de-Sion in 1931. Becoming a teacher in Turkey, Tunisia, and Egypt, in 1971 she decided "to break with any kind of privilege," living in Cairo where she strove to improve the living conditions of the ragmen in the shantytown of Mokattam. Often cordoned off by the mainly Muslim population of the city, these Christians survive by sorting refuse and raising pigs. Sister Emmanuelle's courageous efforts were such that houses, schools, workshops, and a maternity unit were soon being built for the poor. The force of her conviction is contagious: her

Association (ASMAE), created in 1980, has helped nearly 70,000 children worldwide, thanks to the donations she raises. She exported her work, too, creating the same energy whether in the Sudan, Lebanon, Senegal, or the Philippines. France awarded her the Legion of Honor in 2008.

Mother Teresa

1910–1997, Albania/India

Born Agnes Gonxha Bojaxhiu, an Indian nun of Albanian origin, and Nobel Peace Prize winner.

She applied to become a nun in Dublin aged eighteen, before undergoing her novitiate in Darjeeling. In Calcutta, she became director of a school for nuns, but she discovered within her a desire to devote her life to the poor. It took her two years to obtain authorization from the Holy See to work outside the convent. By 1948 she was working in Moti Jheel, a shantytown with a homeless population of one million. What seemed particularly

Mother Teresa in Ethiopia in 1990.

awful to her was the way passersby would step over the dying in the gutter.

In 1952 she opened the first refuge for the terminally ill, Nirmal Hriday, and then founded the Congregation of the Missionaries of Charity. Intervening at an international conference of women in Beijing in 1995, she stated that: "maternity is God's gift to women." Society would be endangered if women refuse to become pregnant and want to work outside the home, she also declared. She took in orphans, opened a care center for leprosy sufferers, and tried to give succor to patients with AIDS. Three hundred and twenty communities of her order have been created worldwide. She was dubbed the Saint of the Slums. Her honors and decorations include, in 1971, the Pope's peace prize; she also received the John Kennedy Prize for humanity; in 1972, the Nehru Prize for International Understanding; in 1975, the Albert Schweitzer Prize; and the Nobel Peace Prize in 1979. In 1985, the secretary general of the United Nations called her "the most powerful woman in the world." She was beatified in 2003 by Pope Jean-Paul II.

Brigitte Vasset

born 1952, France

French doctor, emergency coordinator of Médecins Sans Frontières (MSF), and recipient of the Nobel Peace Prize in 1999. She believes that when one has seen humans emaciated to the point of dying before one's eyes, children washed away by flash floods, men fighting for food, one just *has* to act. Armed with a medical degree specializing in tropical medicine, in 1979 she went on a first MSF mission to Chad, then to Ethiopia in 1985. The following year she joined the permanent staff, before becoming programs director from 1989 to 1992, director of operations until 1998, and since 1999, emergency coordinator. At the head of MSF, she oversees a payroll of more than five thousand and budgets for more than 117 million euros a year. It was in this guise that the Nobel Prize jury found her, just back from Georgia or Sierra Leone. Vasset attacks the French government for its apathy in the face of the horrors of Rwanda, Kosovo, and Chechnya.

Wangari Muta Maathai

born 1940, Kenya

Kenyan academic and first African woman to receive the Nobel Peace Prize, in 2004. In 1964 Maathai became the first woman in East Africa to obtain a degree. An excellent student, she was awarded a grant to study in the USA, where she became aware of the importance of nature for all humankind and of the urgent plight of women. These two questions were to remain at the forefront of her mind when teaching at the University of Nairobi, in 1977. Faced with a corrupt national government, she was harassed, maligned, beaten, and imprisoned in the 1970s and

and "the mother of the trees" has been awarded fourteen international distinctions, as well as the Alternative Nobel Prize. In her speech accepting the (real) Nobel Prize, Maathai stated that "retrogressive traditions, like female genital mutilation" (widespread among the Kikuyu), should be "consciously discard[ed]," saying that instead Africans "should rediscover positive aspects of their culture." The jury was particularly impressed by the way she thinks globally and acts locally.

Vandana Shiva

born 1952, India

Indian physician and pioneer of ecofeminism, winner of the Alternative Nobel Prize in 1993. Shiva is a doctor in philosophy of science, an epistemologist, and alter-globalist. She directs Navdanya, a foundation fighting against patents on life forms. To conserve biodiversity, she has assembled a plant bank

1980s. But she held firm. If the state believed that, by threatening and beating her, she would be silenced, it was sorely deluded: "I have the thick skin of an elephant," she remarked. But all this was not to the taste of her husband, who found her overeducated, too strong, obstinate, unruly—and difficult to satisfy, which is why she took a lover and won the lawsuit her husband took out against her for adultery, obtaining a divorce.

In 2002, this ecologist and feminist militant became an MP and, in 2003, deputy minister for the environment. For a good thirty years, she has been fighting against deforestation in the Green Belt Movement; some 30 million trees have so far been planted by a network of 130,000 women. Her battle in favor of biodiversity has saved jobs and helped improve the image of women in society. Kenyan women have reacted enthusiastically, running to plant trees where the authorities might have laid concrete. Maathai's methods have been exported to Tanzania, Uganda, Malawi, Ethiopia, and Zimbabwe,

that has already furnished more than ten thousand Indian, Pakistani, Tibetan, Nepalese, and Bangladeshi farmers with "organic" seed. Her battle is against "bio-piracy," the appropriation of universal resources by multinational agrochemical concerns. The most harmful of these corporations according to her is Monsanto, which she accuses of pumping out highly toxic herbicides, while its control over seeds gives it control of food production. "More powerful than weapons," Shiva declares.

Donations for rebuilding after the tsunami, she has shown, have been creamed off to construct intensive prawn farms, whose product is destined for export. Calling for a boycott of prawns from the region, Shiva observes that these are precisely the kind of activities that contributed to exacerbate the effects of the tsunami by destroying the natural coastal barrier of the mangroves.

Rashida Bee (right) and Champa Devi (left), survivors of the catastrophe at Bhopal.

Champa Devi

born 1952, India

Rashida Bee

born 1956, India

Indian women, campaigners in an international campaign for justice for the victims of Bhopal; also winners of the Goldman Environmental Prize in 2004.

In December 1984, an unprecedented ecological catastrophe hit India: a pesticide factory run by Union Carbide released 40 tons of polluting gases, killing 20,000 and leaving 500,000 people contaminated. The groundwater now contains heavy metals such as mercury, at one million times the permitted threshold. Who bothers with this Hiroshima of the chemical industry that only struck the poorest people, for the most part illiterate "Untouchables"?

Who would dare to come to grips with a multinational which has since become even more powerful after merging in 2001 with Dow Chemicals, and which flatly refuses to decontaminate the site? The answer is that two women, one Hindu, the other a Muslim, contaminated and sick, who each lost several family members in the disaster, have done so. They even had the audacity to take the affair to a court that condemned Warren Anderson, the plant manager in 1984; though, protected in the United States, he remains free. Devi and Bee began a hunger strike in Delhi before taking their protest to Wall Street. Emboldened, they went further, dumping toxic waste in Dow's offices in India and Holland. Their fight has assumed an international dimension.

Susan B. Anthony

1820–1906, United States

This Quaker teacher started out as a militant against alcoholism and for the abolition of slavery. In 1851, through the journalist Amelia Bloomer, she met Elizabeth Cady Stanton, and in tandem they broadened their campaign to include suffrage, divorce, education, and birth control. Together with the radical Matilda Gage they wrote the six-volume *History of Woman Suffrage*, launched the journal *Revolution* in 1868, and rose to be the first two presidents of the NAWSA (National American Woman Suffrage Association) set up in 1890.

Lecturing widely in Europe as well in the United States, Brownell Anthony nonetheless refused the right to take part in the official ceremony for the Centenary of Independence in 1876. Penning her own Declaration of Rights, she compared women to the once colonized Americans and men to the English. In 1888 she organized the London Congress that led to the creation of the International Council of Women (which was to reach some seventeen countries). Finally in 1920, the so-called Susan Anthony amendment enshrined female voting rights in statute.

Carrie Catt Chapman

1859–1947, United States

Suffragist and pacifist. Elected secretary of the Iowa Women's Vote Association in 1889, she played a predominant role in the successful campaign for women's suffrage in Colorado (1893). She criss-crossed the States petitioning and encouraging women to express their opinions. Becoming a pacifist, in 1901 she published a study on women in industry, her idea being that women could and should help each other to obtain their liberty, no matter in which country they live. In the same vein, having become president of the National American Women's Suffrage Association (NAWSA), she founded the International Women's Suffrage Alliance in 1902. It was her belief that if women had voting rights, all nations would become more civilized and would no longer resort to force. However, during the First World War, she published *The Home Defense* and *War Aims*, demonstrating how even her pacifism could waver in the circumstances of conflict. Once the war ended, she helped to found the Party of Women for Peace and, in 1925, created the National Committee on the Cause and Cure of War. Meanwhile, Chapman had been a militant for women's voting rights and a notable presence on the international scene. Instrumental in the creation of the League of Women Voters, her action made such strides that, in 1918, President Wilson committed himself to further the female vote, the Senate finally voting for a law that was ratified by thirty-six states the following year.

International alliance for women's suffrage, 1914.

Jane Addams

1860–1935, United States

Social militant and feminist. The second woman to receive the Nobel Peace Prize, in 1931. In the outskirts of London, as in the slums of Chicago, she was revolted by the poverty and its grievous moral consequences. In 1889 in Chicago, she set up a shelter ("settlement house") for the poor with a nursery school, library, and clubs. Inviting lecturers, she fought against alcohol abuse and cocaine addiction (a drug sold over the counter to children in pharmacies). She organized a vast network of "social houses," and also battled against child labor and in favor of legislation to protect female homeworkers. With Aletta Jacobs, the Dutch feminist doctor, she founded the International Women's Suffrage Alliance. On May 1, 1915, a group of 1,136 delegates from twelve nations met at a congress in The Hague, demanding not only voting rights, but also the peaceful resolution of the conflict, the right of all peoples to self-determination, the democratic governance of foreign policy, and exclusion of private interest in the arms industry. The congress led to the establishment of an International Committee for Permanent Peace (CIPP), the ancestor of the League of Nations.

She became the first president of the Women's League for Peace and Freedom, created in Zurich in 1919 by representatives from sixteen nations. She had the intelligence to combine the fight for women and for peace in the Women's Peace Party, and the battle for African-American civil rights and against racism by founding the National Association for the Advancement of Colored People. Accused of being in league with anarchists and communists, of being unpatriotic and seditious, Addams ended her life in great solitude, immobilized by physical and psychological problems. Today she is one of the most admired American women of all time.

Banner proclaiming the presence of Jane Addams at Carnegie Hall in New York on February 17, 1913.

Emily Greene Balch

1867–1961, United States

Pacifist, feminist, and anticolonialist, winner of the Nobel Peace Prize in 1946. "Passion, as mother or wife, is not for me," she announced at the end of a life which "was not completely useless."

With a doctorate in philosophy, she was a socialist, not a Marxist. She took part in setting up the first "female trade union," the National Women's Trade Union League of America in 1903, becoming, ten years later, president of the Massachusetts Minimum Wage Commission, which drew up the first law to improve low-pay conditions. In 1926, Balch was appointed to monitor the Marines occupying Haiti; without hesitation, she advised the withdrawal of all shock troops and the establishment of a local government. She was, however, chiefly committed to the feminist cause. She participated in the important International Women's Peace Conference in 1915. With the "Women of The Hague," she was instrumental in establishing the Women's International League for Peace and Freedom (WILPF), becoming its secretary and then its international president. She handed the lion's share of the money awarded by the Nobel Committee over to the league.

Helene Lange

1848–1930, Germany

Intellectual figurehead of the Bund Deutscher Frauenvereine, a woman's league campaigning for voting rights during the first thirty years of the twentieth century. Cofounder and first president of the German Teachers' Organization in 1889, she set up the journal *Die Frau* (The Woman) in 1893. Helene lived with Gertrud Bäumer, with whom she wrote the *Handbuch der Frauenbewegung* (Handbook of the feminist movement).

Hubertine Auclert

1848–1914, France

French feminist, active at the turn of the twentieth century. Having founded the weekly magazine *La Citoyenne* (The Citizen), in 1882 she was already employing the term "feminist" positively—whereas up to that time it had designated an especially effeminate man. She was also the first to fight, not only for equal rights for married women, but also for wives to be allowed to keep their birth name and for language generally to be feminized. But, at the beginning of the twentieth century, the priority was voting rights,

Suffragettes at the National Union for Women's Suffrage in Paris in the 1930s going to pay their respects at the tomb of Hubertine Auclert.

something she demanded with singular energy. In 1901, Hubertine created and plastered about the streets phony election posters in the name of her association "Women's Suffrage." In 1908, she even went so far as to break ballot boxes, and also rushed into the French Parliament with a group of activists. Such eye-catching actions were designed to stoke debate and make a splash in the papers, and were signs of exasperation at the deaf ear that was being turned by male society (not least by political parties and trade unions) to women's demands to be treated as citizens in the full sense.

Séverine

1855–1929, France

First woman to making a living from a career as a reporter. To attain this independence, however, she first had to fire a bullet into her chest! She was born Caroline Rémy. Married at sixteen, she rebelled, and later left her husband and son. Through the receptive, insurrectionary writer and Paris Commune leader Jules Vallès, she managed to become a journalist, publishing reports and investigations in the field in the newspaper he had founded, *Le Cri du peuple*. With the heart of a true woman and the "brain of a citizen," she was intelligent, outgoing, and courageous, editing the popular newspaper after the death of Vallès, and thus becoming the first female editor-in-chief of a French daily. An anarchist who flirted with communism, she remained feminist and subversive, battling against oppression and for justice. She was also pro-abortion and for wage equality between women and men: "Since woman has proved that, as to labor, she can be the equal of man [during the war], why does the male sex earn more?" Her writing was both alert and steeped in irony and her articles hit home. Men often try to bury

Portrait of Séverine by Amélie Beaury-Saurel (oil on canvas, 1893).

women under faint praise: "Garlands we have had for as long as we want!" she counterblasts. "Words we get in profusion! But when it comes down to brass tacks, bye-bye… Our rights! Our rights! Equal pay for the same job—in the moral as well as material sense! Our rights! And cigarettes for women who like to smoke!"

Emmeline Pankhurst

1858–1928, Great Britain

English suffragette. She founded the Woman's Social and Political Union (WSPU) in 1903 with the slogan "Votes for Women" that kick-started the suffragette movement, as much among working-class women as the middle-classes. Aided and abetted by her two daughters, Christabel and Sylvia, and by her husband, the feminist lawyer Richard

Pankhurst, she started by putting pressure on the Labour Party, recently set up to the left of the Liberal Party, though neither wanted to feature votes for women in its manifesto. She then decided to attract attention by other, more visible means. If women were prohibited from entering certain meetings, she would just get them in through the window. In 1906, she even forced the doors of Parliament. In 1907 she led several thousand women into the streets and in 1908 she started handcuffing herself to railings. In 1910, she went even further: together with activists from the WSPU, she threw stones at the windows of the Home Office and broke them. Deliberately seeking out violent confrontations with the police, she was arrested five times between 1908 and 1913.

Condemned for conspiracy against state security, she immediately began a hunger strike so as to obtain the status of "political prisoner," but the government ordered her to be force-fed. Exhausted, she dug deep and undertook her own defense at the trial. If members of the National Union for Women's Suffrage Societies, set up around the same time, remained within the law, the militants of the WSPU often resorted to violence: some destroyed a telephone line; others exploded a bomb in front of the house of the Chancellor of the Exchequer. Many sacrificed themselves courageously. Wrapped in the

WSPU flag, Emily Davison threw herself under the hooves of the king's horse at the Epsom Derby in 1913, and was killed.

It was thanks to actions such as these that Englishwomen aged over thirty obtained voting rights on February 6, 1918. In November 6 of the same year, women candidates were authorized to stand for Parliament, Lady Astor being the first to sit as an MP in 1919. By the year of Emmeline's death, Englishwomen had the right to vote at twenty-one, the same age as men.

Käthe Schirmacher

1859–1930, Germany

German journalist and feminist. She took part in the International Women's Congress at Chicago in 1893 and gave lectures on women's rights all over the world. Leader of the progressive Verband Fortschrittlicher Frauenvereine (League of Progressive Women's Associations), she fought for a decent wage for domestic work. By carrying out mind-numbing tasks that require a vast range of qualities, she argued, housewives facilitate their husbands' access to the labor market—and for free. Unpaid work is unrecognized, despised labor, whereas there is actually "no work more productive than that of being a mother, who alone embodies that preeminent value, that thinking, acting value, called 'being human'." In 1904, she denounced "a 'man-ist' world, created by man, for man, from the man's point of view, and for his sole ends." Women must obtain "equality in difference." In 1909, she protested against the discrepancy between male and female wage levels, with men earning more since they are regarded as the head of the family—receiving a "gender bonus," as she called it—and claimed that such money should be distributed directly to wives. There were many feminists at the time who called for payment for housework and childcare, such as Alys Russell in England or Katherine Anthony in the United States, proclaiming that "maternity is a social function."

Marguerite Durand

1864–1936, France

French feminist. In 1897 she launched *La Fronde*, a paper written and made entirely by women, in whose pages she doggedly fought for women's rights, beginning with the right to vote. Her argument was perfectly logical: "Women contribute by their manual and intellectual labor to the national purse, and thereby claim the right to officially voice their opinion on all questions concerning society and humanity of which they form a part no less than men." She put her weight behind women's demands to be paid the same wages as men and for housewives to be remunerated in recognition of the value of housework. Journalists of *La Fronde* were the butt of much misogynistic sniping, but in 1905, Marguerite went on to launch *L'Action*, followed, in 1909, by *Les Nouvelles*. During the 1914–18 war, she claimed auxiliary military service for women. If they protested as much as they could against the onset of war, once the conflict was under way the majority of feminists were desirous of fighting for their homeland. "Women," wrote Marguerite Durand, "your country needs you, let us be worthy of being citizens." She hoped that to take part in the united front against the enemy, even to risk her life doing so, would prove that women had earned the right to suffrage. Today the Marguerite Durand Library in Paris houses not only her archives but a vast number of documents, books, newspapers, and manuscripts recalling more than a century of feminist struggle.

Constance Markievicz.

Constance Markievicz

1869–1927, Great Britain/Ireland

Irish countess, revolutionary, and feminist and nationalist militant née Georgina Gore-Booth. Constance went to public school, and then studied art at the Académie Julian in Paris. In 1900, she married Count Markievicz, a year after giving birth to a girl. Determined to fight for her country, she refused to live in the shadow of any man. Gallantry, respect for the so-called "weaker sex," she asserted, is a sham; women should rely solely on their own resources.

Coupling the feminist struggle to the nationalist cause, in 1909 she joined the political party Sinn Féin and fought in Dublin in the 1916 Easter Rising. A lieutenant in the Irish Citizen Army, she was condemned to death, a sentence commuted to prison for life. At the elections of December 1918, she was the only woman out of seventy-three Sinn Féin MPs elected, and the first woman elected to the House of Commons. Refusing to sit at Westminster, in 1919 she was minister for labor in the Irish Revolutionary Government. Hostile to the Anglo-Irish Treaty of 1921, she also played a part in the civil war of 1922–23.

Qiu Jin

1875–1907, China

Chinese revolutionary and feminist writer. In 1903, Qiu Jin left her husband and child to go to Japan where she studied and, in spite of widespread distrust of women on the part of the revolutionary leaders, entered politics. "I cannot stifle my desire for revolution, it outstrips my desire to live; and so, fired by this ardor, I will defy these men." Back in China, she founded a newspaper for women, ran a girls' school used as a cover for clandestine military training, and played a key role in propaganda against the Manchu (Qing) Dynasty and foreign imperialism. Her school was then surrounded and taken, and Qiu Jin arrested and imprisoned. Five days later, she was publicly beheaded. In *Stones of the Jingwei Bird*, Qiu Jin pleaded with women "subjected to the despotism of men" not to let themselves be purchased by a husband, but to rise up against ill treatment, to do sport, educate themselves, earn a living—all things that were simply impossible with bound feet. It was against this cruel and debilitating tradition that Qiu Jin fought her greatest feminist battle. Their bones crushed and muscles atrophied, with poor circulation and in atrocious pain, women with bound feet stumbled when they walked and so languished, motionless, captives who often died in childbirth. And all this because men found these crushed "golden lotuses" beautiful.

Marie Elisabeth Lüders

1878–1966, Germany

German militant feminist, one of the first women to obtain a doctorate in political and economic sciences, in 1912. During the First World War, she headed the women's department in charge of female recruitment and the central office that dealt with the welfare of female workers. A member of the Weimar National Assembly, then of the Reichstag, she was arrested by the Gestapo in 1937, but released four months later after an outcry. Later she became a member of the Bundestag (1953–61), and was chair of the German Democratic Party (DDP) in 1957.

Huda Shaarawi

1879–1947, Egypt

Egyptian feminist. When young, she refused to marry her cousin, whose second wife she would have become. By 1922 she had cast off her veil in public, setting up the first women's welfare organization. In 1923, she founded the Egyptian Feminist Union, presiding over it for twenty-four years. It proposed education reform and promoted women's health, succeeding in raising the legal age for marriage to sixteen. In 1944, she established the Arab Women's Federation.

Rose Schneiderman

1882–1972, Poland/United States

American of Polish descent. President of the Women's Trade Union League (WTUL) from 1918 to 1948. Disembarking in New York at the age of eight, she lost her father two years later. Working as a cashier in a department store for almost seventy hours a week, she was paid starvation wages of two dollars. Left-leaning parties and trade unions were starting to defend workers, but remained reticent to lend support to women. Schneiderman understood that workers have to defend themselves and was elected president

Rose Schneiderman.

of a female union in 1904. In 1905 she joined the WTUL, whose objectives were threefold: to unify women workers; to train them in various trades; and to promote laws protecting their rights. Schneiderman was elected vice president of the New York chapel in 1907. Together with workers in the textile industry, she organized the strikes leading to the creation of the International Ladies Garment Workers' Union (ILGWU). When 150 women working for the Triangle Shirtwaist Company died tragically locked up inside their blazing factory, she organized a massive strike movement, the so-called "Uprising of the Twenty Thousand." She strove to promote laws enforcing a minimum wage and limiting the working day to eight hours. "The worker," she declared, "must have bread, but she must have roses too." She strengthened the bonds of solidarity between female workers at a time when men were trying to divide them, and made an important contribution to the foundation of the International Congress of Working Women.

Eugénie Cotton (second from the left) during a journey to Rostov-on-Don in Russia.

Eugénie Cotton

1881–1967, France

Née Feytis, Eugénie Cotton became director of the prestigious École Normale Supérieure college for women at Sèvres. A militant antifascist, she co-founded the Union of French Women and was president of the Women's International Democratic Federation in 1945, as well as vice president of the World Council for Peace.

Nezihe Muhittin

1889–1958, Turkey

First Turkish woman to set up a political party for women (Women's People's Party). As a writer, she published her debut novel in 1909; a teacher, she first became a schools' inspector and then a principal. On May 30, 1923, together with others, she decided to found a political party especially for women in a bid to obtain political, economic, and social rights. The Ministry of the Interior refused its

imprimatur. In 1924, Nezihe founded the Union of Turkish Women, which called for suffrage and the right to stand for Parliament, demands which were eventually granted in 1934.

Ichikawa Fusae

1893–1981, Japan

Leader of the Japanese feminist movement. In 1919, she was one of the founders of the "New Association of Women," whose goal was to draft laws enshrining equality for women and men. An early female journalist, she reported on the dreadful conditions endured by her sex in the workplace. In 1924, she set up a women's alliance for the vote and became editor of the magazine "Women's Suffrage." In 1952, without financial backing or the support of any political party, Fusae succeeded in being elected to the Diet, where she fought against ballot rigging and misappropriation of public funds. She was the founder in 1955 of the New Japan Women's Association, which was to become the Association of Japanese Women Voters. In 1975, she created an action committee for gender equality and against sexist advertising.

Louise Weiss

1893–1983, France

French feminist militant of exceptional strength of conviction, energy, and devotion to her ideas. In 1914, she became one of the first women to become qualified to teach at a French university. Her mother was singularly unimpressed by her achievement: "Louise, I beg you, don't tell your father yet; one piece of bad news in the course of the day is enough!" The first had been the declaration of war.

Suffragettes following Louise Weiss and burning their chains on the place de la Bastille, Paris in 1935.

A suffragette from the outset, and president of the "New Woman" Association founded in 1934, she was the driving-force behind some spectacular actions. Thus, in 1935 she was at the head of a demonstration in which women symbolically burned their "chains." She also handed out socks to MPs reassuring them that, even if their wives got the vote, they'd still do the darning! Candidate for Montrouge at local elections in 1935, her argument ran that "the French woman wants to manage the interests of the city as she manages the interests of hearth and home." Marcel Cachin, the communist leader, agreed to support her, but Léon Blum vacillated: "We only want women to vote if they vote socialist," the head of the women's section, Suzanne Buisson, jibed.

Louise Weiss organized unofficial polling stations with hatboxes for the ballot papers, but these were destroyed by the police. "With heavy heart, I became involved in a fight." She summoned some journalists just before their newspapers were put to bed and posed with her "ballot boxes" in front of the police station, while they snapped photographs of her being frog-marched away by officers. A campaigner for peace, when she realized that war was inevitable she proposed nonmilitary national service for women. A long-time enthusiast for Europe (she had founded *L'Europe nouvelle* in 1918), she entered the European Parliament as a member at the ripe old age of eighty-six, becoming known as "the grandmother of Europe." In her inaugural address on July 17, 1979, she handed over her powers to Simone Veil, an event marked by an historic handshake between two great and courageous women of the twentieth century.

Nawal el Saadawi

born 1931, Egypt

Egyptian feminist militant, doctor, psychiatrist, lecturer, and writer, imprisoned several times, and founder in 1982 of the "Solidarity of Arab Women" association against, among other things, female circumcision, imposition of the veil, and obligatory virginity before marriage, and in favor of secularism and legal abortion. The author of some forty-five works, including *Woman and Sex*, she writes: "Girls' hymens are reconstructed. It would be better to reconstruct the brains of the men who hold virginity in such high regard." A victim of Islamic extremism, in 2007 she had to flee her country and take refuge abroad: she was accused of "disrespect to the principles of Islam and of apostasy" because she wrote that God is neither man nor woman but spirit. The title of one of her plays appeared especially shocking: "God resigns from the summit meeting." The Islamic University of Cairo, Al Azhar, as well as the Egyptian courts, brought a lawsuit against her for "insulting Islam." She has also fought against authoritarianism and the poverty it fosters. She declares: "The woman question is a world question, an economic, racial, political, and state question." "We must campaign together for the freedom of the human being, man or woman."

Nawal el Saadawi.

Cecilia Fire Thunder

born 1946, United States

Amerindian, feminist militant, and the first woman to be elected head of the Oglala (Sioux) tribe in South Dakota in 2004. Born Cecilia Apple, as a child she lived on the Pine Ridge Reservation, until 1960, when her family was resettled in Los Angeles. There she studied as a nurse, before returning to Pine Ridge. Practicing her profession at the hospital on the reservation, she deplored the situation of the women. She set up the Sacred Circle group to combat domestic violence. Becoming well known within the tribe for her energy and commitment, she was elected president, the first time a woman had been so elevated within the traditional hierarchy. Her powers, however, were soon curtailed by the tribal council. In 2006, the State Congress prohibited recourse to abortion completely—even in the event of rape or incest. Cecilia vented her indignation by testifying before a commission at the Federal Senate that one Amerindian out of three in the United States is a victim of rape. She then announced a project to open a family-planning clinic on the Oglala Reservation. The council suspended her from her presidential functions by impeachment and voted for legislation prohibiting abortion on reservation territory. Cecilia and all the pro-choicers are still fighting for a referendum to be held on the law prohibiting abortion.

Shirin Ebadi

born 1947, Iran

Iranian lawyer, winner of the Nobel Peace Prize in 2003 and the first woman of her religion to receive the award. This progressive Muslim had been named judge and then chief justice of the Teheran high court in 1970. She viewed the return of Ayatollah Khomeini in 1979 with approval, but soon realized that the legal situation for women was deteriorating, with the obligatory wearing of the veil and the adoption of an Islamic penal code inspired by Sharia law. Dismissed from her functions, she occupied a secretarial post before retiring. In 1992, women were once again authorized to practice as lawyers, so Shirin Ebadi returned to professional life on a voluntary basis, defending the rights of women and children.

She seeks to draw attention to the most intolerable aspects of Islamic law, but, in the context of a politico-legal system wholly predicated on religion, her successes are perforce infrequent and fragile. It was nonetheless thanks to Shirin that the legal age for marriage for girls was raised from nine to thirteen.

Her notoriety has now reached beyond the borders of Iran. In 1996, she received the prize of the organization Human Rights Watch, as well as the Norwegian Rafto Award for human rights. In 2000, she took part in a trial focusing on the Iranian state security services, discovering her own name in a list of targets to be eliminated in its files. Accused of debasing public opinion, she spent time in the cells of the infamous Evin prison. Even though she was released, Ebadi remains constantly under threat; members of splinter groups related to Hezbollah block the doors to the lecture halls in the (all-woman) university where she teaches law, shouting: "Death to Ebadi." Wives of "martyrs" protest at the fact that she does not always wear the veil abroad, when she is just expressing respect and conforming to the customs of foreign countries.

She learnt of her nomination to the Nobel Peace Prize at a conference in Paris. Even if the government hinted that the award is "not very important," ten thousand Teheranians, mainly women, greeted her at the airport on her return. She feels this prize is meant to encourage her in her nonviolent struggle to advance human rights—especially those of the women and children to whom she donated the money presented by the Nobel Committee.

Asma Jahangir born 1952, Pakistan
Hina Jilani born 1953, Pakistan

Pakistani lawyers and feminists. In 1981 in Lahore, the two sisters founded the first chambers for women lawyers, as well as a women's action forum fighting to change Pakistani law. Hina and Asma Jilani created a refuge in Dastak where each year some three hundred forcibly married women, often battered or

Hina Jilani.

Asma Jahangir.

burned with acid, live under the protection of armed guards. Even being a lawyer does not mean one is exempt from male violence. One day in 1999, Hina ushered into her office a plaintiff, Samia, who was suing for divorce from a husband who physically abused her. Suddenly an armed man rushed into the room, fired a revolver at Samia three times, killing her, and then turned the gun on the lawyer. The whole crime unfolded in the presence of Samia's mother, who, it transpires, had financed the killing—together with her husband—because a divorce would have tarnished the family honor. The assassins were never punished and demonstrations were organized against the Jilani sisters, who are threatened with a fatwa. Only intervention from the Commission of Human Rights saved them—but for how long? The death threats continue but the fight goes on.

In 1998, Asma Jahangir (her married name) was named UN special rapporteur, and in 2004 was appointed special rapporteur on freedom of religion and belief.

Aicha Dabale

born 1957, Ethiopia

President of the association of the women of Djibouti that denounces the wholesale and unpunished rape of Afar women. In 1997, on a humanitarian mission to Addis Ababa, she was abducted by the Ethiopian security services and handed over to police in Djibouti where she was detained. Released in 1998 under international pressure, today she has taken refuge in France and is a member of the Collectif National de Femmes Solidaires (National Collective of United Women), but remains unsure whether to return to Afaristan to provide backing for organizations in the field that fight for the welfare of women and against female genital cutting and infibulation. In certain regions, one woman in two dies of a hemorrhage during childbirth because the midwife has to cut open the sutures, often with a knife that can in any case transmit HIV. Aicha Mohamed Said, the women's rights' delegate to the Federal Afar State, has declared herself ready to launch a campaign against these harmful traditions.

Shukria Haidar

born 1958, Afghanistan

President of the Negar Association, which has been campaigning for women's rights in Afghanistan since 1996. Physical education teacher and member of the Afghan Olympic Committee, Shukria has infuriated the Taliban and is now in exile in France. During the Taliban's rule, girls were prohibited all education and women were forbidden from having careers. Negar was an underground organization: teachers who risked prison and courageous girls met up secretly, studying with fierce determination.

Shukria Haidar on the podium in the conference hall at the Ministry of Communication in April 2006.

Shukria strove to prevent international recognition of the Taliban regime and told the world about the terrible fate of Afghan women. In 2000, she gathered with several hundred others in Tajikistan to affirm a "declaration of the essential rights of Afghan women." In 2003, this charter with 120,000 signatures was presented to the committee in charge of preparing the constitution and was accepted; in principle sexual equality is thus enshrined in the Afghan constitution.

Haidar is now director of physical education and sport at the Ministry for Higher Education and member of the advisory council in the Ministry of Women's Affairs. The battle is far from over yet, though. In 2008, hundreds of Afghan women could see no way out of the inhuman slavery to which their husbands subjected them other than to set themselves ablaze; many of them died.

Sampat Pal Devi

born 1962, India

Indian leader of an all-woman vigilante gang. Like millions of women in her country and elsewhere, Sampat Pal Devi has personally suffered from sexist violence. Married at the age of nine, she became a mother at thirteen. She refused to submit, however, and gathered together a handful of women. The group swelled to hundreds and soon there were three thousand women, all wearing pink saris (earning them the name "Gulabi" or "Pink" gang) and armed with stout sticks, iron bars, and cricket bats. Whenever they learn of a husband mistreating his wife, alleging that she is unable to "give him" a son, they turn up and administer their own special sort of justice, dragging the miscreant out into the public square, humiliating him, and giving him a thrashing in front of the whole community. And they are quite capable of returning a few months later to check that a woman thrown onto the street with her children, for example, has been let back into the marital home. They even lay into police officers who refuse to record rape complaints. They also defend themselves physically against corrupt civil servants who have grown rich on the black market. If Sampat Pal Devi had not organized this militia, doubtless the authorities would have let things go on as they were; she also fights for "Untouchables" abused by Brahmans.

Taslima Nasrin

born 1962, Bangladesh

Committed Bengali writer, victim of a *fatwa* in 1994. Her father is a progressive doctor, of Hindu tradition, but secular. Married and divorced twice, with no children, she is far removed from the submissive position of women in her country, where Islam has been the state religion since 1988 and which is thus governed by Sharia law. As a gynecologist, Taslima is confronted daily with female suffering: beaten by the men of the family, staggering under the burden of repeated pregnancy, their protests stifled. She has taken up her pen as someone else might take up a weapon: articles, poems, stories—all denounce fundamentalism as a "system created by men in which women are enslaved." She has even dared to criticize *purdah* and the traditional veil that women are obliged to wear. "Why don't men wear veils?" she wonders. Religious leaders have threatened her with death. "So I have to pay for the crime of having been born a woman and just have my throat cut in silence?" In 1994, she published *Lajja* (Shame), a novel in which she condemns interdenominational strife between Hindus and Muslims, and accuses the Qur'an of presenting a barrier to modernity. This was too much for her country's justice system: she was indicted for "offences to religious feeling," and a *fatwa* was issued, officially sanctioning her assassination. Crowds of hysterical men flooded onto the streets howling for her head and burning her book. The fact that a woman, Khaleda Zia, runs the country makes no difference, and Nasrin was forced into exile; the experience proved a painful one. In 1998 she attempted to return to Bangladesh to be with her mother who was dying of cancer, but the same year saw the publication of a volume of autobiography, "My Girlhood." The media accused her of "pornography" and it was promptly banned by the authorities; once again she was forced to flee.

Taslima Nasrin at the 20th anniversary of the Editions des Femmes publishing house in Paris in 1984.

Taslima Nasrin strongly denounces the misogyny of all religions. Hence, for instance, in the pre-Islamic Vedic texts of the *Apashtamba-dharma-sutras*, if a man kills a woman, a female vulture, a mongoose, a mole, or a dog, the penance is the same: one day's fast. But Nasrin is considered to be specifically "anti-Islamic" by the extremists who reacted violently in 2007 when she came to the launch of her most recent book in Hyderabad, India. Her head has a price on it of 500,000 rupees. She once thought she might settle in the Indian state of West Bengal, but there she risks up to three years in prison. Despite it all, she continues the fight and appeals to all women: "Women, free yourselves from your gnawing fears, stand tall, straight, and proud. Demonstrate! And if somebody must raise a fist, let it be you!" In 2008, Nasrin received the inaugural Simone de Beauvoir Prize for women's freedom. Though despairing at being treated like an "Untouchable" in India and still persecuted by religious bigotry, this prize has meant the world to her as she confesses that de Beauvoir has been "an inspiration."

Hauwa Ibrahim

born 1966, Nigeria

Nigerian Muslim lawyer, awarded the Sakharov Prize as a human rights' militant in 2006. She crisscrosses the Niger on the back of a donkey, offering to defend the poorest plaintiff for no fee. The first case she pleaded concerned a raped girl who had been condemned to receive one hundred and fifty lashes for "zina" (illicit relations), a punishment meted out in spite of Hauwa Ibrahim's efforts. Her most famous defense is that of Amina Lawal, condemned to stoning for having a daughter out of wedlock. "I have never seen a man condemned for this," Hauwa Ibrahim noted bitterly, "because I've never seen a man have children." Her defense was based on an interpretation of the Qur'an advanced by the Malakite school: a woman can remain pregnant for a period ranging from six months to five years. Amina became pregnant eleven months after her divorce; she might have had "a dormant embryo" within her from earlier conjugal relations. The defendant was saved. This lawyer continues to plead and to fight for education for all, especially in northern Nigeria, where only two percent of the population can read.

Hauwa Ibrahim.

Aminatou Haidar.

Aminatou Haidar

born 1967, Western Sahara

Defender of human rights in her territory and winner of the Sakharov Prize. One day in 1987, she took part in a peaceful demonstration. With six hundred others, she was imprisoned and tortured, detained in secret, without trial, and blindfolded for three years, her family not informed of her whereabouts. Twenty years later, she still finds sunlight painful. "At the time of the 2005 demonstrations, some of us were abducted, stripped, and abandoned in the desert thirty kilometers from where we live." Haidar has since been jailed again. Supported by Amnesty International, she was released in 2006, but still fears reprisals against her two sons or her mother. Nonetheless, she carries on traveling over the world, defending the cause of her people. "As I speak," she protests, "women in Western Sahara are being kidnapped, raped, or held without charge by Moroccan forces." El Ghalia Djimi, abducted and tortured for three years in the same conditions as Aminatou Haidar, is vice president of ASVDH (Western Saharan association for victims of serious violations of human rights perpetrated by the state of Morocco), which she helped set up.

Ayaan Hirsi Ali

born 1969, Somalia

Dutch liberal MP of Somali origin, a campaigner for women's rights and against Islamic fundamentalism. Her mother, driven by shame at having been born a woman, would beat her daughters with a stick. Then one day her polygamous father announced that she had been given to a cousin; though Ayaan Hirsi Ali assures us this is not an unusual childhood in a Muslim country. Her teacher's methods for inculcating the Qur'an were to beat and blindfold her, then smash her skull against a wall. After twelve days in hospital it finally dawned on her that "God is a dream and that to subject oneself to his will is no more, no less than to subject oneself to the will of the strongest." Unwilling to "submit," Ayaan argues that if so many suicide bombers are Muslims, it is because the Qur'an teaches men to be violent and to oppress women, rendering them impervious to reason. "One can affirm unambiguously that present-day Islam is incompatible with the fundamentals of the rule of law in the West."

Tirelessly she denounces all crimes committed against women: the obligation to cover her head so that man, that "billy goat… doesn't jump on her"; this "obsession with maidenhood," which leads to genital mutilation and infibulation, until the wedding day and legalized rape; the manner they are forced to produce sons like "factories"; repudiation and general mistreatment. A law against female excision now bears her name. Aware that girls are often mutilated during the holidays, she advocates a system of regular health checks for all those originating from countries where they may be in jeopardy. The very concept of multiculturalism—which respects cruel practices under the pretext that they are traditional—also gets short shrift. On November 2, 2004, however, Theo van Gogh, who made the film *Submission*, was assassinated in an Amsterdam street. Ayaan Hirsi Ali too has been condemned to death by fundamentalists and has a bodyguard day and night. Dubbed the "Black Voltaire," in 2008 she received the first Simone de Beauvoir Prize for women's freedom.

Ayaan Hirsi Ali in 2005.

Voltairine de Cleyre.

Voltairine de Cleyre

1866–1912, United States

American anarchist and feminist political theorist. This radical freethinker—anticlerical and a believer in direct action—was of the opinion that power exerted on individuals by all the legal and administrative institutions of the state amounted to illegitimate coercion. Giving lectures in Michigan, Great Britain, and Norway, and then in Chicago, where she took active part in the actions of the Industrial Workers of the World (the "Wobblies"), she was to come to the defense of the Mexican peasants following the conflict of 1911. An ardent feminist, she entitled one of her books, *Sex Slavery*: not only is a prostitute an obvious slave, but also, more especially, a married woman "who is a bonded slave, who takes her master's name, her master's bread, her master's commands, and serves her master's passions." Truly radical, she rejected the concept of "conjugal rights." Having a child out of wedlock, a courageous piece of provocation in itself at the end of the nineteenth century, she was rabidly antimilitarist and protested against a war chest that finances "those who choose the trade of homicide." Against the grain of the misogynist bourgeoisie of her age, she was even the victim of an attempted murder. Although seriously wounded, she declared that "it would be an outrage to civilization if he [her attacker] were to be jailed."

Madeleine Pelletier

1874–1939, France

French militant feminist who worked for abortion rights at the turn of the twentieth century. She became an ardent anarchist, but succeeded, thanks to a grant, in studying and becoming the first woman to apply successfully for an internship in a mental asylum. The medical establishment, blocked her at every turn, and it called for a sustained effort on the part of feminist Marguerite Durand to enable Pelletier to gain her diploma in psychiatry. Once qualified, she battled for women's rights and practiced free abortions, believing that to halt a pregnancy should be a woman's inalienable right. She deliberately stayed unmarried because, in a world of "masculinism," any union with a man would act as a constraint.

In the pages of *L'Idée libre*, an anarchist journal concerned with social education, she advocated sex education and birth control. Other suffragettes, however, felt that such positions rendered their demands less credible. Pelletier joined the Communist Party at the beginning of the 1920s, having first supported the French Socialist Party. Finding no movement, no party sufficiently committed to woman's liberation, she founded her own review, *La Suffragiste*. In 1939, she was arrested for undertaking illegal abortions, declared mentally ill, and interned.

Margaret Sanger.

Margaret Sanger

1879–1966, United States

American birth-control pioneer. As a child, she witnessed her own mother dying of exhaustion when confined with her eleventh child. Then, when employed as a nurse in a maternity unit in one of the poorest districts in New York, she would regularly witness women ending their lives on the abortion table. No longer prepared merely to comfort them in their death throes, in 1914 she set up *The Woman Rebel*, in which she preached birth control in the name of family harmony and to prevent terminations—a position that earned her a stint in jail. Repeating her offence on October 16, 1916, she opened a dispensary in Brooklyn, outside whose doors, even before they opened, immigrants, the poor, and the desperate queued up for hours. A month after the business began, however, Sanger was accused of "obscenity," imprisoned, and the establishment closed down. Refusing to pay the fine, she was incarcerated in the City Prison,

Queens, where she spread the message of contraception to her cellmates.

In 1921, she opened the first birth-control clinic in the US. Acquiring national, then international fame, in 1926 this neo-Malthusian organized a major conference on global population in Geneva. In 1931, she launched the *Birth Control Review*. Only in 1950 did Dr. Pincus develop a surefire method of preventing ovulation. Margaret Sanger persuaded him to put his discovery into the service of all women, and in 1960 the Food and Drug Administration authorized the prescription of the contraceptive pill.

Stella Browne

1880–1955, Great Britain

English feminist, and communist, then labor activist. One of the founders of the Malthusian League, which advocated birth control for economic and political reasons, in 1936 she backed the creation of the Abortion Law Reform Association. It is surely thanks to such actions such as these that two years later abortion was permitted in the event of "physical and mental distress."

Marie Stopes

1880–1956, Great Britain

English doctor and founder in 1921 of the Society for Constructive Birth Control and Racial Progress. Basing her ideas on the principles defined by the American Margaret Sanger and on English neo-Malthusians such as Stella Browne, Stopes gave lectures, published books, such as *Married Love* (in

Marie Stopes together with her son.

1918), thus generating a surge of opinion in favor of contraception. Marie wanted women not only to control their reproduction (and hence avoid terminations), but also to develop their sexuality. She founded a clinic in the deprived London area of Holloway from which, in 1939, there sprung more than a hundred contraceptive information centers in England, two-thirds of which were publicly funded.

Nelly Roussel

1884–1922, France

French feminist. In 1904 she was already demanding "maternity pay." A neo-Malthusian, she wanted women to possess a means of controlling their fertility, and campaigned for "conscious maternity," a feel-good expression less negative than "birth control," as employed by Malthus. His point was to prevent the poor from having too many children, whom they could not feed, whereas Roussel's aim was to make women independent and free them from the curse of repeated pregnancy. Their political message was therefore very different. Nelly Roussel and anarchist neo-Malthusians refused to "produce" boys to be used as cannon fodder or be exploited by bosses, or girls to satisfy the lust of bourgeois males.

Gisèle Halimi

born 1927, Tunisia

Celebrated feminist jurist. Originally from Tunisia, aged eighteen, in 1945, she came to Paris to study law and became a lawyer. Her first trial as a court-appointed attorney took place shortly before she went into labor. She also had to endure a painful termination using curettage without anesthetic.

When she defended Djamila Boupacha, a young Algerian militant tortured by French parachutists, many French intellectuals joined the solidarity committee condemning France for doing so little to prevent this "dirty war." With Simone de Beauvoir, among others, Halimi signed the proclamation of

Gisèle Halimi, 1977.

Demonstration in favor of abortion and contraception, Paris, 1979.

343 women who publicly declared that they had had an abortion at a time the operation was still prohibited. As a lawyer, she founded the association "Choisir" that campaigns for the right "to choose to give life." In 1971, while defending a sixteen-year-old, Halimi launched into a tirade against an unjust law that effectively prohibited women not wealthy enough to go to Switzerland from terminating. The accused was released, a verdict backed by a good proportion of French public opinion, thereby making the Loi Veil (a law named after Simone Veil) on abortion four years later easier to pass. Gisèle Halimi thus played a significant role in allowing women to enjoy their "first and most essential freedom." She went on to defend battered women and rape victims. She was elected to represent Isère in 1981, becoming ambassadress to UNESCO in 1985. In 2008, she campaigned for an EU statute to ensure that women's rights in all twenty-seven member states be raised to the same level.

Rebecca Gomperts

born 1966, Netherlands

Dutch doctor and feminist, founder of "Women on Waves" in 1999, a floating abortion unit. Throughout the world, one woman dies in the course of a backstreet termination every six minutes, generally in atrocious suffering. Even in Europe, certain countries still have repressive laws that force women to abort illegally, with all the dangers that this entails. Gomperts decided to act, installing a clinic on a boat sailing in nonterritorial waters so as to help women from countries that outlaw the practice. In 2001, the boat approached the coast of Ireland. Then, in 2003, it was the turn of Polish women to board the ship in spite of violent protests by Christian conservatives. By 2004, Rebecca sailed into view to help the Portuguese, but her path was barred by two warships. The ensuing scandal fueled a debate in Parliament and, following a referendum, abortion was declared legal in Portugal in 2007.

Marthe Richard

1889–1980, France

Frenchwoman who pushed through a law closing brothels. Originally from the Lorraine, where she had worked as a dressmaker, she went to Paris aged seventeen and found herself a wealthy match. She was one of the first women to pilot a plane. During the First World War, she appears to have been a spy for the French. Elected as a city councillor, in April 13, 1946 she got the law bearing her name onto the statute book; it made living off immoral earnings illegal. Abolitionist feminists were in general satisfied with this attempt to eradicate female sex slavery, but, in practice, it simply meant that prostitutes plied their trade on the street instead of in brothels.

Célhia de Lavarène

DOB unknown, France

French journalist, UN mission head. During assignments to South Africa and Cambodia, Célhia uncovered links between humanitarian missions and sex tourism. Under a UN mandate in Slovenia, she became political adviser for Serbian-Croatian relations. For two years in Bosnia from 2002, she led two hundred officers infiltrating people-trafficking and prostitution rings, and carrying out raids. She collected three thousand affidavits from Moldavian, Ukrainian, and Romanian women aged fifteen to nineteen. Five hundred and fifty girls were saved and several brothels closed.

Then in Liberia in 2004, she headed the UN mission in a similar project. Accompanied by an international police team, she discovered that the customers for trafficked females were senior local officials, diplomats, businessmen, members of NGOs, and UN peacekeepers. She had to fight against highly organized supranational networks that recruit their prey from the countryside in former Eastern Bloc nations and from the Maghreb. The borders are crossed illegally, the consignments waved through by "officials." On their arrival in Liberia, the young women are sequestered, beaten, doped, and raped, before being forced into prostitution. At immense personal risk, Célhia de Lavarène has battled to unmask the culprits and save the victims. But it gradually dawned on her that the UN is already aware of the situation and that the networks are well-documented. She was not replaced at the end of her secondment. At this point she wrote a book, *Un Visa à l'enfer* (A visa to hell), telling of her struggle against sex-trafficking. She has also founded an NGO called STOP (Stop Trafficking of People).

Malka Marcovich

born 1959, France

Consultant with the UN and European representative of the Coalition Against the Trafficking of Women (CATWE). She protests against attempts to legalize prostitution, which, she says, gives the green light to "organized crime." Pimps can earn million of dollars and certain brothels are quoted on the stock exchange. Her argument is that legalization does not protect public health, as is often advanced, because it is the women who are controlled and not the customers: nothing forces the men to use condoms and it is this that causes unwanted pregnancies and STDs. To put highly vulnerable bodies at the disposal of the "needs" of men derives from an archaic view of male sexuality. In 2006, she launched a campaign against the upsurge in prostitution at the time of the soccer World Cup in Germany with the slogan: "Buying sex is not a sport!"

Political Leaders

"Women who have wanted to leave
the inner life and make their way
in the outer life, onto the political
platform, are not women; they are
beings without sex, an outrage
to nature even more than to society."

Alphonse Marie Louis de Lamartine
(French poet and statesman, 1790–1869)

November 2008: Barack Obama is elected president of the United States. In the most powerful nation on the planet and in the rest of the world, millions of people shout for joy. And with good reason. His victory is breathtaking: an African-American has attained the highest political post, while his grandfather would not have had the right to eat in many an American restaurant. After centuries of racism, this is a truly historic event.

If **Hillary Clinton** had become president, it would have been much the same thing. For the first time, this nation, illuminated by the light of the Statue of Liberty, would have had a woman at its helm—when her grandmothers did not even enjoy the right to vote. Until recent times, throughout the world (and still in the present day in certain countries), girls have been excluded from schooling, prohibited from receiving higher education or entering many professions, and women in general have been subjected to a kind of apartheid. In a world dominated by men and governed by a system that regards women as inferior, every time a female takes over at the head of a country marks one more step towards justice and democracy. However, the feeling remains that a victory over sexism is not quite as important as one over racism. Could it be because misogyny is even more entrenched? Who put the flag out in 1993 when **Tansu Çiller** became prime minister of Turkey and **Sylvie Kinigi** of Burundi? Who's even heard of **Yanjmaa Sühbaataryn**, president of Mongolia in 1953? And even in Europe, who knows the name **Vigdis Finnbogadottir**, president of Iceland in 1980?

Such women generally become heads of state only after a long line of males, and certain "thinkers" argued long and hard that women could not ever be political beings, as it runs counter to natural law, contradicts their very essence; society as a whole would be doomed were women to leave "their" roles.

In India, little boys stand a better chance of surviving than little girls.

Many men have seen no good reason why women should take "their" place, and fight tooth and nail to prevent women acquiring the prerequisite rights and qualifications. In 1912 an anonymous man spilled the beans: "Female ambition knows no bounds! From the natural partner of man she has turned into an insatiable rival who seems committed to ousting him from all his functions!"

In the final decades of the twentieth, and especially at the beginning of the twenty-first century, about thirty women have beaten the odds and reached the summits of power. It might be late in the annals of history, and they may still be few and far between, but at least these pioneers have shown that it can be done.

A matter of months after the election of Obama, however, some could be heard voicing disappointment: he hasn't changed as much as we hoped.... But this is to confuse two different things. If it is right and just that an African-American can be elected, this does not imply that his policies will be better. It is no less right, and even more democratic—since women comprise half the population—that a woman can be elected. Just as it is right that they appear on the electoral roll, even if, as socialists and radicals feared at the beginning of the last century, they are liable to vote for "the party of the priests." The conquest of power by women is—of and by itself—a sign of progress for humanity. But—and this is another aspect—has the face of the world actually changed? What good is it, pessimists sigh, if, when women are in power, they prove to be if not always worse than their male counterparts, in any case very like them, since they too are only human beings.

Sheik Hasina Wajed and **Khaleda Zia**, regularly swapping places at the head of Bangladesh, spend their time sending in the troops against one other, while their people languish in poverty and misery. Moreover, these women are often not independent entities. Wajed is a "daughter of" a former male leader; Zia is a "widow of," just as **Indira Gandhi** was a "daughter of," **Benazir Bhutto** an "orphan daughter of"; in the Philippines Cory Aquino was a "widow of" and **Gloria Macapagal-Arroyo** an "orphan of," while **Bandaranaike** from Sri Lanka (and the first woman to be a true head of government in the world in 1960) was the widow of an assassinated leader. This then is the first general tendency of women in power, frequent in feudal countries: they embody a clan, they are Bhuttos, Gandhis; a bit as Marie and Catherine in Renaissance France were first and foremost de Medicis. They wave the flag or the sword of revenge in an allegory that propels them to the summit, goddesses both adored and martyred. With an iron fist, they hold down a starving and ignorant people.

In the nation of Indira Gandhi, there is a shortfall of some 60 million women. They are killed either in the womb, at birth, when little girls, or even after marriage. Today, in the country of the late Benazir Bhutto, girls can receive death threats if they persist in trying to go to school, and women are doused with acid if they betray the least inclination for freedom. Their leaders, be they women, belong to the dominant caste, and have little concern for the common good. Exactly like so many male leaders. There is, though, an historical difference: often, for a woman to gain access to a domain reserved for menfolk, the sphere of political power, for instance, since she starts at such a disadvantage, she often has to play dirty. She may then turn her back on her feminine side and forget, even look down on her fellow women.

Hillary Clinton and Barack Obama: the fact there was a choice between these two candidates for the Presidency of the United States in itself constitutes a huge leap forward for democracy.

A meeting between eurozone leaders in 2008: women are the exception.

The three major women pioneers who headed their nations—**Indira Gandhi**, **Golda Meir**, and **Margaret Thatcher**—were all scrappers, "Iron Ladies" intent on displaying their "virility." But, as distinct from the "male" attitude embraced by these heads of state, **Ellen Johnson-Sirleaf**, for example, shepherds Liberia like a good mother, scolding her children when fractious, but helping its victims and the weak; she is known as "Old Ma." And **Mame Boye Madior**, prime minister of Senegal, declares: "They wait for me with a sword, I answer them with a smile." In putting an end to the terrible civil war in Liberia, **Ruth Sando Perry** said she made the most of her sensitivity as a mother and a woman.

This was an argument often employed by women during their struggle for the right to vote and to enter politics: we can manage our families, so in the same way we could run the country. In the West, where, not without setbacks, it has gradually become possible for women to acquire an education and enjoy rights not dissimilar from those of men, female leaders can attain power though intrinsic merit. For how many women leaders were there in Europe between Thatcher in 1979 and **Angela Merkel** in 2005? (Note in passing the telltale difference in style between the thrusting British PM, obsessed by the idea of not appearing to belong to the so-called weaker sex, and the German Chancellor, who seems quietly oblivious of gender difference.) Between the two lies a gray zone, with **Mary Robinson** in Ireland in 1990, **Edith Cresson** in France, and, farther afield, **Kim Campbell** in Canada in 1991—none particularly effective. It was not before 2006 that a woman, **Myung-Sook**, led South Korea, while on the continent of machismo, there appeared the headline-grabbing **Michelle Bachelet** in Chile, joined the following year by **Cristina Kirchner** in Argentina. Pragmatic leaders, realists, hard working, unhampered by grandiose ideology, but capable of making concrete advances, in the Merkel vein. Still, by the end of 2008, a photograph of nineteen leaders of the eurozone showed eighteen men and just one woman, the Bundeskanzlerin. Women at the top remain the exception.

But do women exert power in a different way? Would a more mixed world be a more civilized one? Or is this an illusion? **Julia Kristeva**, the great Franco-American-Bulgarian thinker, thinks not: "The particular impact of women within political life would allow us, were it to come to pass, to revalorize that buried part of our psychological experience that helps us put the life of the mind before thought as calculation. Because they can carry life within them and they have to let it go, women are more attentive to life in general." Let us hope so.

After all, female access to political power is so recent that it is far too early to assess its effects. Perhaps one clue comes from Scandinavia. Nordic women—leading countries where more than just lip-service is paid to male/female equality—can take power without being ashamed of their femininity and without hiding their feminism, yet also without having to ape men or pretending to be goddesses, icons, or saints. Thus the Finn **Tarja Halonen** leads her country and is still involved in organizations militating for cultural diversity, social justice, against the death penalty and the war in Iraq, and all the while actively backing the Council of Europe's campaign against violence on women. With women like that, a different world is possible. And then there's **Gro Harlem Brundtland**, today president of the World Health Organization, who led Norway for ten years from 1981, the first leader in Europe to form a cabinet with an equal sex ratio, and who devised and implemented sustainable development as early as 1983. Today, of course, that idea is all the rage. And it was the American Al Gore who received the Nobel Prize in 2007 for having drawn attention to the topic. "The problem in politics," the vigorous former prime minister of New Zealand, **Helen Clark**, protests, "is that often more attention is paid to what women wear than to what they say."

It is high time to listen to them, to see them as they really are, and to find a place for their inventiveness and vitality.

UNESCO's first female president, Irina Bokova, takes office on October 23, 2009.

Alesandra Kollontai

1872–1952, Russia

Born Domontovich, she was the first woman in the world to become a member of a government, in the USSR in 1917. Daughter of a Ukrainian general in the Imperial Army and of a wealthy Finnish woman, at sixteen she graduated, obtaining a teacher's certificate and marrying an engineer at nineteen, giving birth to a boy, before divorcing and joining the social democrat movement in 1889. She backed working-class strikes and studied abroad, returning to Russia to join the Mensheviks in 1906 and then the Bolshevik Party in 1917: she was an active propagandist and sat on the Central Committee of the Communist Party. Shortly after the October Revolution, she became the first woman to be elected onto the Executive Committee of the Soviet of Petrograd, before Lenin appointed her people's commissar for social affairs (the equivalent of a minister). Although mildly dissenting from the party line, since she supported workers' opposition movements, she became a diplomat, representing the USSR in Norway, Mexico, and then Sweden. Her presence must have come as a surprise in what was an entirely male-dominated political world.

The new Soviet government, however, was wary of her feminist convictions; she believed that the alienation of women was a political problem and, in "Make Way for Winged Eros," voiced a novel conception of the relationship between the genders. She would have liked to have lived in a "free union" with Pavel Dybenko, the head of the Baltic mariners, but was forced to conform to party morality and marry.

Once in government, Kollontai was instrumental in promulgating the "Code of the Family," which established total equality with regards to parental authority over the children and allowed women to to keep their maiden name. She believed that the State should liberate women from housework and child-rearing: "The separation between kitchen and marriage is no less significant for women than that between Church and State." As Minister for Health in 1920, she legalized abortion, and for two years directed Jenotdel, the woman's section of the Central Committee of the Communist Party, assisting women to take on a full role in political life (obliging men to pay alimony, applying recruitment quotas for women, fighting against illiteracy and prostitution, setting up training courses and career guidance for female workers, who in turn are encouraged to teach what they learn).

Margaret Bondfield

1873–1953, Great Britain

Member of the Labour Party and the United Kingdom's first woman cabinet minister. At fourteen, she apprenticed in a draper's shop, but with the help of a customer who befriended her, she educated herself and became involved in politics. By 1921, one million women had joined unions.

Bondfield became president of the Trades Union Congress (TUC) and Labour minister in the government of Ramsey McDonald in 1929.

Suzanne Lacore among the government headed by Léon Blum in 1936.

Suzanne Lacore

1875–1975, France

French under-secretary of state for public health in 1936, during the left-wing Popular Front. She was a pioneer, like Irène Joliot-Curie and Cecile Brunschvicg, even if they were not yet permitted to speak in the Parliament at the Palais-Bourbon. Once an elementary teacher in the Dordogne, she was a socialist and a feminist and introduced district nurses to improve child welfare.

Cécile Brunschvicg

1877–1946, France

Under-secretary of state for National Education, appointed by Léon Blum, in 1936, at the time of the left-wing Popular Front (with Irène Joliot-Curie and Suzanne Lacore).

A feminist with intellectual middle-class roots, she worked as a visiting social worker, feeling growing indignation at the working conditions of women. She believed their exploitation resulted from isolation and encouraged them to join or form unions.

In 1917, she helped set up a college for women factory overseers. Brunschvicg defended women's right to work, demanding wage equality with men, though not in the most arduous jobs. Moderate and pragmatic, she kept faith with this at once egalitarian yet differentiated stance. President of the Union Française pour le Suffrage des Femmes (campaigning for votes for women), she penned hundreds of articles advocating women's voting rights in the newspaper, *La Française*, which she edited.

Her concern with such social questions made her an obvious choice for the under-secretary of state for National Education, a post she held until June 1937, then becoming vice president of the Upper Council for Child Welfare and of the Upper Council for Social Hygiene. French families owe her a thousand school cafeterias and a training program for teachers specializing in children with special needs. Cécile Brunschvicg threw her weight behind the League of Women Voters at the Society of Nations in 1919, organized the Tenth Congress of the AISF (International Association for Women's Suffrage) in Paris in 1926, collaborated on the International Institute for Intellectual Cooperation, and took an early interest in the development of a united Europe.

Cécile Brunschvicg (center) rewards the devotion of nurses at the Paris region compensation office in the 1930s.

Louise Schroeder flanked by her advisors in Berlin in 1948.

Louise Schroeder

1887–1957, Germany

Female politician and a militant in the Social Democratic Party (SPD), she became the first woman to enter the Bundestag in the Weimar Republic and helped found the Arbeiterwohlfahrt (Institute for Worker's Welfare). Highly active in this movement, in the 1930s and 1940s the Nazis harbored suspicions over her socialist opinions. She was even dismissed from the then German Faculty of Politics, where she had been lecturing since 1925. After 1945, she fought to restore democracy to Germany as a member of Berlin City Council. In 1947, she was eloquent in denouncing the Soviet blockade and became mayor of Berlin. Indefatigable, she also sat on the committee that founded the Freie Universität of Berlin and, after the division of Germany, served as mayor of West Berlin from 1948 to 1951. She became a member of the European Parliament, but also edited the journal, *Das sozialistische Jahrhundert* (The Socialist Century) from 1946 to 1951. Her courage and popularity earned her the award of Great (Federal) cross of Merit, and she was given the freedom of the city of Berlin in 1957.

Anna Kéthly

1889–1976, Hungary

First Hungarian woman to enter Parliament, in 1922, during an extremely conservative regime. Joining the Social Democrat Party (the sole left-wing party permitted), she was the only woman member. She was committed to supporting women's rights, in particular in the fight for female voting rights, which had been defended since 1903 by the Feminist Association founded by Agnes Szabo.

En route for New York, Anna Kéthly stops off in Frankfurt in 1956.

Ana Pauker

1893–1960, Romania

First female foreign minister in Romania from 1947 to 1952. Aged twenty-four, she joined the Romanian Communist Party, and at twenty-nine she was elected onto the Central Committee. In spite of the execution of her husband during the great Stalinist purges of 1938, she became a member of the Secretariat of the Central Committee and then foreign minister, the first woman to hold the post, and finally vice prime minister. She was deposed for "cosmopolitanism" and "deviationism" and arrested in 1953, a victim of Stalin's anti-Semitic purges, no doubt due to her Jewish and bourgeois origins.

Ana Pauker defending herself at a trial against the Communists in 1936.

Germaine Poinso-Chapuis

1901–1981, France

First female minister for public health and population in France, in the government of Robert Schuman in 1947. Lawyer, onetime Resistant, and a moderate feminist of Christian Democrat leanings, she tabled laws on child welfare. She fought against alcoholism and prostitution and named a true equal opportunities staff: five men and five women. She remained in the post for less than a year (from November 1947 to July 1948). The next female minister, Simone Veil, would also hold the public health portfolio some twenty-six years later.

Alva Myrdal

1902–1986, Sweden

First woman to head the Commission of Social Affairs at the UN in 1949; first woman ambassador to India in 1955; minister for disarmament in 1966; first female head of a delegation to the Geneva Conference on Disarmament from 1962 to 1973. She was awarded the Nobel Peace Prize in 1982.

Myrdal exerted a strong influence on the pioneering and progressive policies promoting women implemented by the Danish Social Democrat government that has held power since 1932, introducing maternity leave in 1936 and making contraception available in 1938. A sociologist by training and a dyed-in-the-wool feminist, Alva strove to free women from the scourge of unwanted pregnancy, but also to provide adequate conditions for mothers-to-be (with crèches and free canteen meals). In *Crisis in the Population Question*, she demanded a sustained program of sex education, family benefits, contraception, and abortion practiced legally and without danger by qualified doctors. She went on to tackle the problem of war, in 1961 founding the SIPRI, an international institute for peace research, which attracted scientists from the whole world to pool their researches in the quest for disarmament.

Throughout her life she has concentrated on a specific problem per decade: "In the 1930s, I devoted myself to family policy, in the 1940s to education policy, in the 1950s to the politics of Third World aid, in the 1960s to questions of disarmament, and in the 1970s to the relationship between Church and State." Aged eighty, she once again sounded the alarm declaring that war is an assassination, and that the purpose of contemporary military preparations is mass assassination. She went on to predict that in the century of the atom, its victims would be counted in the millions, claiming the century in which she lived deserved but one name: the age of barbarism.

Federica Montseny

1905–1994, Spain

First female minister in Europe in 1936. An anarchist and militant with the FAI (Iberian Anarchist Federation), affiliated to the CNT (National Confederation of Labor), she became a member of the latter's National Committee. It was so rare to see a Spanish woman mounting the platform during meetings that she was called "the woman who speaks." During the Spanish Popular Front, a left-leaning government, she was appointed minister for health by Largo Caballero. She outlined an ambitious program of health care and prevention. A convinced feminist, in October 1936 she legalized abortion, setting up training centers for women (directed particularly at prostitutes), and placing women in key positions in the health services. She was also a prolific author.

Nafisa Sid Cara

1910–2002, France

Algerian woman who was a member of the French government from 1959 to 1962, the first female minister in the Fifth Republic. She was in this sense a pioneer, as she was when a militant activist for women's social rights and head of a movement to suppress the veil for Muslim women. Her commitment to French Algeria, however, ran counter to the flow of history. (She was the sister of Chérif Sid Cara, co-president, with General Massu of the committee that led the putsch attempting to unseat President de Gaulle). A French teacher, and in 1958 elected member to the French National Assembly representing a constituency in Algiers, she was named by Michel Debré "secretary of state for social questions in Algeria and for the development of the personal status of Muslim law." She then became inspector general for social affairs (until 1975), before in 1979 joining the National Committee studying problems faced by French Muslims. She was made a commander of the Legion of Honor in 2001.

French Premier Michel Debré presenting his government to Général de Gaulle. Nafisa Sid Cara (second row, third from the right) is the sole woman.

Margaret Thatcher and President François Mitterrand at the European summit in Rome in 1990.

Margaret Thatcher

born 1925, Great Britain

Born Margaret Hilda Roberts, she was prime minister of the United Kingdom from 1979 to 1990 (the first such in Europe).

Thatcher's father ran a corner shop, providing his daughter with a window onto the workings and benefits of the market economy. Receiving a grant to study chemistry at Oxford, "Maggie" quickly became the leader of the Conservative student body. She married the wealthy businessman Denis Thatcher, giving birth to twins. She meanwhile studied law and in 1959 was elected as a Conservative MP. Working tirelessly, she slept no more than three or four hours a day. The "Iron Lady," as she came to be known, was much admired for her elephantine memory, but her aloof and over-bearing manner made her enemies.

In 1962, she became under-secretary of state for social security, then for housing, the treasury, and energy. As minster for education in 1970, she made a name for herself by putting an end to free milk in schools. The press had a field day, giving her a reputation for insensitivity. Rising to the head of the Conservative Party in 1975, she trumpeted a creed of liberalism she never abjured: people must be able to work without state hindrance, to spend what they earn, to own a house, to climb the social ladder through courage and hard work, and to enjoy their success as individuals. Clearly her ambition—rooted in drive, conviction, indomitable will, and intelligence—was to lead her country. She had done nothing to keep her right-wing agenda under wraps and it was not long before she was putting it into practice: privatization and the reduction of the role of the state, even if this meant three million unemployed.

In 1981, Irish militants of the IRA demanded to be treated as political prisoners instead of criminals. This demand was turned down and a hunger strike started, resulting in the death of prisoner Bobby Sands. The European media were much exercised by his death and ten thousand people joined his funeral cortège. Thatcher, though, did not waver and eight further deaths followed. Her "coolness" was further demonstrated following the IRA attack in Brighton in 1984, when she and her cabinet were the intended victims; the Conservative party conference which was being held continued as planned.

Economic recession and high unemployment weakened support for her government, but she rallied the population behind her thanks to an outside enemy: the Argentine generals who attempted to claim the Falklands Islands, British overseas territories. Declaring war, UK forces crossed the Atlantic and, with support from the Chilean president General Pinochet, crushed their

Argentine adversaries. To the winner, the spoils: thus it was that she triumphed in the 1983 elections and again in 1987.

Thatcher eventually resigned, having lost the support of her party, in November 1990; she had enjoyed the longest continual period in office of any British prime minister since the nineteenth century.

Simone Veil

born 1927, France

Née Jacob, she became the first female minister for health in France in 1974. She was brought up in Nice, in a perfectly assimilated, non-observant Jewish family. Sitting for her baccalaureate on March 28, 1944, on March 30 she was arrested by the Gestapo: she was only sixteen years old. She experienced the full horror of the Drancy holding camp and of Auschwitz-Birkenau. Her mother died of exhaustion and typhus. Once released, Simone

demonstrated remarkable courage in not showing hatred for her torturers.

On the prison board, she made efforts to improve living conditions in penitentiaries, especially in Algeria. At the directorship of civil affairs, she drafted a law on adoption "in the interests and for the benefit of the child." As minister for health, she strove to improve living conditions for the old and the disabled and was instrumental in extending maternity leave and creating parental leave. Later, in 1976, she widened the social security net to cover the population at large. In 1979, at the head of a (relatively conservative) RPR-UDF list, she became president of the European Parliament, occupying this post up to 1982, before becoming a member of the Constitutional Council (until 2007).

In 2008, she was only the sixth woman to be elected to the French Academy. Her greatest achievement remains the 1975 law that bears her name, which authorized abortion under certain conditions. In the French National Assembly in 1974, Veil had already shown strength and clarity in defending contraception funding and its untrammeled access for minors.

It is thanks to her that the law on contraception, voted on at the end of 1967, was accepted democratically. In Parliament in November 1974, a posse of furious men pelted her with abuse, predicting that she was going to unleash civil war and kick off a steep decline in morality. She determinedly pursued her path, however, demanding that the voices of women—the distressed, ostracized, traumatized, and mutilated women, victims of backstreet abortions—be heard, denouncing the hypocrisy of those who ignore the hundreds of thousands of abortions that take place every year, and highlighting the injustice of penalizing poorer women, while the rich just cross the border to Switzerland; a feminist, she wanted women to be liberated from the curse of constant pregnancy, to live as fully fledged individuals with a part to play in society.

Vigdis Finnbogadottir

born 1930, Iceland

President of Iceland in 1980; re-elected in 1984, 1988, and 1992; first woman president of a democratic nation. Vigdis studied French literature and theater at the Sorbonne, history of theater in Copenhagen, and finally English literature and educational science back in Iceland.

Divorced and mother of an adopted daughter, she has proven a great innovator. A defender of women's rights, she promotes ecology and advocates access to a thorough multilingual education. In 1996, she rejected the notion of standing for a fifth time, becoming instead president of UNESCO's World Commission on the Ethics of Scientific Knowledge and Technology. She founded the International Council of Young Women, whose mission is to promote women's rights across the globe.

Edith Cresson

born 1934, France

The only woman to date to have held the post of French prime minister (1991–92). As minister for agriculture, in 1981, and then as head of the government, she was often the butt of misogynist insults. She named five women ministers. Appointed as a European commissioner in 1994, she was accused of mismanagement and obliged to resign.

Vigdis Finnbogadottir and Ronald Reagan at the Reykjavik summit in 1986.

Vaira Vike-Freiberga

born 1937, Latvia

First female president of Latvia from 1999 to 2007. Her father drowned shortly after she was born. Her family fled massacres perpetrated by the Red Army and often went hungry. From 1954 to 1998, she lived in Canada, where she obtained a Masters in psychology and taught at the University of Montreal. She was chiefly concerned with youth education and with the identity and future of her native Latvia. She became vice president of the Science Council of Canada and a member of the "Council of Women World Leaders" at Harvard. In 1998, she was made director of the Institute of Latvia. Latvia has since joined NATO and the European Union on her watch.

Gro Harlem Brundtland

born 1939, Norway

First female prime minister of Norway, in 1981. As a child, she wanted to be a doctor, like her father; she qualified as a physician becoming director of the school health services. At seven, her father had registered her with the junior section of the Norwegian Labor Party; she went on to lead the party to victory on three occasions. If her father was her model, she outstripped him, though she never forgot to show solidarity with other women, remaining a self-declared and effective feminist.

Gro studied in the United States, obtaining a Masters in public health and receiving a grant from the Harvard School of Public Health. Back in Oslo, she worked with the Ministry for Health from 1965, as well as at the national hospital. Her reputation for competence began to make waves and she became minister for the environment from 1974 to 1979. At forty-one she attained the upper reaches of executive power, becoming prime minister at the head of a social democrat government in 1981, being re-elected in 1986 (until 1989) and again in 1990 (until 1996). In her government the quotas of the two genders are exactly equal. As prime minister, she set up a reserve fund for the future generations, thus making her mark as a pioneer of sustainable development. In 1983 she headed the UNO Commission for the Environment and Development, which submitted a report entitled: "Our Common Future," better known simply as the Brundtland Report. In it one can already read what governmental authorities have only just begun to notice some twenty-five years later: energy demand in Asia will increase by 50 percent; 1.2 billion people live on less than a dollar a day; 20 percent of the population uses 80 percent of the world's resources, etc. The only solution is sustainable development, clearly defined as "development which meets the needs of present generations without compromising the ability of future generations to meet their needs." The Brundtland Report led directly to the 1992 Earth Summit in Rio.

From 1998 to 2003 Gro led the World Health Organization, the first woman to fill what is a post of the highest responsibility. Not only did she spearhead the fight against nicotine addiction, she is also conscious that population explosions impoverish countries and that repeated pregnancies weaken, even kill, those very women who might act as a driving force for stability and progress. She worked diligently for the liberalization of abortion, realizing that "every year, twenty million dangerous terminations are undertaken." At an international conference on population and development in Cairo in 1994, to howls of protest from Muslim and Catholic fundamentalists, she took to the podium to demand that abortion be decriminalized worldwide. She asks hard questions of the supposed "pro-life" lobby: "Morality becomes hypocrisy if it means accepting mothers suffering or dying in connection with unwanted pregnancies. The same conference saw the adoption of the concept of "reproductive health." At the UN, Brundtland declares that the role of the organization should be "the reduction of human suffering" in all lands. In this respect her contribution has certainly proved telling.

Ruth Dreifuss

born 1940, Switzerland

The first female president of the Swiss Confederation in 1999. A graduate in economic sciences from the University of Geneva, she is a journalist, reader at her university, and secretary of the Swiss Trades Union Congress. In 1993, she was elected to the Federal Council after a demonstration by ten thousand Swiss women. She supports maternity benefits, health, and old-age insurance, and opposes restrictions on rights for foreigners. She is also the first Jewish woman to sit on the Federal Council.

Ludmila Jivkova

1942–1981, Bulgaria

Bulgarian minister for culture from 1975 to 1981. She studied history of art at Oxford and in Moscow, became head of the Committee for Arts and Culture in 1975 and a member of the politburo of the Central Committee of the Communist Party. For the six years her ministry lasted, she promoted Bulgarian culture throughout the world.

Johanna Sigurdardottir

born 1942, Iceland

Prime minister of Iceland in 2009 and the first openly homosexual world leader. Mother of two adult sons, since 2002 she has been married to Jonina Leosdottir, a writer. A onetime trade unionist, and five times minister for social affairs, Sigurdardottir has held her seat in the Icelandic Parliament, the

Althing, since 1978. This ex-air hostess became head of the Icelandic government at a time when its economy had slumped dramatically and when many people were losing their savings as bank after bank went into receivership. Months of sometimes turbulent demonstrations had ousted the then right-of-center government. Heading a left-of-center coalition, the Social Democratic Alliance, that leant on the leftist Green party, Johanna promptly launched an attack on those behind the crisis. Proclaimed acting prime minister on Sunday February 1, 2009, by February 2 she was demanding the immediate resignation of the three governors of the Central Bank. The two main nationalized banks are now headed by women and gender parity is total in the government.

Tarja Halonen

born 1943, Finland

First woman to be elected president of Finland, in 2000; re-elected in 2006. This feminist, pacifist, and Third World activist who became head of state was the first to obtain a degree in her family. She has campaigned since her youth for the Rom and Lapp minorities and for cultural diversity, social justice, also chairing an organization defending the rights of homosexuals of both genders.

Tarja Halonen (center) at a meeting with other women leaders on climate problems in Copenhagen in 2009.

A member of the Finnish Social Democrat Party since 1971, she practiced as a trades union lawyer and jurist, before serving as private parliamentary secretary to the prime minister in 1974 and 1975. Her political career really took off in 1977 with her election on to the Helsinki City Council, and then to Parliament (where she sat for more than twenty years).

Tarja was the first Finnish woman to become minister for health and social affairs (from 1987 to 1990), minister for justice in 1990–91, and finally for foreign affairs from 1995 to 2000. A happy unmarried mother, living with a man who was not the father of her child, the couple decided to marry due to problems of protocol when traveling on official business abroad.

In a religiously observant country, where the Lutheran Church is almost a state faith, she has protested against the fact that women cannot be ordained. She is a self-confessed free-thinker, taking a stand against the death penalty and campaigning for the construction of a socially just Europe. "Red Tarja," as she is called, has frequently called for a "fairer globalization."

Mary Robinson
born 1944, Ireland

First female president of the Irish Republic, from 1990 to 1997. The positions she took up during her twenty years as a senator sent shockwaves through this very religious country: in favor of divorce, contraception, and rights for homosexuals, and against discrimination towards illegitimate children. And yet, in what was a moment of high symbolism, Robinson was duly elected the first woman to the post and the first from the Labour Party. In Ireland, however, the powers of the president of the Republic are limited. In 1997, Robinson stepped down to become UN high

Mary Robinson at a congress in Washington on April 13, 2008.

commissioner for human rights until 2002. She was critical of the war in Chechnya and also of the detention camp at Guantanamo.

Hanna Suchocka
born 1946, Poland

First Polish female prime minister, from 1992 to 1993. She focused especially on getting her country into NATO, that "pillar of security and stability in Europe" and a "genuine military power," and rolling back women's rights. Even after the end of her mandate, she continues to exert an influence, mobilizing Christian Democrat deputies at the Council of Europe in an effort to reinforce the position of the pope. The Holy See has opposed a request from the UN to make contraceptives freely available and improve the conditions for women forced to undergo abortions. Like the pope, Hanna Suchoka does not appear to be swayed by the fact that there are 50 million women undergoing abortions each year, many of whom are likely to die on the operation table or suffer serious aftereffects. Indeed for Suchocka, who can be termed a reactionary, they should not be entitled to what the UN calls "reproductive health," which includes control over their own fertility.

She has published a book called *La Caccia* (The Hunt) describing her pursuit of war criminals, in which she accuses the Albanian leaders of Kosovo, including the current (2009) prime minister, Hashim Thaçi, of having been involved in a terrible organ trafficking scandal. In 1999, three hundred Serb prisoners are said to have been transported from Kosovo to Albania and locked up in "private clinics," where surgeons removed their organs before they were killed. At the time the lack of firm evidence made it impossible for her to open an enquiry. But today, after becoming acquainted with the charges in her book, Serbia has asked the ICT to launch an investigation.

Carla del Ponte

born 1947, Switzerland

President of the International Criminal Tribunal (ICT) from 1999 to 2007. Swiss attorney general, she was named co-prosecutor on the Rwandan ICT from 1999 and 2003, and then chief prosecutor for ex-Yugoslavia. Succeeding the Canadian Louise Arbour, she indicted some of those behind the Rwandan genocide, and continues to track down war criminals. In a report submitted in October 2007 to the European ministers for foreign affairs, she notes that Serbia had not sufficiently cooperated on the arrest of leader Radovan Karadžić and Serb General Ratko Mladić, accused of genocide in 1995 for the massacre of around eight thousand Muslims. Her life is under constant threat and she remains one of the most closely protected personalities in the world, but no threat could make this woman of exemplary courage and probity fail in her duty. On January 1, 2008, having reached the end of her mandate, she became Swiss ambassadress to Buenos Aires.

Emma Bonino

born 1948, Italy

A feminist militant since the 1970s, she fought for the legalization of abortion, and in 1978 the Fascist law of 1932 framed to "protect the race" was finally repealed in Italy. Emma was elected to the Chamber of Deputies from 1976 to 1994. In 1995, she was European Commissioner in ECHO (humanitarian aid). In 2007, she became minister for European Affairs and Foreign Trade in the Prodi government.

Mary MacAleese

born 1951, Ireland

Second woman to become president of Ireland (after Mary Robinson), but the first to be born in Northern Ireland. A lawyer, she taught law and criminology before heading a television station and an electricity company. A fervent Catholic, a nationalist and a conservative, she proved extremely popular. She was the first woman to be appointed vice chancellor of Queen's University, Belfast. Elected president of Ireland in 1997 (in what was a rare state of affairs in politics, she not only succeeded a woman but was also pitted against three female rivals), she was re-elected in 2004. She calls herself a feminist, hopes that women attain executive positions and that they can be ordained as priests, but she is utterly opposed to abortion and divorce. She has declared herself in favor of Church control over education, but her powers are limited.

Irina Bokova

born 1952, Bulgaria

The first woman to be elected Director-General of UNESCO in October 2009, she carried the vote on the fifth poll by eliminating the Egyptian Farouk Hosni. Daughter of a leader of the Bulgarian Communist Party, she studied at the Institute of International Relations and became an adviser at the UN headquarters in New York, and then coordinator of relations between her nation and the European Union, as well as Bulgarian ambassadress to France. She was a member and then vice-president of the Commission on Foreign Affairs from 2001 to 2005. Her involvement with UNESCO dates from 2005 with the position of ambassadress, before joining the Executive Board in 2007. Divorced, she is the mother of two children, and possesses a perfect command of English, French, Spanish, and Russian. Almost as soon as she was elected, this friend of Simone Veil's attended the Women's Forum at Deauville (a female "Davos"), thus demonstrating that her priorities include gender equality.

Ségolène Royal

born 1953, France

French female politician. President of the Poitou-Charentes region, in 2007 she became the first woman in France to reach the second round of a French presidential election. A graduate in economics from the University of Nancy, and then from the prestigious "Sciences Po" in 1978, she joined the Socialist Party the same year, before entering the Ecole Nationale d'Administration (ENA, whence many professionals in the French civil service are recruited). There she met François Hollande, who became her companion.

She acted as an official representative during the general secretariat of President Mitterrand in 1982. In 1988 she was elected member for the Deux-Sèvres constituency and in Parliament campaigned in particular for a bill aimed at preventing violence against women, and another opposed to the commercial and degrading use of the human body in advertising. Minister for the environment in 1992–93, she became minister delegate for secondary education from 1997 to 2000. In 1999, Ségolène Royal authorized school nurses to prescribe the morning-after pill to girls "in a situation of distress or in an extreme emergency." Minister delegate for the family and childhood with Élisabeth Guigou between 2000 and 2002, she created nearly 20,000 child-minding places, as well as introducing a fortnight's paternity leave. In 2004, she was successful in the region of Poitou-Charentes, the then prime minister's stronghold. She is not the first woman to become president of a region, but in 2004 she was the only one in France. She refused aid to firms that delocalize and make workers redundant while turning a profit or damaging the environment. When she announced her candidature for the presidential election, one fellow Socialist exclaimed: "But who'll look after the children?" (Her companion was busy as first secretary of the Socialist Party). Her bid, however, failed, and Nicolas Sarkozy was elected in her stead.

Angela Merkel
born 1954, Germany

In 2005 she became the first female chancellor of a united Germany. Accepting the prevailing communism of the time, her father, a vicar, and her mother, an English teacher, were not involved in politics. After the fall of the Berlin Wall she joined the Democratic Awakening party and quickly rose to

become a recognized political force, the fact that she grew up in East Germany and that Germany was intent on rapid reunification proving a help. She was also aided by the support of Helmut Kohl, who in 1991 named her minister for women and youth, and then, in 1994, minister for the environment. But the woman Kohl dubbed "the girl" was soon to show her teeth and her thirst for power: when her patron went through a sticky patch, she turned the knife and, in 2000, succeeded him as leader of the Christian Democratic Union (CDU).

The first German woman to attain the top governmental position of chancellor (aged only fifty-one), she leads a coalition government implementing firm and not particularly popular—but ever prudent—austerity measures. Governing as close as possible to the center, and especially not too far to the left, she is prepared to accept immigration provided that "mosque domes are not built ostentatiously higher than church steeples." No less intransigent when Germany took over the presidency of the European Union, if she criticized Bush for

Guantanamo, she also rebuked Putin for perverting democracy in Russia. A convinced European, her politics is all patience, toughness, and pragmatism. She was re-elected in 2009.

Dalia Grybauskaité

born 1956, Lithuania

The first female President of the Republic of Lithuania, in July 2009. An economics graduate from the Institute of Finance and Economics in Leningrad (LFEI) in the USSR in 1983, she gained an economic science doctorate from the Academy of Sciences in Moscow in 1988, pursuing her studies in the US (Georgetown University, Washington D.C.).

Multilingual, she speaks Lithuanian, Russian, English, French, and Polish. A karate champion and teacher in Vilnius, she acted as vice-minister for Foreign Affairs in 2000–2001, Finance Minister between 2001 and 2004, European Commissioner for financial programming and budget between 2004 and 2009. Scarcely had she been elected than she virulently attacked the preceding government for failing to tackle inflation, accusing it of "feasting during a cholera epidemic."

Iula Timochenko

born 1960, Ukraine

A key figure in the Orange Revolution of 2004. Pro-Western President Viktor Yushchenko named her prime minister in 2005, only to dismiss her seven months later. In September 2007, once again allied to Yushchenko, she won the early parliamentary elections, her party, Biot, obtaining 32 percent of the votes—ten points more than at the previous elections—and beating the outgoing pro-Russian prime minister, Viktor Yanukovych, to become prime minister once again in December 2007. This pretty woman has made a fortune in the gas trade and is studious in her defense of the interests of the Privat group. Since the Orange Revolution, this consortium has extended its tentacles throughout the economy and into the energy and metallurgical industries, as well as into the financial sphere, earning her the moniker of the "Gas Princess."

Lívia Járóka

born 1972, Bulgaria

First Rom member of the European Parliament in 2004. Given that Gypsies have tended to be regarded as second-class citizens in Bulgaria, it is very encouraging that a woman from the Rom community (by her father; her mother is Jewish) has been elected—on a right-of-center platform.

Lívia Járóka.

Elected as a deputy on a Liberal ticket, Prime Minister Trudeau named her minister for science and technology. She was thus the first woman from Quebec to serve in a federal government. In 1974, she became minister for the environment and then minister of transport from 1975 to 1979. In 1980, Jeanne Sauvé was elected to preside over the House and thus became the first woman Speaker in the federal legislature. Imposing bilingualism, she observed that her appointment represents a significant move forward for women throughout the country. A recipient of many awards, at her death she was honored with a state funeral in the Cathedral of Marie-Reine-du-Monde.

Jeanne Sauvé.

Jeanne Sauvé

1922–1993, Canada

Governor general of Canada from 1984 to 1990, the first woman in the post for 116 years. Née Jeanne Mathilde Benoit, she was dubbed the "woman of the firsts," even when she was at Notre-Dame-du-Rosaire in Ottawa. For twenty years, she held down a career as a journalist, before launching out into politics in 1972, rapidly climbing the slippery pole without apparent effort, driven by an ambition to make the most of her talents.

Lise Payette

born 1931, Canada

Hailing from Quebec, she became the first minister for women in 1976. A feminist journalist, she gave stay-at-home housewives, whom she considers too passive, the ironic nickname of "Yvettes." It was these women who came out against the minister, refusing to vote "yes" in a referendum that could have led to independence for Quebec from the Canadian Confederation. She can be seen as a leader who, desirous of enforcing equality, sought to minimize the important traditional place of women, which also has its part to play in the construction of national identity.

Madeleine Albright

born 1937, United States

First female US secretary of state, the highest political post ever reached by a woman in the history of the

United States. Born Marie Korbelová, into a Czechoslovakian Jewish family, she speaks seven languages. An American citizen since 1957, she is a graduate in political science, holds a doctorate in public law, and helped frame much of President Jimmy Carter's policy from 1978 to 1981. In 1993, she joined the Clinton administration, who named her ambassador to the United Nations. Although she subsequently clarified her remarks and expressed regret for her hasty words, she met with much criticism when she rejected the term "genocide" for events in Rwanda and appeared to disregard the possibility of half a million Iraqi children dying due to sanctions. From 1997 to 2001, as secretary of state, she flew around the world praising democracy and human rights.

Madeleine Albright.

Nancy Pelosi

born 1940, United States

The first woman in the US to rise to the much-coveted post of leader of the House of Representatives, in 2007. Her father was mayor of Baltimore, her husband is a real-estate magnate and they have five children. She speaks for the Democratic Party in northern California and is a staunch defender of social justice.

Progressive, she supports the right to abortion, non-custodial sentencing, and is opposed to school prayers and to the maintenance of troops in Iraq. But in 2001 she voted for the Patriot Act, which, under the pretext of combating terrorism, allows for arbitrary detention.

Representing the eighth district of California at Congress since 1987, she has been the figurehead of her party in the House of Representatives since 2002.

Nancy Pelosi.

Kim Campbell

born 1947, Canada

First female minister for justice in Canada, in 1990; first female minister for defense in 1993; first woman prime minister from June to November 1993, the only female head of a national government in North America. Holder of two baccalaureates (majoring in arts and law), she obtained a doctorate in government from the London School of Economics. She taught political sciences at the University of British Colombia and at Vancouver Community College.

As member and minister, she battled to head the Progressive Conservatives—she is more of a "traditional" conservative herself. She started out as a very popular prime minister, but she eschewed innovative measures and her term ended in defeat. She went on to become president of the Council of Women World Leaders.

Hillary Rodham Clinton

born 1948, United States

Sixty-seventh US secretary of state. As first lady, Clinton stood firm behind her husband, Bill, even when, as president in office, he was accused of sexual harassment. At the same time, as a renowned lawyer, a militant Democrat, and a defender of the rights of the child, she tried to force through a Social Security program for the poorest in society. Democrat senator for New York since 2000, Clinton was the leading candidate for the Democratic presidential election in 2008, though she was not the first female candidate to run for the presidency of the United States, since Victoria Claflin Woodhull had had that honor in 1872 (Woodhull was the translator of the *Communist Manifesto* in America and an advocate of free love, a pioneer who acquired the nickname "Mrs Satan" as well as a spell in prison). Clinton lost at the Democratic primaries to Barack Obama, who, on his election, chose her as his secretary of state for foreign affairs.

Hillary Clinton during the Presidential election campaign in January 2008.

Michaëlle Jean

born 1957, Canada

Condoleezza Rice

born 1954, United States

First African-American woman to become a presidential adviser (to George W. Bush), in 2001, and then secretary of state in 2004. Born in Birmingham, Alabama, a segregated state in the southern United States, when she was a fifteen-year-old coed her father, a preacher, told her she would have to do "twice as well" as a white person to attain the same privileges. Doctor of political science, she joined the staff at Stanford University. Condoleezza Rice impressed President Bush, who appointed her head of the National Security Council in 2001. In 2004, she became the first African-American secretary of state. She basically piloted United States foreign policy, in particular with regard to Eastern European countries, in which she is a specialist.

The American secret services played a role in regime change in Ukraine and Georgia, the so-called "soft revolutions." Rice justifies the coherence of the war in Iraq as an effort to import democracy—just as Europe was "saved from chaos" at the end of the Second World War.

Of Haitian origin, she became governor general of Canada in 2005. Originally from Port-au-Prince, Jean has lived in Quebec since the age of eleven, when her family fled the dictator Duvalier. A naturalized Canadian, she possesses perfect command of five languages (French, English, Spanish, Italian, and Creole), entering teaching and then becoming a journalist and TV presenter in Quebec, notably on a news show called *Les Grands reportages*.

She worked for eight years for an association aiding female victims of marital violence and carried out a major investigation entitled "Wounded Sexuality" that made an impact in the National Assembly. She is not the first immigrant woman governor, being preceded by Adrienne Clarkson, but she is the first black woman to be called "Her Most Honorable Excellency," to represent the Queen of England, and to be commander in chief of the Canadian armed forces. Barack Obama's first visit abroad after his election as president of the United States was to Michaëlle Jean, and they spoke about Haiti. Even if the post of governor is primarily ceremonial, Jean, a living symbol of Canadian cultural diversity, performs it with gusto and humanity.

Mary Eugenia Charles

1916–2005, Dominica

First woman to be prime minister of Dominica—in 1980, reelected in 1985, and from 1990 to 1995 (more than twelve years in total), and the first female prime minister in the Caribbean. A lawyer by training, she was a co-founder of the Freedom Party. The "freedom" concerned was chiefly that of the press, and later, when she had attained the top post in the executive, of the larger banana growers. Finally, she was also a champion of the free circulation of capital. It is due to her policies that the island of Dominica has been transformed into a fully-fledged tax haven.

Janet Jagan

1920–2009, Republic of Guyana

Prime minister (from March 1997 to December of the same year) and then president of the Cooperative Republic of Guyana from December 1997 to 1999, succeeding her husband, Cheddi Jagan, in the post. American-born, white, Jewish, Marxist (at her beginnings), she had founded, with her husband, the Communist newspaper *Mirror* in 1943, the Progressive People's Party (PPP) in 1950, and helped the country free itself from its British overlords. Leader of the PPP, she was elected president of Guyana aged seventy-seven, but she was unable to improve the situation in a country decolonized in haste and torn by racist strife and widespread corruption.

Janet Jagan.

Lydia Gueiler-Tejada

born 1921, Bolivia

President of Bolivia from 1979 to 1980. An accountant and a member of the Movimiento Nacionalista Revolucionario, she sat as a member of the Congress of Bolivia from 1956 to 1964. After a coup d'état, she lived in exile for nineteen years. On returning in 1979, she was elected leader of the House and then became acting president. Gueiler was subsequently overthrown by a third coup d'état, though this did not prevent her from serving as ambassador to Germany and Venezuela. She is a self-declared feminist and has published *Woman and the Revolution*.

Portia Simpson-Miller together with Hugo Chavez in 2007.

Portia Simpson-Miller

born 1945, Jamaica

First woman to be prime minister of Jamaica, in 2006. Although born in a shantytown and having had little schooling, she became a Member of Parliament in 1976. Once in charge, her popularity swelled: a woman of the people, it was felt only she could save the population from their abjection. Between 1989 and 2001, she was minister several times, including of Labour and of Sports.

Violeta Chamorro

born 1929, Nicaragua

First female president in Central America, she was president of the Republic of Nicaragua from 1990 to 1997. Chamorro is the widow of Pedro Chamorro, an opponent of the regime led by the dictator Somoza and editor-in-chief of the anti-governmental *Prensa*. An anti-Sandinista (the Sandino revolution defended peasants and workers), she took over the reins of the paper after her husband was assassinated in 1978. The Sandinistas suspected her of receiving money from the United States so as to unseat the government. When she took power after a civil war lasting ten years, she abolished military service, put thousands of weapons out of commission, and reduced the armed forces by 25 percent, though this did little to stop the Contras, armed by the United States, from perpetrating further atrocities.

Mireya Moscovo de Aria

born 1946, Republic of Panama

President of the Republic of Panama from 1999 to 2004. Widow of the former president, she has been known to muzzle the press and her opponents alike. Her country continues to exist under the influence of the United States, which exerts direct control over the customs and transport, due to the Panama Canal. She has been discredited by corruption scandals.

Michelle Bachelet

born 1951, Chile

In 2006 she became the first woman to be elected president (for four years) by universal suffrage in all South America. Bachelet was just twenty-two when Socialist President Salvador Allende was overthrown by General Pinochet. Her father, a general in the air force, Alberto Bachelet, was arrested and tortured to death by his fellow officers. Michelle committed her cause to that of the Socialist Youth and was soon undertaking covert actions, as was her mother, a free-thinking archaeologist and advocate of women's liberation. Both were arrested, tortured, then permitted to go into exile, ordeals that proved character-forming for Michelle, a highly energetic woman who never thinks of herself as a victim.

Her private life has often been at odds with the standards of the Catholic Church, all-powerful on the continent. Marrying a Chilean comrade while they were both in exile in the GDR, in 1977 she had a son and in 1984 a daughter, but shortly afterwards left her spouse. She had a relationship with a member of the armed branch of the Communist Party, and then with a doctor with right-wing leanings with whom she had a daughter in 1992. As divorce was prohibited until 2004, she thus had a child by a lover while still married.

Adviser to the Ministry of Health, and the only woman to enter the National Academy of Strategic and Political Studies, being top of her year, an adviser for the Ministry of Defense, she became defense minister in 2002, the first woman in the post in Latin America. She then made a bid for the top position. Energetic, wreathed in smiles and straight-talking, she carried the day due to her manifest competence and hard work, and a gift for listening to the people that made "Michelle" hugely popular. The government she put in place in March 2006 had an equal number of men and women, with the latter in the key positions of defense and the economy.

In Chile, a land where 18 percent of the population lives below the poverty line, Bachelet did her best to improve life for the least able: hospital care was made free for the old, numerous child-minding places were created, and the minimum pension increased. She also did much for the large numbers of young Chilean girls (14 percent) who become pregnant, making it possible for them to take the morning-after pill without parental consent. Catholic reaction was virulent (and in the end it carried the day: in April 2008, the Constitutional Court prohibited the open sale of this type of contraception), while feminist associations reproached her for not seeking to authorize abortion. Caught between a rock and a hard place, some cannot forgive her for holding back, while others think she has gone too far. In August 2007, a huge demonstration, organized by a powerful workers' confederation of 150,000 people, took place, objecting to the neoliberal economic policies followed by the government. Although Bachelet scored 80 percent approval ratings in a 2009 poll, she was unable to stand again in the 2010 presidential elections, due to the Chilean constitution's one-term restriction.

Cristina Fernández Kirchner

born 1953, Argentina

First female president of Argentina in 2007. She was a direct successor to her husband Nestor Kirchner, who, in power since 2003, had promoted economic growth in his country. Having announced that she would continue to pursue her husband's policies, the Argentines voted in droves for her, electing her in the first round with 45 percent of the vote. In what is still a rare state of affairs in the world of politics, her main competitor was also a woman, Elisa Carrió (who polled 23 percent of the vote).

Nicia Maldonado Cruz

DOB unknown, Venezuela

Amerindian from Venezuela, in 2006 she was named minister for indigenous affairs. Many of the country's 3,200 indigenous communities are suffering from serious malnutrition, the first urgent problem confronting the minister. The minister then organized the first bilateral meeting between "the brothers of Venezuela and Colombia," laying the foundations for "indigenous socialist communities."

Casimira Rodriguez Romero

born 1966, Bolivia

Quechua Amerindian and minister of justice in Bolivia since 2006. A house servant aged thirteen, she looked after fifteen people for eighteen hours a day, unpaid. Finding the strength to rebel, in 1987 she founded the Domestic Workers' Trade Union. She managed to forge an alliance together with agricultural workers' organizations, miners, coca planters, and indigenous groups. She is backed by the movement of Evo Morales; when he gained power, she found herself being offered the justice portfolio. Overwhelmed and overawed, she finally accepted so as to walk "with head held high" among her community. The tough world of politics proved very different from the mainly female environment of self-help associations, however. Yet Romera has kept going. "So many children shouldn't be unable to go to school or have unhealthy diets, like when I did when I was a little girl. Our *wawas* (children) also suffer from mistreatment, violence, and rape. I would like to see the day when Bolivian children are able to grow up with parents who love them and eat enough not to be hungry."

Casimira Rodriguez Romero.

Qingling Song and her husband in 1924.

Qingling Song
1893–1981, China

Vice president, honorary acting president, and one-time president of China. Her parents opposed her relationship with Sun Yat-sen, founder of the Republican and Nationalist Party, and, afraid that she might become his concubine, kept her in Shanghai. Qingling escaped to Japan where she married Sun Yat-sen who had just obtained a divorce. Thus, aged twenty-two, she became the new president of China's wife, and then his widow, when he died in 1924. Two years later Qingling Song was elected to the Kuomintang Central Executive Committee. While her elder sister, Ailing,

became one of the richest businesswomen in China, her younger sister, Mei Ling, married Chang Kai-shek, the general and statesman. Ever industrious, especially in the area of women's rights, Qingling, who founded the Chinese Defense League, joined the Communists, finding herself in conflict with her sister. Mao Zedong appointed her vice president of the Central Popular Government, and in the 1950s, she was an unofficial ambassadress to India, Burma, Pakistan, and Indonesia. After a miscarriage that left her unable to have children, she focused on social concerns, especially the welfare of mothers-to-be and infants. She set up the magazine *China Reconstructs* (now *China Today*) and was acting vice president (chair) from 1968 to 1972. Although critical of the Central Committee, shortly before her death she was named honorary president of the People's Republic.

Yanjmaa Sühbaataryn
1893–1963, Mongolia

In 1953–54 she became the second female head of state in the world (after Anchimaa-Toka, in the Tuvinian People's Republic). Actually, she was only acting president and, like many female leaders after her, owed her position to widowhood. Interestingly, having kept her patronymic (as is common for Mongolian women), she took her husband's name only after he was killed. This allowed her to appear as her late husband's reincarnation and also as a "heroine" ("baatar" means "hero"). She nonetheless had merits of her own, since she had been a member of the Politburo of the Revolutionary People's Party from 1940 to 1954; secretary of the Central Committee from 1941 to 1947; member of the Presidium of the Lesser Khural (executive committee of the State Great Khural, or national assembly) from 1940 to 1950, and member of the Great Khural from 1950 to 1962.

Vijaya Lakshmi Pandit

1900–1990, India

The first woman to be elected chief delegate at the United Nations General Assembly.

Daughter of a president of the National Congress and sister of Prime Minister Jawaharlal Nehru, she was cosseted and educated by home tutors. Playing a part in political life, she joined the civil disobedience movement and spent three stints in prison. A member of the Legislative Assembly of the United Provinces, in 1937 she became minister for health in the provincial government.

High commissioner for India in London, ambassadress to the Soviet Union and then to the United States, Ms. Pandit was an active campaigner for women and children's rights. From 1941 to 1943 she chaired the All-India Women's Conference, creating and becoming president of All-India Save the Children.

Sirimavo Bandaranaike

1916–2000, Sri Lanka

Prime minister in 1960 and first female head of government in the world. Like many powerful Asian women, she replaced her husband after his assassination. From 1960 to 1965, and from 1970 to 1977, she was prime minister; it was during this term that Ceylon changed its name to Sri Lanka (in 1972), and then again, from 1994 to 2000, while her daughter was president. She came from a Buddhist family but, although educated by Christian nuns (as so often in very wealthy families), her political orientation was resolutely socialist: she oversaw the nationalization of banks, insurance, and oil companies, as well as partnerships with the Soviet Union and Maoist China. As with Golda Meir, it was said that she was the "only man" in the government. Yet, instead of trying to settle the grievous Tamil question, which soon turned into a civil war, and faced with the ambitions of her daughter, Chandrika, she strove to hold onto the reins of power at all costs. In the end, though, she was destined to fail. Resigning in August 2000, she executed her electoral duties and died two months later. She holds the longevity record for a head of government (eighteen years over three terms).

Mao Zedong shaking Sirimavo Bandaranaike's hand in 1963.

Nehru and his daughter Indira Gandhi in 1959.

Indira Gandhi

1917–1984, India

Prime minister of India from 1966 to 1977 and 1980 to 1984 (sixteen years over two terms). She was the second female head of government, after Sirimavo Bandaranaike in Sri Lanka. Her name is deceptive, as she did not descend from the famous Mohandas Gandhi, who fought to free India from colonialism. She is in fact the daughter of Nehru, the founder of independent India, and leader of the country after 1947.

When young, she was an enthusiastic nationalist and was imprisoned by the British. Her family belonged to the higher caste of the Brahmans, and Indira Nehru studied at top institutions in Calcutta, and then in Europe (Geneva and Oxford). Gandhi is the name of her husband, a lawyer she married, even though he came from a lower caste, and with whom she had two sons: Rajiv (in 1944) and Sanjay (in 1946).

Widowed at forty-three, she grew increasingly close to her father, becoming indispensable to him,

both as an acute, even authoritative adviser on political matters, and as a female figure who accompanied him on his diplomatic travels. Becoming better known abroad, at home she was elected as a member of the powerful Congress Party in 1938, becoming its head in 1959, before being appointed minister of information. Finally, in 1966, she obtained power in the "biggest democracy in the world."

Within the country, she wielded power with an iron fist that stifled opposition, in particular from the Communists, though she proved quarrelsome abroad. In 1971, she entered the so-called War of Bangladeshi Liberation. India's victory resulted in the splitting off of East Pakistan, which became Bangladesh. The resultant tensions and conflicts remained unresolved, however, and the two historic adversaries embarked on a nuclear arms race. Moreover, Gandhi invaded and annexed the tiny Himalayan state of the Sikkim. This victory, and the first nuclear test in 1974, made her into a kind of "war goddess." In a country where women are often considered inferior to men, Indira began by being extremely popular. A sort of incarnation of a deity in the Hindu pantheon, she appeared as the embodiment of power and also as a mother figure, with her graying hair neatly concealed beneath the traditional veil. Indirama, she was called: "Indira, our venerated mother." But her policies could not feed her famished people and rebellions were sparked, indignation fired by a program of enforced sterilization that aimed to reduce India's population explosion. (According to UN experts, a policy of birth control was absolutely essential. Doctor Nayyar, Indira Gandhi's personal physician, and a woman, became the minister for health and family planning responsible for its implementation.) Indira Gandhi responded to such grievances by proclaiming a state of emergency, underlining the dictatorial appearance of her governance still further.

Beaten in 1977, she returned to power in 1980, now lending an ear to astrologers and soothsayers

Indira Gandhi in the 1970s.

Corazon Aquino

1933–2009, Philippines

First female president of the Philippines in 1986. A successful student in New York, Corazon (Cory) Cojuango married Senator Benigno Aquino. As an opponent of the dictator, Marcos, he was imprisoned, then exiled. On returning in 1983, he was assassinated as he alighted from his plane, his funeral being followed by a million people. When his supposed assassins were acquitted, popular indignation knew no bounds. The fifty-three-year-old widow and mother of five stood at the presidential elections in 1986, enjoying great popular support. Marcos won the elections thanks to massive fraud, but enormous demonstrations, strikes, and powerful popular movements forced him to flee. Cory Aquino was proclaimed president, attempting to restore justice to a country eaten away by corruption, its treasury plundered by Marcos and his wife. Doing her utmost to kick-start the economic recovery of a country in which more than half live in abject poverty, she was also popular in the West, negotiating to reschedule the debt and to attract investors, women especially. By the end of her mandate in 1992, the situation in the Philippines had not improved a great deal, but the country had succeeded in ridding itself of dictatorship.

in her decisions. But she was suspected of electoral fraud, embezzlement, and of attempting to promote her son Sanjay as her successor to ensure the dynasty. When the Sikhs revolted and took refuge in the holy city of Amritsar, she repressed their demands for independence with savagery, even ordering troops to take the hallowed Golden Temple. The army fired into the crowd, including on unarmed women and children. Shortly afterwards, she was herself assassinated by one of her bodyguards, a Sikh.

Governing such a poor country, with its castes, languages, and religions was no easy task. It has to be noted, however, that the path of nonviolence so courageously employed by a man, the "Mahatma" Gandhi, was succeeded by recourse to violence and war, used without scruple by a woman, Indira Gandhi. Nowadays, Indian women continue to be burned alive when their family cannot raise a dowry, female fetuses are still aborted, and newborn girls killed, to the point that in the India of 2007 there were 50 million more men than women.

Pratibha Devisingh Patil

born 1934, India

Becoming president of India on July 19, 2007, she was the first woman to fill this post (Indira Gandhi was prime minister). With three husbands, two children, thorough studies, and a faultless career, she trained as a lawyer, became a member of the Congress Party, and was easily elected as an MP. Deputy minister of education in 1967, she held the tourism and social affairs portfolios, acting as minister of state from 1972 to 1978. Above all, she became the first female governor of the state of Rajasthan. She was designated as a candidate for the presidency at the instigation of Sonia Gandhi, thanks to her long fidelity to the Nehru-Gandhi family, and won the election following a rather hard-hitting campaign, declaring that, once president, she would not sit on her hands.

Han Myung-Sook together with Jacques Chirac, at the Élysée Palace, Paris in 2006.

Han Myung-Sook

born 1944, South Korea

First active woman prime minister of South Korea in 2006–07. (She was not exactly the first in this post as she was preceded by Chang Sang, who, however, only lasted twenty days, from July 11 to 31, 2002).

Han Myung-Sook is an upstanding figure and a convinced feminist who studied Christian theology and French literature (in June 2006, she inaugurated the Korean garden planted on the roof of the new University of Paris VII).

In the 1970s, she fought against the dictatorship of General Park Chung-hee and was tortured and imprisoned. In 1987 she set up the KWAU (Korea

Women's Association United) and, in 2001, she was appointed minister of sexual equality, before, in 2003, becoming environment minister. She succeeded in repealing a law that had subjected the wife entirely to the head of the family. She travels a great deal to keep up good relations with many countries, especially those useful for her country's economy. Nigeria is one such, since Korea has no oil of its own and imports large quantities in exchange for modernizing that country's rail network. As she has declared, Seoul is intent on tripling its assistance to Africa. For all that, Han has not neglected contacts with Kazakhstan, Uzbekistan, and the United Arab Emirates, and was glad of the visit by the European Parliament aimed at improving Korea's relationships with its neighbors, Japan in particular.

Makiko Tanaka

born 1944, Japan

Japanese politician and first female foreign minister, from April 2001 to January 2002. She studied at Germantown Friends School in the United States, obtaining a BA from Waseda University. Daughter of Minister Kakuei Tanaka, at a very young age she was working in her father's Etsuzankai Organization. Hugely popular, she took on the role of "first lady" when her mother fell ill.

She was elected to the Diet in 1993 on the demise of her father. Aged fifty-seven, Prime Minister Koizumi appointed her foreign minister, but she was forced to step down by the ruling Liberal Democratic Party amid controversies and accusations of daring to criticize Koizumi. In 2002, Tanaka resigned from the Diet on suspicion of having purloined money from one of her secretaries. The Tokyo Court of Justice found in her favor,

however, and she later ran as an independent candidate for the Diet, though she now supports the Japanese Democratic Party. It cannot be denied that as a politician she possesses a fiery tongue. On a visit to the United States, Tanaka made waves when she called George W. Bush "an asshole." In Japan, a country where equality between women's and men's rights dates from only 1986, women make up less than 10 percent of the members of the Diet. Makiko, however, who kept her maiden name on marrying Naoki Suzuki in 1969, has declared that the Japanese would be prepared to accept a woman prime minister.

Chandrika Kumaratunge Bandaranaike

born 1945, Sri Lanka

First female president of the Republic of Sri Lanka in 1994. More than just "her father's daughter" (her father was prime minister of Sri Lanka from 1956 to his assassination, by a Buddhist, in 1959), she is the daughter of Sirimavo Bandaranaike, who, in 1960, became the world's first female prime minister. Chandrika studied political science in Paris, took part in the protests in May 1968 and worked for the prestigious daily, *Le Monde*.

Returning to Colombo, she was prime minister for four months in 1994, and then president from 1994 until 2005, naming her mother as prime minister when she became president. Her husband, a Sri Lankan movie star, was also murdered. She lost an eye in an assassination attempt by the Tamil Tigers in 1999, though she was no more effective than her mother in negotiating with these rebels who have long demanded a separate state.

Chinese Prime Minister Wen Jiabao meeting Khaleda Zia in 2005.

blows. Unfortunately the majority of the population still lives in abject poverty and its women remain downtrodden and disadvantaged. In 2007, she was arrested for corruption in a procurement and contract award scandal, and jailed.

Khaleda Zia

born 1945, Bangladesh

First female prime minister of Bangladesh, from 1991 to 1996, and again from 2001 to 2006. Widow of the assassinated General Ziaur (Zia) Rahman, she replaced him at the head of the conservative Bangladesh Nationalist Party, fighting against his assassins. She was imprisoned on several occasions but, supported by the entire family clan, still managed to become prime minister. Election campaigns in Bangladesh are often extremely violent: her camp and that of her rival, Hasina Wajed, repeatedly came to

Megawati Setiawati Soekarnoputri

born 1946, Indonesia

President from 2001 to 2004 and the first woman to head the largest Muslim country in the world. Like many other female leaders, she is a "daughter of" a famous ruler. Her father was the country's first president after independence and it was the name Soekarno (Sukarno) that propelled her to power. She was elected to the People's Representative Council in 1987 and became president of the Indonesian Democratic Party in 1993.

Sheik Hasina Wajed

born 1947, Bangladesh

She governed Bangladesh between 1996 and 2001. Almost her entire family was assassinated by the military in 1975. Her father was prime minister. Replacing him at the head of the political party he created, the Awami League, she became prime minister in turn in 1996. She kept up a constant rivalry with Khaleda Zia and accused her of fomenting a grenade attack at a public meeting in 2004. Unleashing the troops on the capital Dacca, casualties ran into thousands, with many dead. Hasina also accused Khaleda Zia of having swelled the electoral roll in her favor by creating 14 million phony voters. It is hard to see the benefits Bangladeshis might have reaped from her stint at their country's helm. She was imprisoned for embezzlement in July 2007 but became Prime Minister once again in 2009.

Sheik Hasina Wajed in the 1990s.

Gloria Macapagal-Arroyo

born 1947, Philippines

First female vice president of the Philippines from 1998 to 2001 and the second female president in 2001, reelected in 2004. As with so many leading Asian women, she is a "daughter of"—namely of former President Diosdado Macapagal, known as "the Incorruptible." She studied in the US (at Georgetown University, at the same time as Bill Clinton). Aquino appointed her under-secretary of state for trade and industry from 1989 to 1992. A Member of the Christian Democrat party, Macapagal-Arroyo was then elected as a senator, until 1998. Made vice president in 1998, she acted simultaneously as secretary of state for social affairs and development.

As president-in-office, accused of aggravated corruption, she fled, leaving the vice president (who, allegedly, may also have embezzled funds) to keep the seat warm. For her second mandate, things became even murkier with accusations of ballot-rigging. Even Aquino asked her to stand down, and ten of her ministers resigned. She remained immovable, arrogant, and self-assured.

In 2006, this fervent Catholic, whose self-appointed roles include "defending God and moral values," signed a statute abolishing the death penalty. But who is responsible for the violence, political assassinations, and kidnappings? Who killed 180 journalists and political opponents during 2006 alone? Macapagal-Arroyo has accused the military, who are old hands at arranging coups d'état. In 2007, a contingent tried to mount a seventh mutiny, asking the army "no longer to support Mrs Arroyo, whose presidency is contrary to the Constitution," but they found themselves behind bars. Then, when women took to the streets in celebration of Woman's Day, she ordered the police to disperse them with truncheons.

Benazir Bhutto

1953–2007, Pakistan

Prime minister of Pakistan for a total of four and a half years from 1988 to 1990 and 1993 to 1996. First female governmental head in a Muslim country.

Her father, Zulfikar Ali Bhutto, was hanged in 1979 (she was also the granddaughter of the founder of the most important political party in 1947). Her father brought her up to believe she had a great political destiny, and she studied in the same universities he had attended—the best in the United States and in England (she became president of the Student Union at Oxford)—and appointed her as his assistant, so that she met Gandhi in 1972.

After his exile, she returned to head the party founded by her mother, the begum Nusrat Bhutto. When the Pakistan People's Party (PPP) won the elections, she became prime minister, quite legally, though the impression was that Pakistan had become a

monarchy. As a fine-looking woman of thirty-five, who faced Islamists head-on, she earned esteem, though she was soon being accused of "corruption and incompetence," dismissed, and her husband imprisoned. Yet she was to return, with the aid of the Pakistani military and the Afghan Taliban, and was complicit in the shameless enrichment of her husband, whom she had no hesitation in promoting to the Ministry for Investment. Once again, she was removed from power in 1996, leaving a parlous economic situation behind her. But from her exile in Dubai and London, in 2007 this skillful politician heard the news that the Pakistan government of President Pervez Musharraf had lifted the charges against her; realizing that he needed her, her popularity, and her powerful party, the PPP, she returned to Karachi in October and was acclaimed in her stronghold by nearly a million of her supporters. They threw rose petals at her Jeep, singing and shouting: "Bee,

Bee!" (her initials in English). A suicide attacker tried to kill her shortly after her arrival, but she escaped because she had bent down in the back of her armored vehicle to loosen a sandal just as the bomb exploded. The resulting massacre left 139 dead.

On December 27, 2007, she was indeed assassinated in another suicide attack at a meeting in an Islamabad suburb. Who did it? The military? Islamic fundamentalists? She had protested against the latter who, she claimed, "from the peaceful nation it once was, [have] converted my homeland into a violent society of Kalashnikovs, heroin users, and radicalized Islam," despite the fact that they had been instrumental in helping her attain power in 1996 and worked hand in hand with the army and the secret service. She had predicted that, if anything happened to her, "I will make Musharraf responsible." Still, the then president (who took power in a putsch) himself had connections to Jamiat Ulema-e-Islam, a right-wing religious group with immense influence in Pakistan, helpmates to the Afghan Taliban and another pawn on the American checkerboard. It was on record, she recalled with indignation, that an Islamist like Osama bin Laden was keen to undermine her power under the pretext that "a woman should not be permitted to head a country." But was this reason enough to make her into an "icon," into a "pasionaria of democracy," an innocent "martyr"? Many young, non-religious Pakistanis are of the opinion that she, in spite of the lack of social justice, would have been the lesser of two evils.

Facing page, bottom
Benazir Bhutto in December 2007, shortly before she was assassinated.

Above
Benazir Bhutto during elections in Islamabad in 1990.

Kumari Mayawati.

(our sister). "The queen of the pariahs" stands at the head of a state with 180 million inhabitants, but one of the poorest in the country. "We will make Uttar Pradesh into a state free of injustice and crime," she promised. But by 2008 there were still no roads and no wells, and poverty-stricken women complained they could see no change on the horizon. Meanwhile, Mayawati was busy trying to land the post of prime minister of India at the May 2009 elections. An Indian political analyst had already declared: "Mayawati's victory could spark a social revolution in India." But she failed to secure the position.

Kumari Mayawati

born 1956, India

An Indian of the "Untouchable" caste, the Dalits, and minister-president of the state of Uttar Pradesh in 2007. Her father was employed in telecommunications, while she went to school, though she still had to milk the cows every evening. Obtaining a BA in education science, she continued her studies (law) and became a teacher. Steely and ambitious, she started out in politics with the hope of rolling back the open discrimination against the Dalits.

In the elections of May 2007, her party, the BSP (or "party of the masses") carried all before it. Aged thirty-nine, Kumari Mayawati was thus elected as the head of her state for the first time, being subsequently re-elected three times. Pragmatic and opportunistic, she had no hesitation in forging alliances, with the caste of the Brahmans, Muslims, or even with the BPJ, the ultra-nationalist Hindu party. Extremely wealthy and suspected of embezzling two million Euros, accused of corruption during each of her three mandates, she retorted that the money came from her supporters, who call her "behanji"

Malalai Joya

born 1979, Afghanistan

She was elected in 2005 as the youngest female member of the Afghan Parliament, but was removed from office in 2007 for having dared to criticize a Parliament she lambasted as "worse than a stable." Her outspoken remarks alluded to the insults and invectives with which her colleagues often replace rational argument: an old mujahideen one day even hit her with his crutch. She has also reproached the government for having "pardoned" the war criminals and drug lords that reign supreme in her country without any semblance of trial. She accuses the Northern Alliance of being as brutal, undemocratic, and repressive in the name of religion as the Taliban. Words like these have put her life on the line and she has survived no less than four assassination attempts. She can go outside only when accompanied by armed guards, for whom she can no longer pay now her parliamentary status has been revoked.

She has traveled to many European countries to plead the cause of secularity and women's rights.

Golda Meir

1898–1978, Israel

Prime minister of Israel from 1969 to 1974. Born Golda Mabovitch, in the Ukraine, during the reign of Tsar Nicolas II, she suffered persecution as a Jew. An unemployed carpenter, her father emigrated to the United States, where Golda helped her mother in the small grocery store she managed to open, only to leave home at fifteen to study as a primary school teacher. She paid for her studies by working as a laundress, at the same time joining up as an active Socialist Zionist militant. At nineteen, she married Moritz Meyerson. A delegate to the American chapter of the World Jewish Congress, she emigrated to Palestine in 1921. Then came three years on a kibbutz, the birth of two children, followed by divorce. Golda occupied a leading position in the Zionist Women Pioneers' Organization before becoming executive secretary in the Histadrut (a trades union confederation). She was one of the people who signed the declaration of the creation of the state of Israel in 1948.

She served as Israel's ambassador in Moscow and, in 1949, became parliamentary member for the left-wing Mapai party. She was named minister for labor until 1956 (a crucial period which saw millions of emigrants flooding in to the country), and finally prime minister in the government of David Ben-

Gurion. "You are the only man in my cabinet," he told her. In 1956, Golda Meir (the Hebrew form of her name) became foreign minister, a post she held for ten years. By 1966, she was secretary general of Mapai, and, in 1969, aged seventy-one, she agreed to head a government. A living symbol of the state of Israel and "grandmother of the Jewish people," she believed in the infallibility of the Israeli army. Tough and unyielding, in the aftermath of the 1967 Six Day War she rejected all talk of withdrawal from the Occupied Territories. Her conviction was a simple one: "There are no Palestinians!" With Moshe Dayan, she carried the can for the setbacks of the Yom Kippur War in 1973. Though she went on to win the subsequent election, she resigned in 1974.

Another "Iron Lady", she liked saber-rattling and had little time for women's rights; when she opened an estate in the region of the Sea of Galilee, she lambasted the architects for not positioning the kitchens so that the housewives might admire the view. When the government planned forbidding Israeli women from going out at night to reduce the number of rapes, she retorted: "It's the men who ought to be locked up. It is they who attack women. Not the other way round."

Tansu Çiller

born 1946, Turkey

First woman prime minister of Turkey in 1993. She undertook secondary school studies at the American College, obtaining a BA in economics from the University of the Bosphorus, and a doctorate at the universities of Connecticut and Yale. Teaching economics at the University of the Bosphorus, she has published nine books in her field.

She entered politics in 1990, joining the conservative Right Way Party (DYP), quickly ascending the hierarchy: in 1991 she was elected member for Istanbul, going on to become economics minister. President of the DYP, she obtained a majority at the Party Congress and became prime minister. During her term, however, she failed to address the problems and issues important to women. Non-religious, from 1995 to 1997 she had nonetheless to enter into a coalition with the Islamic Party. Her rule was overturned by the army and she has been accused of corruption.

Tzipi Livni

born 1958, Israel

Israeli female politician. She has had an impressive career: minister for regional co-operation in 2001; minister for agriculture in 2002; minister for immigrant absorption from 2003 to 2006; minister for housing and construction in 2004–05; minister for justice in 2005–06. Her parents claimed they perpetrated murderous attacks in British Palestine, while, by twenty-one, after serving in Betar (an extreme right-wing youth organization), their daughter became a Mossad (secret service) agent. A member of Likud, she has moved to the center ground, and is

Tzipi Livni, 2009.

one of the founders of the Kadima Party. In 2008, promoted to the all-important post of head of Israeli diplomacy, she backed a further bloody incursion into the Gaza Strip.

Masouma Mubarak

DOB unknown, Kuwait

First female minister in Kuwait in 2005. Professor of international relations at the University of Kuwait, she is a Shiite and represents the religious minority in the government as minister for planning and as secretary of state for administrative development.

At the Women's Forum in 2006. Michèle Alliot-Marie, French Defense Minister, greeting Masouma Mubarak (right).

Elisabeth Domitien

1925–2005, Central African Republic

Prime minister of the Central African Republic in 1975–76, the first female PM in Africa. Having fought for the independence of her country, she became vice president of the (only) party, Bokassa later appointing her prime minister. Although illiterate, she was active on the trade and agriculture fronts. Convinced of the notion that women are the mainstays of African development, she was dismissed by Bokassa for not agreeing with his elevation to emperor, and was arrested, imprisoned, and finally rehabilitated.

Ruth Sando Perry

born 1938, Liberia

President of the State Council for the National Transitional Government of the Republic of Liberia in 1996–97. She was proud to consider herself as the first female African president, though she was not actually elected by the inhabitants but designated by her peers in the Council of State. She was chosen after the failure to implement peace agreements signed in Abuja, and as the country continued to be overrun by armed and extremely vicious gangs. She herself expressed few doubts as to her abilities, claiming that she knew she could govern these men.

She speaks of the factional chiefs as lawless, immoral warlords and of the thorny task of disarming them. Ruth Perry was far from being wet behind the ears, though, as she had served on the Committee of African Women for Peace and Development, and had been a member of the Democratic National Party of Liberia since 1985, all the while finding time to set up the Peace Now,

Peace for Liberia movement, and becoming a founder member of the Women's Development Association of Liberia and of the Liberian Women's Initiative. She took up the gauntlet, asking for assistance from the UN. She has conceded that the sad reality of child-soldiers illustrates the onerous task to be undertaken. She succeeded in holding free elections in 1997, calling upon all to place themselves in the service of the community, the church, and the home. Unfortunately she made the mistake of handing over power to Charles Taylor, a warlord who has stood accused of numerous war crimes and crimes against humanity.

Ellen Johnson-Sirleaf

born 1938, Liberia

President of Liberia since 2005 (at the same time head of state and of the government), the first woman democratically elected to the presidency of an African state.

A graduate in economics from the University of Colorado and a holder of a Masters in public administration from the University of Harvard, she is a member of the Alpha Kappa Sorority, an interdependent organization of African American women. Secretary of state for finance in Liberia of 1972 to 1978, then minister for finance in 1979–80, and president of the National Bank. In 1980, though initially supporting the coup d'état of Master Sergeant Samuel Doe, she soon opposed the corruption that underpinned his dictatorship. She was imprisoned and condemned to death, escaping and opting for exile in the United States, where she was employed by Citibank and various international organizations, including the IMF and the World Bank.

The script was repeated in 1989: she initially backed Charles Taylor, before rising up against him when he turned into a bloodthirsty dictator. She stood for election in 1997, but without success. Returning from exile once more in 2003, she discovered a country in ruins, totally devastated by a murderous civil war that lasted fourteen years: 250,000 died, torture was rife, women were raped and contaminated by AIDS, there were tens of thousands of child-soldiers and victims of atrocious wounds, yet those who had waged the war remained in a position to do harm and senior officials were still corrupt.

Johnson-Sirleaf began in 2004 heading the Commission on Good Governance for a transitional government set up after the escape of Charles Taylor, accused of war crimes. In 2005, aged sixty-seven, she headed the Party of Unity, winning the elections on November 8, 2005, with nearly 60 percent of the vote, against George Weah, the ex-international footballer. Ellen took the oath in front of dozens of delegations from the world over, declaring that she must make women from Liberia, Africa and the whole world proud. She named women in several significant posts in her government, including as finance minister who faced a debt thirty times the national budget. Johnson has promulgated a law criminalizing rape, in the hope that the hundreds of Indian police sent to reinforce the quota of the UN peacekeepers in 2007 are able to impose it. She is perfectly aware that she will need the UN if she is going to be able to pull her people out of stagnation. "I don't make any excuses about being pro-Western," she has remarked, since it "contributes to the development of [the] country." She has also requested the lifting of sanctions on diamond exports and prevailed upon the United States to write off the Liberian debt. Adroitly putting over her point of view with firmness in the presence of the (overwhelmingly white) governing authorities of the IMF and the World Bank, she listens to complaints from the poorest of her fellow citizens.

Described by some as an "Iron Lady", she has become a mother figure to her people, taking care of them and preventing them from resuming fighting. No easy task when former warlords sit in a Parliament in which her party does not even enjoy a majority. She also has to counter unemployment affecting some 80 percent of the population, widespread illiteracy, and ethnic strife (she herself belongs to the very small minority of former African-Americans, freed slaves who created Liberia, which is now 95 percent home to other indigenous groups). Her program is focused on security, the rule of the law and the preponderance of the state, on kick-starting the economy and rebuilding the infrastructure. She has promised that never again in this country should a person or group of individuals feel so excluded that they have to resort to force in the name of justice.

Mame Boye Madior

born 1940, Senegal

Prime minister of Senegal in 2001–02. She started out as minister of justice in 2000 before President Abdoulaye Wade appointed her head of his government. "They wait for me with a sword, I answer with a smile," she remarked. "Tata" strove to reduce poverty and promote peace, focusing on public education. During her mandate, the National Library of Senegal was set up and inaugurated in 2002, and she named several women ministers. She was hustled out of office following her alleged dismissal of government responsibility in the shipwreck of the *Joola*, an accident that left 1,800 dead due to the army's delay in rescuing those aboard the capsized vessel.

Aminata Traoré

born 1947, Mali

Minister of culture in Mali from 1997 to 2000. Like Léopold Senghor, she studied at the University of Caen in Normandy, obtaining a PhD in social psychology and a diploma in psychopathology. In 1963, she moved to the Ivory Coast, her husband's native land.

In Abidjan, from 1975 to 1988, she taught at the Institute of Ethno-sociology, before joining the staff of the Ministry for Women. From 1988 to 1992, she worked for various regional and international organizations that aim at promoting the role of women in water and public hygiene. She was named Mali minister for culture, but resigned after three years. Since then, as a militant on the international stage, she has voiced her indignation at seeing Africa "plundered and marginalized," denouncing the Bretton Woods institutions (the IMF and World Bank) for impoverishing the people of the continent with their "cynical world order."

In 2006, Traoré directed the World Social Forum; she was also instrumental in setting up FORAM (Forum pour un autre Mali [Forum for Another Mali]) and in 2007 its "Migrances" festival, as well as the Amadou Hampâté Bâ Center, the Malian national performing arts center.

Aminata Traoré.

Sylvie Kinigi

born 1952, Burundi

First woman to be prime minister of Burundi in 1993–94 (for seven months), in the first democratically elected multiethnic government in the nation. She was named by President Melchior Ndadaye in the belief that a female Tutsi might better be able to reconcile that community to the Hutu, but he was later assassinated together with six of his cabinet. It is this act that sparked the genocide. During the resulting civil war, Sylvie Kinigi found herself acting president at the head of a country devastated by massacres. Issuing repeated calls for peace and reconciliation, she attempted to form a new administration. In 2007, she became senior political adviser and coordinator of programs to the special representative of the UN secretary general for the Great Lakes.

Agathe Uwilingiyimana

1953–1994, Rwanda

Prime minister of Rwanda in 1993–94 (for just over eight months). A teacher of mathematics and chemistry, she became trade minister in 1989, and minister of education in 1992. In this latter post, trying to ensure justice, she abolished the ethnic quota system, thereby attracting hatred on the part of Hutu extremists. Amid extreme instability in the country, President Juvenal Habyarimana's airplane was shot down by rockets on April 6, 1994. On the following day, Agathe and her husband were assassinated by the presidential guard.

Luisa Diogo Dias at the opening of the United Nations Economic and Social Council summit in Geneva, 2006.

Luisa Diogo Dias

born 1958, Mozambique

Head of the government of Mozambique in 2004, and the first female prime minister in the country. Studying in England, she obtained a Masters in economics. Minister for finance in 1980, she also worked for the World Bank. The country is devastated by AIDS and its debt is colossal. "This country is poor," she points out, "and every cent the nation pays out is one less for the inhabitants of Mozambique."

Helen Clark

born 1950, New Zealand

Second female prime minister in New Zealand, elected in 1999 and re-elected in 2002 and 2005. A Labour MP since 1981, Helen Clark was minister for the environment and housing by 1986 and then for health and work. An antimilitarist, the prime

Jenny Shipley
born 1952, New Zealand

First woman prime minister of New Zealand (itself the first country in the world to introduce female suffrage, in 1893) from 1997 to 1999. She joined the National Party of New Zealand, which won the elections in 1990, holding the post of minister for social welfare (where her measures were essentially neoconservative), and then minister for health (where she reduced state cover and encouraged people to make private provision), and finally for women's affairs, a job she left as soon as she was able to take on the portfolio for state-run businesses. (It was the prime minister, Jim Bolger, who brought her into his Cabinet, but she made the most of his absence in Scotland to take over at the head of the Party, which promptly designated her as prime minister).

minister opposed the war in Iraq. She also made good progress on both the trade and social fronts, with a low unemployment rate, improved rights for families and the old, and advances in education and health. Ecologically minded, she has implemented sustainable development and was a pioneer in the battle against climate change. She has also served as minister for arts, culture and heritage. In 2009, she became the first female administrator of the UN Development Programme and was president of the UN Group on Development. Her promotion was marked by a remarkable Maori ceremony. Indeed, during her three mandates as head of New Zealand, she has furthered reconciliation with the indigenous population and been an advocate of multiculturalism.

Jenny Shipley, 2007.

Intellectuals
and Scientists

"Females of every stripe are
intellectually, physically,
and ethically inapt for medicine."

The Medical Society of San Francisco, 1874

In 1924, an international meeting of female doctors was held in London with eighteen countries represented by three hundred women. **Safiye Ali** was the only representative from Turkey. Not much of a surprise considering she was the only female doctor in the country. At the end of her speech, she declared: "It is not the female physicians of Turkey today whom I represent here, since they do not have the right to study medicine, but future generations of women doctors." She is a perfect example of a pioneer: she had to fight to get the same access to science as men; she succeeded, but was still thinking of the women who would come after her. Safiye also devoted her efforts to poor children suffering from malnutrition, being one of the prime movers behind special milk distribution. Her emancipation is not hers alone; it is an effect of civilization.

To be in an intellectually demanding profession, to carry out cutting-edge research, to work at a high level of scholarship, to become a scientist at all, that is not easy for anyone—but it is doubly hard for a woman. Prohibitions and obstacles litter her path: difficulties in studying and undertaking research, in finding jobs and obtaining recognition. In the early days, places to study were quite simply prohibited to girls. The Hungarian physicist **Mileva Einstein-Marić** (married to Albert Einstein), for example, managed to get into the only science university open to women, in Zurich in 1896. In France, at the beginning of the twentieth century, there were student-teacher demonstrations around the Sorbonne to the cry of "No women!" and "Science is a man's job!" In Italy, girl pupils were kept cooped up in the classroom while the boys ran around during recreation. When **Maria Montessori** started studying medicine, she was not permitted to attend dissection classes, so had to wield her scalpel at night in secret. In 1938, the Englishwoman **Rosalind Franklin**, whose contribution to the understanding of the structure of

DNA is a capital contribution to biology, was authorized to teach in a women's college at Cambridge, but she had to give up all hope of marriage because only single women were eligible for grants and she chose science as her preeminent goal. The American **Dorothy Reed** (a pioneer in biological medicine) shamed her family by entering the school of Johns Hopkins Medicine ("our daughter is on vacation," her mother would tell visitors). The fact that this single university would accept coeds was the fruit of the action of a handful of women who worked tirelessly and endowed it with bequests.

Among students and teachers, misogyny reigned, and women would often suffer harassment. Thus Reed herself was accused of "unhealthy sexual curiosity" when simply doing an internship, the argument being that in the wards she ran there would be black patients waiting to rape her, and so it would be her fault if this incitement to "interracial sex" got out of hand! The German **Maria Goeppert-Mayer** (future winner of the Nobel Prize for Physics) lived when young in Göttingen, the so-called "mathematics center of the world," surrounded by scientists. Yet the gynecologist directing the university clinic for women thought that one wanting to be a scientist

Women had a long hard fight before being permitted to study medicine.

went "against nature," and the mental activities required would endanger "the maternal instinct" (Maria wasn't listening and had two children). Even though Oxford University had admitted women since 1920, **Dorothy Crowfoot Hodgkin** (future winner of the Nobel Prize for Chemistry) ran foul of the regulations that stipulated that the number of women should not exceed a fifth of the number of men. It was thus at the all-girl Somerville College that Crowfoot studied and gained her research fellowship.

Then comes the next hurdle: once a woman has succeeded, not without some effort, in undertaking the studies she wants to, it is much harder for her to acquire a post than for her male colleagues. Thus, when Karl Cori was named at the University of Buffalo, his wife **Theresa Gerty Cori** (future Nobel Prize-winner for Physiology), gladly left her native Czechoslovakia for the United States in the belief that, due to the high level of development of "biochemical methods" there, she was sure to be able to devote herself to research, and they would continue to work together. On her arrival, however, she was advised not to hamstring her husband's career by trying to work with him. The unspoken rule of "no women at the top" discouraged her and, when the Coris became American citizens in 1928, her husband was offered prestigious positions, while she had to be satisfied with unpaid "associate" posts. Attempts were even made to prevent her from joining the research staff of Cori's own lab. Theresa was supposed to while away her time peering at amoebae extracted from excrement (she discreetly replaced the color-stained feces under the microscope with paramecia). But for sixteen years, Gerty remained a research associate, then a "research associate professor," and it was only after she was awarded the Nobel Prize that she finally became a full professor of biochemistry and member of a host of scholarly societies.

Zurich University: the only university where Mileva Einstein-Marić was authorized to study in 1896.

In 1896, **Annie Cannon Jump** entered the observatory at Harvard, where director Edward Pickering asked her to take on the gigantic task of classifying some 250,000 stars. Pickering found working with women ideal because only they were prepared to accept the paltry wages, and he alone could earn glory and satisfaction from the results they provided! Among those dubbed "Pickering's Women," **Williamina Fleming** (1857–1911) developed a classification system of stellar spectra which, after nine years of work, was adapted to reorganize the Henry Draper Catalog of ten thousand stars. She also discovered white dwarf stars. The success of this much-neglected pioneer was all the more extraordinary, since she had first entered Pickering's service as a domestic servant.

North America, however, generally offered one last hope for many female scientists, who emigrated there and obtained US nationality, either fleeing persecution and the dangers of war, because of superior working conditions (this goes for men too), or because gender equality could be more advanced there than in certain European countries. Yet, in the new continent, as elsewhere, it seemed that academic males were seized by a kind of panic at the idea of women doing things (at least) as well as themselves.

A graduation ceremony in the 2000s at Harvard University, Cambridge, Mass. Less than a century ago coeducation had been unthinkable.

"What is the greatest revolution since the war that we have witnessed?" wondered Gustave Cohen, professor at the Faculty of Arts of Paris, in 1930. "It is the invasion of the university by women ... to the point that one asks oneself with concern if, after having once been our mistresses, they will not one day become our masters."

The third stage: have scientific women, educated and tireless researchers, enjoyed the same level of recognition for their discoveries as their male colleagues? We rather doubt it. When **Marie Curie** discovered radioactivity, with the assistance of Pierre Curie, who joined her in her work, journalists found it impossible to get their mind round the fact that she was not her husband's assistant. It was she, after all, who had been the first woman to pass the state teaching exam in physics; it was she who, in 1900, became the first woman teacher of physics at the all-girls' École Normale at Sèvres; and it was she who was the first woman to obtain a science doctorate, on June 25, 1903, when she sat for her viva at the Sorbonne. But she was still just a woman. And when the Curies went to collect their Nobel Prize for Physics in 1903 in Stockholm, Marie had to take her seat among the onlookers because only men were allowed to speak at the Academy of Science. After Marie Curie, the next female winner of a Nobel for Physics was to be Maria Goeppert-Mayer, some sixty years later.

Why have so few women won Nobel Prizes? Perhaps because the Royal Science Academy in Stockholm, which attributes the awards for physics, chemistry, and economics, numbers just forty women out of five hundred members, and that the committees appointed to shortlist the candidates are mainly composed of men. Female scientists who do win the prize do so often flanked by two men on either side. Thus **Christiane Nuesslein-Volhard**, **Theresa Cori**, **Maria Goeppert-Mayer**, **Gertrude Elion**, and **Rosalyn Yalow** all received the prize sandwiched between two male colleagues. Today it even appears that **Simone de Beauvoir** was placed second in the French national philosophy exam and Jean-Paul Sartre first, only because the jury did not dare to put a girl at the top ahead of a young man.

Sometimes the supreme prize, the Nobel, has even been "stolen" from female scientists. **Jocelyn Bell**, the British astrophysicist, discovered the first pulsar, but it was her thesis supervisor who walked off with the Nobel Prize for Physics in 1975. Marianne Grunberg-Manago (born in 1921), a French biologist and the first woman to head the International Union of Biochemistry in 1985, discovered an enzyme, which transformed genetic research and threw new light on DNA ... for which her lab director was awarded a Nobel Prize. **Lise Meitner** carried out all her research on radioactivity with Otto Hahn. When Austria was annexed by the Nazis in 1938, she had to go into exile. During this interlude, Hahn—alone—received the Prize. It is said that this piece of "silliness" was due to scientific ignorance in a Sweden isolated by World War II. It was **Nettie Stevens** who described chromosome differentiation using the symbols "X" and "Y," markers determining the gender of every human fetus. The impact of this discovery has been enormous worldwide, and yet only her male colleague, Thomas Hunt Morgan, was to receive the Nobel Prize for work on genetics. In similar fashion, **Mileva Einstein-Marić** cosigned the article featuring the famous formula: $E=mc^2$, with her husband, yet only Albert became a global celebrity. And what can be said of the English chemist **Rosalind Franklin**, from whom a colleague, Maurice Wilkins, stole (the word is not too strong) a photo and a report formulating the hypothesis of a helix structure for DNA, sending it to two coworkers, later receiving the Nobel Prize with them? It was (female) historians of science who got her recognized for her role and extracted her from the trashcan of history.

But does discrimination no longer exist in the twenty-first century? The **Irène Joliot-Curie** Prize (the eponymous scientist tried on several occasions to be elected to the French Academy of Science, without success) was set up expressly to promote the place of women in research and technology in France. That was back in 2001, a year in which there were 10,700 women for 146,000 men on the books of the CNRS (the French national research program). In 1981, the Japanese scientist **Saruhashi** created a prize of the same name awarded each year to her female colleagues to encourage the scientific creativity of women. She made it perfectly clear that the prize is necessary because Japanese women are often handicapped in science as compared to their male coworkers. This situation does not seem to have changed, because, in 2007, the prize was given to **Yukari Takayabu** from the Center for Climatology Research at the University of Tokyo for her work on cumulonimbus clouds and global warming. Who would have learnt of her if she had

not received what has become one of the most prestigious prizes awarded to Japanese female scientists? The UN Organization for Education, Science and Culture has denounced "a long-term imbalance between men and women in science research." Not only do women remain underrepresented in the scientific professions, but those wanting to make a career in the sciences receive less support and have fewer opportunities for advancement than their male peers, a situation liable to reduce the potential of civil society, it summarized. Every year an international jury now decrees a prize (the sum in 2004 was 100,000 dollars) to female researchers whose innovative work has made a substantial contribution to the advancement of knowledge. And Rosalyn Yalow (Nobel Prize for Physiology and Medicine), conscious of her value as a woman, declares that "the world cannot afford the loss of the talents of half its people if we are to solve the many problems which beset us."

Marguerite Perey, the first Frenchwoman to be elected to the Académie des Sciences, March 14, 1962.

Top, *Maria Montessori with some schoolchildren, c. 1951.*
Bottom, *Maria Montessori teaching a course in Rome in the 1930s.*

Maria Montessori

1870–1952, Italy

Italian pedagogue and first female doctor in Italy, in 1896. Assistant psychiatrist and holder of a chair first in hygiene, then in anthropology (1904) at the University of Rome. In 1900, a league for the education of children with disabilities appointed her head of a model teacher-training school. Starting from concrete methods, based on the stimulation of the senses, which initially she deployed with "backward" children, she invented a revolutionary scientific method for the education of all that has spread throughout the world. Instead of "training" children as if they were animals, the teacher brings

out their personality and awareness with games, building blocks, balls, and rings—tools routinely used nowadays in crèches and nursery schools everywhere. The first Casa dei Bambini (Children's House) opened in Rome in 1907, and in 1909 she published the book that made her famous, *Scientific Pedagogy as Applied to Child Education* (a method translated into twenty languages). Benito Mussolini named her Inspector General of Schools, but in 1936 she was expelled from her homeland.

Melanie Klein

1882–1960, Austria/Great Britain

Founder of child psychoanalysis. Strongly influenced by her mother, Melanie studied medicine like her father before taking the bold and unusual step for a woman at the time of specializing in psychiatry. She undertook an analysis with Ferenczi in Budapest, and then another in Berlin with Karl Abraham. A member of the Psychoanalytical Society in 1923, and of the British Psychoanalytical Society in London (where she finally made her home), she published findings that met with a mixed reception from her colleagues, who were soon ferociously divided with regard to her discoveries. Klein published *The Psychoanalysis of Children* in 1932. Disputing the absolute primacy of the relationship of child to father in the theory of compulsions advanced by Freud, she proposed instead that what determines the individual is primarily determined by the relationship of the nursling to its mother. Ambivalent relationships, of love and hate, of desire and fear, are sentiments experienced by both boys and girls.

In *Envy and Gratitude* (1957), she explains how the suckling breast represents for the nursling something that possesses all it wishes for; it is an inexhaustible supply of milk and love; and is thus the first object

Melanie Klein.

her love for her mother, her darling Sonni, she felt aggression towards her father. Her mother urged her to study medicine, a career path rarely recommended to girls in 1906. The death of her mother in 1911 and the birth of her own daughter threw her into such turmoil that she undertook an analysis, later becoming a psychoanalyst herself.

That the mother-daughter relationship is the strongest seems obvious once one recalls that women, just like men, live prior to birth within their mother's belly. As Horney saw it, boys suffer from their inability to produce children, and misogyny is a kind of "revenge" for this inability. Fleeing Nazism, she went into exile in the United States where she published *The Flight from Womanhood*, a text that resulted in her expulsion from the American Psychoanalytical Society. The importance of motherhood has been taken up by psychoanalysts such as Luce Irigaray, who is, however, wary of overstating the female capacity for motherhood as "something extra," as a privilege, because "sexual difference is not quantifiable as it falls outside the economic sphere."

envied by the child. This feeling does nothing but intensify its hatred and demands. Unlike Freud, who founded gender difference on the girl's penis envy, Klein's approach is that it is the boys who are tortured by the desire to become pregnant. According to her, penis envy should be linked to the fundamental desire for the maternal breast, which the infant would like to be inexhaustible and omnipresent, belonging to a mother who is able to protect the subject against all and any suffering. Klein also worked on female sexuality, throwing new light on what Freud termed the "dark continent."

Karen Horney

1885–1952, The Netherlands/United States

The first psychoanalyst to question the notorious concept of "penis envy" from which, according to Freud, girls are meant to suffer. But did she have an "inverted" Oedipus complex herself? Combined with

Hannah Arendt

1906–1975, Germany

The best-known female philosopher of the twentieth century (with Simone Weil) and the first woman to serve as professor at Princeton University. Her thinking is imbued with the dilemma of Jewish difference. Early on, collecting evidence of Hitler's anti-Semitic propaganda, she was arrested by the Gestapo, before being released. Fleeing her country, in 1933 she went into exile in France. Her position was for the creation, not of Israel, but of a federal mixed Judeo-Arab state in Palestine. Interned in a camp in the Pyrenees, she

Hannah Arendt.

somehow got away, managing to reach New York in 1941. Her exile, during which she had to work as a home-help, was initially tough. Taking American nationality in 1951, she lectured in the universities of Berkeley and Columbia and held a professorship in social thought at Chicago. From 1967 to her death she also taught political philosophy at the New School for Research, New York. *The Origins of Totalitarianism* is a major work of contemporary thought (for the first time Nazism and Stalinism were placed on the same footing) that prepared the ground for *Eichmann in Jerusalem. A Report on the Banality of Evil*, compiled from articles she wrote for the *New Yorker* covering the ten months of the Nazi henchman's trial. The analysis she provides— according to which, in certain circumstances, anyone at all is capable of sinking into a similar moral and political quagmire—makes for uncomfortable reading.

Germaine Tillion

1907–2008, France

Groundbreaking ethnologist, Resistant, and committed fighter against injustice. On her first mission to the Aures Mountains in Algeria when just twenty-seven, she studied kinship relationships in a seminomadic tribe (between 1934 and 1937, and in 1939–40). From June 1940 she helped set up the "Musée de l'Homme" Resistance network, taking over operations on the arrest of its early leaders. Attempting to go to their aid, she was betrayed by a priest and snatched in turn, together with her mother, on August 13, 1942. Imprisoned in the city jail, and then at Fresnes (where she started to write her thesis), she was deported to Ravensbrück, a camp in which 90,000 prisoners perished, being detained from October 1943 to April 1945. On learning that the SS had gassed her mother, she lost the "visceral desire to live."

Once released, Germaine Tillion was again saved—but this time by work, research, and writing. In 1946 she published *Ravensbrück*; in 1960, *France*

Germaine Tillion, 1985.

and Algeria: Complementary Enemies; in 1966, *The Republic of Cousins*, that analyzes female oppression. She founded an ethnology based on the strongly endogamous Mediterranean world, as distinct from the ethnology of Lévi-Strauss, who studied mainly exogamous Amerindian societies. Appointed by Mitterrand to look into the fate of the civilian population in Algeria, she was an attaché in the Soustelle cabinet and set up social centers to combat the discrimination that hit the poor especially hard. During the Algerian War, she became committed to finding a solution to the "Algerian tragedy," campaigning against torture and advocating education for all to strengthen social ties. At the age of 100, she described herself as still "searching for truth and right."

Simone de Beauvoir, at a conference in Japan in 1966.

Simone de Beauvoir

1908–1986, France

French novelist and philosopher and pioneer of the new feminism. Flanked by a mother who took her to Mass every day, telling her that, "the body is entirely vulgar and repugnant," and a father who declared "Simone has the brain of a man," the young woman launched on a dazzling intellectual career. Second overall in the national competitive exam in philosophy in 1929, she embarked on a lifelong relationship with Jean-Paul Sartre, which was more of a success in the field of ideas than on the sexual plane. In 1949, she published that bible of global new feminism, *The Second Sex*. Written quickly over a space of a few weeks, the book created an immense fuss in France, and in the Vatican, which put it on a blacklist, whereas on publication in the United States in 1953 it became a runaway bestseller. The philosopher describes the female and maternal biological functions: periods, defloration, pregnancy, and childbirth, in gruesome

terms expressive of her loathing for having been born a woman. In fact the book's byline—"one is not born a woman, one becomes one"—is misleading. She strives to prove how women can and should struggle to escape such natural hindrances and not see them as their inevitable fate. *The Second Sex* calls for an ongoing process of women's liberation so that women and men, equal and different, can finally love, free of alienation.

The Mandarins (1954), a novel that won the much-vaunted Prix Goncourt, shows her penchant for introspection, even if the author never conceived of "fiction as otherwise than informed by an idea, by a philosophy." Endorsing existentialism as formulated by Sartre, she adapts it in *The Ethics of Ambiguity* (1947), into the credo that "wanting to be free means wanting others to be free too."

She also was concerned with the plight of oppressed and colonized peoples, took a stand against the Franco-Algeria conflict (signing the "manifesto of the 121") and the Vietnam War. In 1971 she signed the proclamation of the 343 women who confessed themselves "guilty" of having an abortion, because "freedom, for a woman, starts with the womb." Her four-volume autobiography, *The Memoirs of a Dutiful Daughter*, appearing in 1958, met with resounding success. She then threw herself into the feminist cause, becoming president of the Ligue Française du Droit International des Femmes (French League for the International Rights of Women) that highlights sexist discrimination.

Françoise Dolto

1908–1986, France

Psychoanalyst and pioneer of psychologically based childcare; founding member of the French Society of Psychoanalysis and the French Freudian School. Born Françoise Marette, as a child she adored her father and he was her role model. On the other hand, she viewed her mother as worthless and spiteful, forgiving her only because she was "sick and so not responsible." She had to overcome many of the prejudices of her time, because she wished not only to be a wife and a mother, but also to study and become a "doctor of education." In 1939, she presented her thesis on psychoanalysis and psychiatry, the same year becoming a founder member of the Society of Psychoanalysis in Paris; later she nailed her colors to the Freudian school headed by Jacques Lacan. Her main finding was the fabulous, if today self-evident, discovery that a baby is a person, a linguistic entity, who is bathed in a whirlpool of language from birth, and even in the womb. One should "speak true," even to the newborn.

At the beginning, Dolto was met with incredulity, even superciliousness, from colleagues and the general public alike. But, forsaking the ivory tower in which too many analysts immure themselves, she made a series of daily programs on the national radio station, France Inter, where she replied on air to parents' letters about how best to bring up their children. She spoke naturally, without jargon, but forfeiting none of her analytical rigor. Dolto believed that if only parents would make clear what is forbidden and teach their children the essential law of never harming others—without terrorizing or abusing them—so that they channeled their aggressive impulses into socialized drives, young people would not commit so many self-serving acts of cruelty. For the growing infant each loss should harbor the promise of further development: forgoing the quiet of the maternal womb, it can breathe; abandoning the pleasures of suckling, it can speak; no longer a hermaphrodite, it can take pleasure in its genitals. "We can only be of one sex and can only conjecture about the pleasures and desires of the other sex. That is why men and women never truly meet," she declared in one of her most widely read books, *Lorsque l'enfant paraît* (When the child appears).

Françoise Dolto.

Michelle Perrot

born 1928, France

Professor emeritus of contemporary history at University Paris VII Denis-Diderot and pioneer in women's history. A qualified teacher of history, she taught at a school in Caen. A communist "fellow-traveler", she campaigned for the peace movement and in the Union des Femmes Françaises (Union of French Women), and then in the Communist Party from 1954 to 1956. Beginning her research on working-class history, she did not at that time dare to deal with a subject concerning women head-on. Having earned a doctorate "d'État," she became interested in the penitentiary system.

Meanwhile, the protests, strikes, and riots of May 1968 gave her the courage to launch the great debate: "Do women have a history?" If today this question raises a smile, at the beginning of the 1970s it was regarded by "revolutionaries" as an irrelevant distraction from the central challenge of the class struggle.

Michelle Perrot thus truly paved the way for a "gendered" approach. The high point was in 1991–92 when Michelle Perrot edited (with Georges Duby) the monumental *History of Women in the West from Antiquity to the Present-day* (Plon; Harvard), which opened up a truly pan-European perspective. She has not, however, confined her research to the history of women and womanhood alone. She was also appointed general editor of another huge collective enterprise (*The History of Private Life*) and anchored a radio program on France Culture.

This now celebrated woman—chevalière of the Legion of Honor and officer of the National Order of Merit, to name but a few—has lost none of her open-mindedness and solidarity with her fellow women.

Elinor Ostrom giving a press conference in Stockholm, 2009.

Elinor Ostrom

born 1933, United States

Winner, together with Oliver Williamson, of the "Nobel" prize for economics in 2009, she shows how "commons" (collective goods) can be effectively "governed" by associations of users in collaboration with companies. In a break with the credo of unregulated liberalism and privatization, she demonstrates that the aim of communities that manage (and often create) such communal property can be the collective interest. In work closely associated with environmental protection, Ostrom has particularly studied groups who exploit natural resources such as fish, forests, and lakes. Professor of Economics at the University of Indiana, she was the first woman to receive the prize established in 1969 "in memory of Alfred Nobel."

Kate Millett (right) with Delphine Seyrig at a press conference on their return from Iran in 1979.

Kate Millett

born 1934, United States

American intellectual, writer, and celebrated feminist militant. Published in 1968 *Sexual Politics*— a counterblast against a patriarchal system that oppresses women and suffocates their sexuality— which soon became a bestseller. Unafraid of attacking the big names of Anglo-American literature (Norman Mailer, Henry Miller, D. H. Lawrence), her analysis was a provocative breath of fresh air and was soon taken up by feminists the world over. When she decided to come out, the scandal reached fever pitch: lesbianism was still largely taboo. A *Time* magazine cover presented her as a real virago. Expelled from university and disinherited, she hit back with a manifesto of bisexuality, *Flying*, in 1974. Theorist and major figure in the women's liberation movement "NOW," she was also a painter, setting up a community for women artists. Everywhere she lives—New York, Japan, Iran—she fights to improve the female condition. Millett has voiced her disquiet at the rising tide of anti-feminism.

Julia Kristeva

born 1941, Bulgaria/France

Semiologist, linguist, psychoanalyst (member of the Psychoanalytical Society of Paris), novelist. Julia Kristeva is a professor at University Paris VII, where she heads the doctorate school of "language, literatures, images," and at the Institut Universitaire Français; she teaches at the University of Columbia, the New School of New York, and the University of Toronto; doctor honoris causa from eight universities; president of the French National Disabled Council; member of a brains' trust associated with the French Economic and Social Council; chevalière of Arts and Letters in 1987 (French award); decorated with the Order of Merit in 1991 and the Legion of Honor in 1997; Holberg Prize in 2004 (the "Nobel" for essays).

Born in Bulgaria, she left the Black Sea for France in 1966; wife of author and critic Philippe Sollers, they have a son, David, born in 1976. She lives and works in France and in the United States, where the great majority of her work has been translated into English, bringing her international fame. This cosmopolitan citizen of Europe is a "creator without borders" endowed with a theoretical rigor and a dazzling virtuosity of thought that is never purely abstract, since its aim is to "question thought in the flesh." Since *Sémiotikè*, her first book, and *The Revolution in Poetic Language* (1974) (on poets Lautréamont and Mallarmé), she has been delving into the drives, impulses, rhythms, and ruptures that the symbolic (order) strives to repress in constituting "signifiance." Julia Kristeva constantly explores pleasure and pleasuring, the unsaid and the repressed in society, expressing her views through female exemplars: playwright and fellow feminist Olympe de Gouge (*The Chinese*), revolutionary heroines Charlotte Corday and Madame Roland (*Seule une femme*), St. Teresa of Avila (2008), not forgetting three "female geniuses" and "insubordinates": Hannah

Julia Kristeva, 1997.

Arendt, Melanie Klein, and Colette; as well as Anna Comnena, the first female intellectual in Europe, a character in her scholarly yet humorous thriller, *Murder in Byzantium*. Kristeva plumbs "that part of humankind [woman] which remains largely neglected," thereby countering Simone de Beauvoir, who thought that motherhood stupefies women. In her novel *The Samurai* (a response to de Beauvoir's *The Mandarins*), she dances with words, buoyant, gravid with a new cosmos, "circulating energies and languages between diverse identities: nature-culture, me-other, life-death." In 2006, Kristeva gave the sum received for the Hannah Arendt Prize for political thought to Afghan women who see no way out of their predicament other than to set their body ablaze. In 2008, she created the Simone de Beauvoir prize for women's freedom.

Annie Cannon Jump

1863–1941, United States

American astronomer. A trailblazer in more ways than one: the only woman to be an honorary member of the Royal Astronomical Society; first woman to be awarded an honorary doctorate from the University of Oxford; first woman to receive the Henry Draper Medal from the National Academy of Sciences in 1931. Cannon was the name of her father (a senator), and Jump that of her mother, a passionate stargazer, who had three daughters of her own as well as bringing up her husband's four children. The source of the young Annie's vocation is not hard to find. Graduate in astronomy and physics from Wellesley College in Massachusetts by 1884, she traveled to Europe, but sadly went deaf in 1894. She then lost her adored mother and returned to Wellesley, where she held a teaching post in physics, though it was astronomy that really attracted her. In 1896, she entered Harvard College Observatory (HCO), whose director, Edward Pickering, asked her to devise a classification for 250,000 stars. Examining primarily Southern Hemisphere stars, she was soon listing about five thousand a month. To proceed at such a rate, she would first examine photographic plates and pick out the spectral types up to magnitude 9. These results she would dictate in the form of alphabetic code to an assistant who recorded the values in a notebook.

The fruit of her work, as well as that of a posse of women astronomers in the group, is now contained in the Henry Draper Catalog, issued between 1918 and 1924. The alphabetic code she used in identifying types of spectra forms the backbone of the Harvard classification system and is still employed to indicate stellar spectra.

Antonia Maury

1866–1952, United States

American astronomer and discoverer of stars. Born in New York, she obtained a BSc in astronomy from Vassar College in 1887, becoming a part-time assistant at the Harvard College Observatory between 1888 and 1896 (teaching sciences in a school in Cambridge, Massachusetts, between 1891 and 1894), and joining the HCO between 1918 and 1935. Her work centered on stellar classification. Specializing in the stars of the Southern Hemisphere, she was notably responsible for analyzing the spectrum of the star Sirius. She played a key role in the compilation of the Henry Draper Catalog and in 1943 received the Annie Jump Cannon Prize from the American Astronomical Society. With neither husband nor children on the horizon, her life was wholly dedicated to exploring the depths of space.

Henrietta Leavitt

1868–1921, United States

American astronomer. Headed the important photometry service at the Harvard College Observatory, directed by Pickering. She discovered 2,400 variable stars in 1912, facilitating a precise evaluation of the distance between various stellar clusters and galaxies. An asteroid bears her name.

Cecelia Payne Gaposchkin

1900–1979, Great Britain

British astronomer. She obtained a PhD from Radcliffe (Harvard) in 1925. In her thesis, "Stellar Atmospheres, a Contribution to the Observational Study of High Temperature in the Reversing Layers of Stars," she used spectrometry to determine the composition of stars and the sun, proving that they possess an abundance of hydrogen and helium, their composition being radically different to that of the earth. Until that time, it was thought that if the earth were as hot as the sun, it would present an identical spectrum. In 1977 she was invited to the prestigious Henry Norris Russell lectureship of the American Astronomical Society.

Claudie Haigneré, 1999.

Claudie Haigneré

born 1957, France

Scientist and first French woman astronaut in 1996. Qualifying as a medical doctor aged twenty-four, she practiced at the rheumatology clinic at Cochin Hospital. In 1985, she was selected by the Centre National d'Études Spatiales (National Center for Space Studies) from a thousand other candidates, obtaining a DEA (MSc) in biomechanics, followed by a doctorate in neuroscience. In 1990, she oversaw the physiological and medical components of the space program. In 1992, she headed scientific coordination for the Altair Franco-Russian mission. She was frequently seconded to Star City near Moscow and then to the Russian space center in Kazakhstan. In the meantime, she lived among the twenty-two other European astronauts in Cologne. In 1996, she was named on the Cassiopeia mission, orbiting in the Russian Mir space station for seventeen days, running experiments in biology and neurosensory and cardiovascular physiology. To understand how human beings and animals react in the weightless laboratory, she had aboard an egg-laying salamander—a revealing experiment which earned her the "Grand Siècle" prize. In 2001, she went on the Andromeda mission: after nine months' training, she was the first French astronaut to fly aboard the International Space Station, undertaking some novel experiments (earth observations and studies of the ionosphere, in particular). These exploits did not prevent her from having a daughter, Carla, with husband, Jean-Pierre Haigneré, also an astronaut. In 2002, she was named by the Raffarin government in the post of minister delegate for research and new technologies, then as minister for European affairs in 2005. She was made commander of the Legion of Honor in 2007 and is president of Cité des Sciences et de l'industrie in Paris.

Hertha Marks Ayrton

1854–1923, Germany

German physician whose work on the electric arc was to open the door to plasma physics. Her father died when she was seven and she had to earn a living when at Cambridge. In 1885 she married William Ayrton and they worked together. She was the first woman to read a paper at the Institute of Electrical Engineers in 1899, becoming a member of the institution that same year. When, at the request of the Ministry for the Navy, the couple studied the little arc lights used in studios, only her husband was paid. Hertha began to make observations of the indentations left by waves shifting over the sands. In 1904, she was the first woman to speak before the Royal Society on "The Origin and Growth of Ripple Marks" (in 1901 her paper had been read by a man). Finally, in 1906, she received the Hughes Medal from the Royal Society. During the war, she developed a device to ventilate the trenches of mustard gas.

Marie Curie

1867–1934, Poland/France

Franco-Polish physicist and chemist, a woman pioneer par excellence. The first woman on the staff at the teacher-training school at Sèvres in 1900; the first to teach at the Sorbonne; the first to earn a science doctorate from the same institution. The first prizewinner of either gender to be awarded two Nobel Prizes: the first in 1903 for Physics and the second in 1911 for Chemistry; the first woman to be interred at the Pantheon in Paris.

Losing her mother at eleven, her father was a mathematics and physics teacher. She immersed herself in her studies to the tertiary level (prohibited to girls). Having left Poland for France, in spite of the obstacle of a new language and her lower level of attainment compared to the other students, by working relentlessly for two years she was listed first among the BSc (physics) candidates in 1893, before obtaining another degree in mathematics in 1894. In 1895, she married the physicist Pierre Curie. Both had simple tastes, enjoyed nature, and regarded science as a kind of priesthood. They had two daughters: Irène in 1896 and Ève in 1904. Marie took her maternal duties seriously.

Undertaking her thesis on the "uranic rays" discovered by Becquerel, together with Pierre she toiled in a wretched clapboard hut, analyzing tons of ore, crushing, dissolving, and filtering it, and isolating the radioactive component. (She invented the term "radioactivity"). After several years, the Curies managed to isolate a single decigram of

Pierre and Marie Curie in their laboratory in 1898.

radium salts, a discovery for which they received the Nobel Prize for Physics (shared with Becquerel).

Her life was plagued by misogyny. When Pierre died in 1906, she inherited his post at the Sorbonne and thus became the first woman university professor in France. On the other hand, in 1910, Édouard Branly purloined her place at the Academy of Science. Then when her liaison with Paul Langevin was exposed, she had to face the press, her colleagues, xenophobia, even violence. Increasingly she took refuge in her research, publishing a Treatise on Radioactivity in 1910, isolating one whole gram of pure radium and becoming the first person to establish radioactive standards. For this work, she received an unprecedented accolade: a second Nobel Prize, this time for Chemistry, and for her alone.

When war broke out, she devoted herself to the defense of her adopted homeland. Fitting twenty cars with X-ray apparatus, she passed her driving license and drove to the front herself to treat the casualties, rapidly training a radiology nursing corps. At the end of the conflict, she became head of the Institute of Radium, where she schooled many young researchers, including her daughter, Irène.

One day she was visited by an American journalist who enquired into her needs. Thanks to subscriptions from the women of America, funds were gathered together to invite the now celebrated physicist to the United States where President Harding received her at the White House and presented her with a gram of radium.

Continuing her work and transmitting knowledge to future scientists from all over the world was exhausting work and she became extremely ill, suffering from incurable lesions and requiring several eye operations. Without openly admitting it, she suspected that the cause of her sickness was radioactivity and she died from leukemia associated with X-ray exposure. Her daughters refused an elaborate ceremony, so their mother was buried at Sceaux cemetery. On April 20, 1995, however, the remains of Pierre and Marie Curie were transferred to the Pantheon, Marie being the first woman to be given the honor of a funeral at the French national monument for her achievements.

A truly exceptional woman, Marie Sklodowska-Curie devoted her life to science. Her discoveries revolutionized physics and their applications have opened new possibilities in cancer treatment.

Albert Einstein, Mileva Marić, and their son in 1904.

Mileva Einstein-Marić

1875–1934, Hungary

Hungarian physicist. She had both a passionate love affair as well as an intellectual collaboration with Albert Einstein, but Mr. Einstein senior forbade Albert from marrying a non-Jew. As Einstein's career continued to thrive, Mileva became pregnant and in 1902 had a daughter in secret whom she was forced to abandon. She chose not to hand in her thesis. When Einstein senior passed away, she could officially become Mrs. Einstein, and the couple had two children; she alone brought them up, which was a tough job as the son was mentally handicapped, prone to violent outbursts, and required numerous spells in clinics. A specialist in theoretical physics, Marić eventually returned to research in tandem with her spouse, and together they published several articles in a prestigious Leipzig journal, *Annalen der Physik*. One of their many papers contains the famous formula $E=mc^2$. This article was jointly

signed and Milena Marić's contribution was surely significant as she had studied quantum physics in Heidelberg. In 1921, however, only Albert was to receive the Nobel Prize for Physics. Although separated from Marić since 1914, he handed every penny of the prize money over to her.

Lise Meitner

1878–1968, Austria/Sweden

Physicist who discovered the mechanism of nuclear fission. Meitner obtained a doctor's qualification in 1906 from Vienna University. The following year she attended lectures by Max Planck in Berlin and, although women were not accepted at the Physics Institute, worked there clandestinely. In 1917, Lise Meitner discovered the existence of protactinium, in

1923 nonradiative transition (Frenchman Pierre Auger was to "discover" it himself some two years later, so the phenomenon bears the name "Auger effect"), and in 1932 the isomerism of uranium 239.

Meitner undertook all this research on radioactivity with Otto Hahn, working discreetly by his side for thirty years. Of Jewish origin, in 1938 she had to flee to the Netherlands and Denmark, settling finally in Sweden. She continued to work, however, with the little means at her disposal, publishing a key paper on uranium fission in 1939. While she was in exile, Hahn alone was awarded the Nobel Prize. She was, however, the first woman to gain the Fermi Prize decreed by the Atomic Energy Commission, and today element 109 is called meitnerium.

his surname to that of his wife) the Nobel Prize. Professor at the Faculty of Science of Paris in 1937, Irène was the only female member on the scientific committee of the French Atomic Energy Commission (Commissariat à l'Énergie Atomique) and she played a central role in the manufacture of the first atomic battery, the ZOE. She founded the new Orsay-Physics Institute where a synchrocyclotron was installed.

During the Popular Front, she spent a few months as secretary of state under Léon Blum, the first, with two other women, at such an elevated post. A firm opponent of war, during the First World War, when just a girl of seventeen, she had gone up to the Front with her mother to X-ray casualties. She was in addition a member of the National Council for Peace and National Committee of the Union des Femmes Françaises.

Irène Joliot-Curie

1897–1956, France

French physicist, winner of the Nobel Prize for Chemistry in 1935. She was also under-secretary of state for scientific research in 1936; director of the Institute of Radium in 1946. Daughter of Pierre and Marie Curie, who were both awarded Nobel Prizes, she followed in their footsteps with a B.Sc. in mathematics and physics from the Sorbonne and a thesis on alpha rays in polonium in 1925. Assisting her mother at the Institute of Radium from 1919, she designed a gold-leaf electroscope to measure radioactivity in fertilizer. At the time, scientists thought that chemical elements arising from atomic transmutations were stable and non-radioactive. After making tests with boron and magnesium, Irène and Frédéric Joliot-Curie demonstrated that further radioactive elements can be produced artificially. It is this discovery that was the subject of a report to the Academy of Sciences and earned the couple (in which the husband had remarkably enough joined

Maria Goeppert-Mayer

1906–1972, Germany/United States

Physicist, winner of the Nobel Prize for Physics in 1963. The first woman to win the award for theoretical physics. In spite of her family's misgivings, Maria married J. E. Mayer, an American physicist from the Rockefeller Foundation, who supported her when she submitted a thesis on theoretical physics in 1929, in which she showed the existence of two-photon absorption (TPA). Its first application dated to some thirty years later with the appearance of the laser, spawning many other practical developments. She was to have a daughter, Marianne, in 1933, and a son, Peter, in 1938, all the while undertaking cutting-edge research (she published *Statistical Mechanics* in 1940).

From Germany, where it had become impossible for her to teach, she left for the United States, being employed far below her qualifications at Johns

Hopkins University in Baltimore and Columbia. Her early research concerned isotope separation, then nuclear physics and the development of the atomic weapon. In 1946, she was appointed professor in the department of physics and at the Institute of Nuclear Studies in Chicago. In 1959, she became the first physicist at the Argonne National Laboratory and professor of physics at the Fermi Institute in Chicago. Subsequently she joined the National Academy of Washington and the Heidelberg Akademie des Wissenschaften. By 1948, she was advancing a theory on the layered structure of spin-orbit interactions at the atomic core, publishing her findings only at the end of 1949 in Physical Review. The Nobel was rightly presented to her "for her contributions to the theory of the core of the atom and elementary particles." In 1960, she was given a physics chair at San Diego.

Dorothy Crowfoot Hodgkin applauded by Princess Christina, Queen Louise, King Gustav Adolf , and Princess Sibylla on December 10, 1964.

Dorothy Crowfoot Hodgkin

1910–1994, Great Britain

British scientist who won the Nobel Prize for Chemistry in 1964. Born in Cairo to an archaeologist father and botanist mother, she spent her childhood in the Sudan, then in Jordan, finally studying at Oxford where she continued her research and taught. Her childhood vocation and lifelong passion was to "see" atoms using X-ray crystallography, something she managed after many years of work. Endowed with a wonderful eye, Dorothy could determine a crystal's structure simply by examining a photograph.

Her research also laid the foundation for cellular biology. Thanks to X-ray crystallography, one can obtain the chemical formula for a compound almost without any other physicochemical observations. She analyzed the structure of some important substances: cholesterol in 1937, penicillin, vitamin B12 in 1954; insulin in 1969, with her female students B. Low and K. Dornberger-Schiff; lactoglobulin, ferritin and the tobacco-mosaic virus.

Yet she neglected neither family life nor the non-academic world. Marrying Thomas Hodgkin, a communist teacher, in 1937, she had three children, between 1938 and 1946. During the Cold War, she forged scientific contacts between researchers in East and West, campaigned at and then chaired the Pugwash Conferences against nuclear weapons (Nobel Prize for Peace in 1995). She provided expertise in X-rays for biomedical ends to North Vietnam. In China she worked with students on artificially synthesizing insulin. Her awards include: the Florence Nightingale Prize, the Order of Merit, Copley Medal of the Royal Society, Lomonosov Medal, and the Lenin Peace Prize.

Katsuko Saruhashi

born 1920, Japan

Japanese geological chemist, specialist in natural radioactivity at sea. The first woman graduate in chemistry from Tokyo University (1957) and a member of the Science Council of Japan (1980). In the waters of the Pacific she made technical measurements of CO_2 concentration, studied the propagation of residues from nuclear tests (1954), and the diffusion and absorption of CO_2. Director of the Geotechnical Laboratory of the M. R. I. (1979–80) and then of the Geochemistry Research Association (1990–98), she has been a recipient of the Miyake Prize (1985) and the Tanaka Prize (1993).

Rosalind Franklin.

Rosalind Franklin

1920–1958, Great Britain

English chemist, whose major contribution to the history of biology paved the way for the understanding of the DNA that codes for the genome in all living things.

Obtaining a doctorate in 1941, from 1946 to 1951 she was a researcher at the CNRS in Paris, and then at King's College, London. She designed and built an X-ray machine that enabled her to make excellent images of the diffraction pattern of deoxyribonucleic acid (DNA), a finding that has had a crucial impact, as DNA is key to all current research on cloning and genetically modified crops. Maurice Wilkins, who was working with her, purloined one of her photos and a report demonstrating the hypothesis of a helical form for DNA (double-helix structure), dispatching the precious documents to the American James Watson and the Briton Francis Crick. The three male researchers

put the finishing touches to the model and walked off with the Nobel Prize in 1963 for "their" discovery, without Rosalind Franklin's name even been mentioned (she had died four years previously, aged only thirty-seven years).

Ada Yonath

born 1939, Israel

Nobel Prize for Chemistry in 2009, with the Americans Thomas Steitz and Venkatraman Ramakrishnan, for work on establishing a detailed description of ribosome, the cell's protein factory: this is the molecule that decodes DNA and thus is crucial to the existence of life. Such research may lead to the development of new antibiotics.

Born in Palestine during the British Mandate, Ada came from a poor family who possessed very few books. One day coming across the biography of

Marie Curie, she was fired with enthusiasm and became determined to devote her life to research. Her father, a rabbi and grocer, however, died when she was but ten years old. Managing nonetheless to read chemistry at the Hebrew University in Jerusalem, she obtained her master's in 1964, before presenting a thesis in crystallography at the Weizmann Institute and, in 1970, setting up the first protein crystallography laboratory. She is also a graduate of the Massachusetts Institute of Technology, Boston, and the Carnegie Mellon University. Professor of structural biology at the Weizmann Institute, she also heads a section of the Max Planck Institute, Hamburg.

A pacifist, on Palestine military radio she has fought for the release of Palestinian prisoners on the basis that their incarceration only increases the desire for vengeance and prolongs the conflict. A feminist, she has also supported the cause of her fellow women, arguing at the award ceremony of the Oréal-UNESCO Women in Science Award in 2007 that, since women constitute half the population, humanity loses half its brain capacity if it fails to encourage women to enter the sciences and add to the storehouse of knowledge.

Jocelyn Bell

born 1943, Great Britain

British astrophysicist. The first, in 1967, to observe pulsars, though it was Antony Hewish who received the 1975 Nobel Prize for Physics for the discovery. A student at Glasgow University and then at Cambridge, Bell graduated in science in 1965, and began a thesis under the supervision of Hewish. For the first two years of her doctorate, she assisted him in building a radio-telescope that came on stream in 1967; it used interplanetary scintillation to study quasars. Jocelyn Bell discovered the existence of neutron stars that revolve extremely quickly, emitting strong electromagnetic fields in the direction of their magnetic axis. Their pulsations are extremely regular and their position constant on the celestial sphere.

Honored with a CBE, in 1986 she received the Beatrice M. Tinsley Prize. Dean of Science at the University of Bath between 2001 and 2004, she was president of the Royal Astronomical Society between 2002 and 2004.

Nettie Stevens

1861–1912, United States

American geneticist, who in 1905 showed that an X chromosome determined the sex of female and the Y chromosome that of male embryos.

Bachelor of Arts in 1899 and Master of Arts in 1900 from the University of Stanford, she studied biology (specializing in cytology) at Bryn Mawr College, where she obtained a doctorate in 1903. She was soon investigating embryo differentiation and deepening her understanding of the chromosome. She first isolated the Y chromosome on a coleopteran, the Tenebrio, deducing that sexual differentiation depends on its presence or absence. In her article "Accessory Chromosome," she presented chromosome differentiation with the symbols "X" and "Y." This finding tackled head-on the prevailing idea that gender was a question of fixed heredity. The impact of the discovery was enormous worldwide. However, only Thomas Hunt Morgan (1866–1945), with whom in 1904 she had cosigned one of the most highly esteemed articles in this field of research, was to receive the Nobel Prize for his work on genetics—and not Stevens.

Florence Sabin.

Florence Sabin

1871–1953, United States

The most highly regarded American woman scientist of her era, the first female tenured professor of histology in a university. She published the seminal *Atlas of the Medulla and Midbrain* in 1901. At the Rockefeller Institute for Medical Research, she orientated her investigations more towards the immune system and tuberculosis. Such research needed to be undertaken on living tissue—a first. For thirteen years she headed the Department of Cell Studies. In 1944 the Colorado State authorities appointed her to chair the health side of the postwar planning committee. She succeeded in shepherding through a raft of health reforms, soon dubbed the Sabin Program. She was also chair of the Board of Health and Hospitals in Denver. Sabin received many prizes and awards and the State of Colorado set up a statue of her in the Capitol.

Dorothy Reed

1874–1964, United States

American pioneer in biological medicine. In 1901, she showed the specific role of a cell in Hodgkin's Disease. Battling for routine pre- and postnatal monitoring, she was elected by the US Children's Bureau and crisscrossed the United States raising awareness on pregnancy, childbirth, and the newborn infant.

Gerty Theresa Cori

1896–1957, Czechoslovakia/United States

Born Radnitz, the first woman to receive the Nobel Prize in Physiology or Medicine in 1947, with her husband Karl Cori (and Bernardo Houssay), for their discovery of the physiological implications of biochemical reactions. Studying medicine at Prague University, she graduated in 1920 with a love of microscopes and research on thyroid hormones, but became a pediatrician at the Karolinen Hospital in Vienna. Her family often went hungry and she had the greatest difficulty obtaining a place worthy of her talents.

At last, she and her husband managed to publish an article in 1923 analyzing the correlations between cancer and carbohydrate metabolism, thereby clarifying one of the essential characteristics of the metabolism of cancerous tissues. They went on to elucidate the metabolism of glycogen and, in 1936, the functions of glucose-1 phosphates (Cori esters), finally working on the enzymes responsible for the formation/disintegration of the glycogen molecule, the exchange of sugar and lactic acid between muscles and the liver (Cori cycle). But who precisely made the discovery that earned them the Nobel Prize? "Two voices uttered thoughts formulated by a single brain," is how they saw it.

Thereafter, Gerty Cori studied pathologies in sugar metabolism particularly affecting children, proving for the first time that a disease could be due to an inherited enzyme deficiency. Her work-rate never faltered, toiling away in her lab in temperatures of nearly 40°C until the term of her pregnancy (she had a son in 1936), and she was still hard at it when she came down with myelofibrosis, an extremely painful and incurable disease.

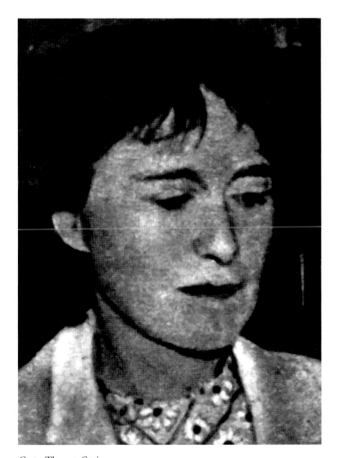

Gerty Theresa Cori.

Helen Taussig Brooke

1898–1966, United States

American surgeon and head of the heart clinic in the Harriet Lane Home from 1930 to 1963, she made one of most significant medical advances of the twentieth century. She devised a procedure for surgically correcting heart defects that redirected blood flow to the lungs, thus saving the lives of many so-called "blue babies."

Safiye Ali

1900–1952, Turkey

The first female doctor from Turkey. Her father and grandfather were senior palace officials. She received an excellent education, carefully orchestrated by her family, finishing at the American college in Istanbul in 1916. From childhood she had always dreamt of becoming a physician. Her parents sent her to study medicine in Germany at Würzburg and she became the first Turkish woman to study at a German university. She qualified as a gynecologist and pediatrician in 1921. Marrying a German ophthalmologist, both opened their practice in Istanbul. Safiye represented Turkey at international symposia on medicine on three occasions.

Barbara McClintock

1902–1992, United States

American biologist, winner of the Nobel Prize in Physiology or Medicine in 1983 (the third woman to receive it). Discovered "wandering genes" or "transposable elements."

Channeling her immense energies into scientific research, she possessed a toughness, stamina, daring, and eagerness to go when none had gone before that enabled her to do a thirteen-hour day. As long as she was learning, investigating, proposing hypotheses and exhaustively checking them, she was a happy woman. Studying relentlessly, "giving herself lessons" when she lacked money or when misogyny stood in her way, aged twenty-five she obtained a PhD in botany and was named postgraduate instructor at Cornell in 1927. Particularly interested in microscopic cell study, she was a pioneer in cytogenetics. With the assistance

Barbara McClintock in New York, October 1983.
She had recently been awarded the Nobel Prize for Medicine.

of a student, Harriet Creighton, and working herself to the bone, she dealt with corn (maize) seedlings and confirmed what Morgan had discovered in 1911: chromosomes are indeed what carry the genes.

In 1930, McClintock was the first to describe the crossing-over of homologous chromosomes during meiosis; then, in 1931, again together with her assistant, she proved the link between crossing-over and the recombination of genetic traits. She published the first genetic map for corn in 1931, a discovery universally recognized at the Sixth International Congress of Genetics in 1932. The third woman to become a member of the US Academy of Sciences, she was the first to preside over the Genetics Society of America. Receiving many prizes, she never obtained a post worthy of her attainments, first occupying an assistant professorship at the University of Missouri, and then, aged thirty-nine, working in the genetic research center at Cold Spring Harbor. Nonetheless, she advanced daring hypotheses based on the changes she observed in corn plants. After seven years' research, McClintock arrived at the conclusion that genes can have a regulating activity on genome expression and that in addition certain sections of the genome can move about on the same chromosome and even jump to another one (transposition). The announcement of her discovery was met with total incomprehension by her colleagues. Yet all these jumping, shifting, combining genes had a rejuvenating effect on evolutionary science and, by the 1970s, not a single expert was still advocating the immutability of genetic inheritance.

Learning that she had been awarded the Nobel Prize on the radio, she felt overwhelmed by an honor that came so late that it seemed merely to interrupt the research she was then undertaking. She modestly declared that what is known as scientific knowledge is actually a huge joke; according to her, one manages to establish many correlations, but not the truth, and life is much more marvelous than science can enable us to discover.

Rachel Carson

1907–1964, United States

American biologist and pioneer in ecology. A graduate in zoology and marine biology, she very quickly recognized the extent to which the chemical industry pollutes the environment. She enjoyed a remarkable career, less for her own benefit than to alert public opinion as to the risks incurred, especially in terms of health. Her essay, Silent Spring, which appeared in 1962, a good twenty years before ecology became trendy, denounced, among many things, the dangers of toxic chemicals.

In 1969 she returned to her native Italy, which awarded her the title "Grande Signora della Scienza." Directing the Institute of Cellular Biology in Rome, she entitled an overview of her life published in 1988, *In Praise of Imperfection*.

Gertrude Elion

1918–1999, United States

American biochemist, winner of the Nobel Prize in Physiology or Medicine in 1988, with Sir James Black and the American George H. Hitchings. The daughter of immigrants of Lithuanian and Polish origin who had been ruined in the crisis of 1929, she had to work while pursuing her doctorate. A chemistry graduate from Hunter College, she got a job as a voluntary lab technician. In 1944 she was

Rita Levi-Montalcini

born 1909, Italy

Neurobiologist, winner of the Nobel Prize in Physiology or Medicine in 1983. Rejecting her "destiny" of housewife and mother, she always wanted to be a doctor. In the face of fatherly opposition, she studied at the University of Turin, becoming passionately interested in that "jungle," the nervous system, but when Mussolini seized power, it became impossible for her to practice. Deep in the Italian countryside, she undertook research in her bedroom, using chicken embryos, and also worked as a nurse in refugee camps. As the situation was becoming extremely perilous she went into exile to St. Louis, USA. There, aided by a young biochemist, she isolated the nerve growth factor (NGF), thereby elucidating the transmission of nerve signals to cells, for which she earned her Nobel Prize.

The discovery has facilitated an approach to tumors that hopefully may one day lead to therapy for diseases such as Alzheimer's and Parkinson's.

Gertrude Elion.

taken on by the Wellcome Laboratories, collaborating with Hitchings on clarifying the differences between the metabolism of nucleic acid in healthy and in cancerous human cells. She has PhDs in science from George Washington University, the University of Michigan, and Brown University, and is science research director and head of the department of experimental therapy at Burroughs Wellcome. She also teaches at Duke University, Durham. Her discoveries include: cytostatic purinethol against leukemia and pyrimethamine against malaria (1952), aziathioprine that limits transplant rejection (1962), allopurinol against gout (1966), a broad-spectrum antibiotic (1969), the antiviral acyclovir against herpes, and azidothymidine (AZT, 1974) used in the treatment of AIDS.

Rosalyn Yalow.

screening technique for newborn babies has been routine since 1980.

Rosalyn Yalow

born 1921, United States

Winner of the Nobel Prize in Physiology or Medicine in 1977 (shared with Roger Guillemin and Andrew Scally). As a teaching assistant in physics at the University of Illinois, she was the sole woman among four hundred teachers. After running a radioisotope service in a hospital in the Bronx for more than twenty years, she worked with Solomon Berson, their research enabling them to make the revolutionary invention of radioimmunology. This laboratory technique allows the measurement of any biological substance present in the blood or urine in the most negligible quantities (down to one million-millionth of a gram). The identification and proportion of hormones in the hypothalamus can be used to monitor cancers and diagnose allergies. For example, hormonal treatment for thyroid insufficiency in newborns can forestall serious disablement. In France, this

Christiane Nuesslein-Volhard

born 1942, Germany

German research geneticist, winner of the Nobel Prize in Physiology or Medicine in 1995 with the Americans Edward B. Lewis and Eric F. Wieschaus. Formed in the laboratory ran by Walter Gehring, she runs the genetic division at the Max-Planck Institute for developmental biology in Tübingen. Divorced and childless, she is frank, uncomplicated, wonderfully energetic, and, although she says she can be lazy, is in fact indefatigable once a subject grabs her interest. She has received many prizes including the Albert-Lasker Award for basic Medical Research, (1991), the Louis-Jeantet Prize for Medicine (1992), the Nobel itself, and the Oréal-UNESCO award (2006) for women in science. Her

Christiane Nuesslein-Volhard, 1995.

Lihadh Al-Gazali

DOB unknown, Iraq/United Arab Emirates

Prizewinner in 2008 of the Oréal-UNESCO award for women in science, for the UAE. In a region where marriages between blood relations create havoc, she set up the first office to register birth defects, demonstrating the importance of prenuptial consultation. In institutions where education is traditionally separated by gender, she can be seen wearing trousers teaching students dressed in robes.

Linda Buck

born 1947, United States

American biologist and winner of the Nobel Prize in Physiology or Medicine in 2004 (together with Richard Axel) for her work on smell.

Linda Buck obtained a psychology and microbiology diploma in 1975 from the University of Washington, completing a PhD in immunology at the medical center of the University of Texas. For her post-doctoral research, she explored the operation of the olfactory system, the least studied of the five senses, whose basic mechanisms make it possible to memorize some ten thousand odors. The importance of odor perception was recognized by Linda Buck when working in the Fred Hutchinson Cancer Research Center, Seattle.

Starting from analyses of the DNA of mice (which possess more olfactory receptors than humans), combined with physiological and genetic studies, she discovered the existence of a thousand different genes that code for smell receptors in the mammal genome. Located in the epithelium, each receptor is capable of detecting several molecules to compose a broad palette of odors. Once detected, the nervous system

center of interest is how a cluster of cells through a modicum of organization can become an embryo. She and the two American researchers were rewarded for enabling the molecular decoding of the complex mechanisms of embryogenesis and the root causes for a series of defects. Already identified for the drosophila fruit-fly, these mechanisms that control the cellular and tissue transformations of the egg to the point of complete organization can now be seen as valid for all living species, and therefore for mammals and humans. The three Nobel laureates identified, described, and classified the genes that play key roles in controlling development. In spite of much potential for misuse, this research has opened the door to treatment of various genetic anomalies.

Linda Buck at a press conference at the Wyndham Hotel, Washington, on December 1, 2004.

transmits the information to the brain for analysis. Starting in 1980, Buck's work was published in 1991. Prior to winning the Nobel Prize, Linda Buck was named professor in the neurobiology department at the Harvard Medical Center in 2001 and then member of the National Academy of Sciences in 2003. Her work has proved a springboard for further genetic and molecular analysis of the mechanism of smell, and on the pheromones so essential for communication and the source of many forms of sexual and social behavior.

of Science Prize, the King Faisal International Prize for Medicine, the Research and Medicine Prize from the Institute of Life Sciences, and the International AIDS Society Prize. She was made officer of the Order of the Legion of Honor in 2006. The Nobel Prize was announced while she was at the Fifth Health Congress at Phnom Penh, as she is director of ANRS (the French agency that researches on AIDS and hepatitis) in South-East Asia, a post that represents a chance to develop cooperation with countries in the south. She has devoted herself without stint as much to applied as to fundamental research in immunology and virology, so as to make a meaningful impact on human health problems. She became aware of the dramatic nature of the situation when traveling in the Central African Republic in 1983. If, at that time, people were unaware of the scope of the pandemic, she and her team made a first description of HIV, calling it LAV. Today, after research lasting a quarter of a century, and noting the devastation it has caused, she has redoubled her efforts, turning to the disease's innate regulatory mechanisms, by studying the early telltales on the molecular scale in order to detect the first effects of the development of the virus (observed especially in primates).

Françoise Barré-Sinoussi

born 1947, France

Winner of the Nobel Prize in Physiology or Medicine in 2008 with Luc Montagnier for their discovery of HIV. Less familiar than that of her colleague, the name of Françoise Barré-Sinoussi, laboratory head and senior professor at the Pasteur Institute and director of and senior professor at INSERM, has been associated to date with 216 original publications in international scientific reviews. The professor has received the Sovac Prize, the Körber Foundation Prize, the French Academy

Françoise Barré-Sinoussi.

Elizabeth Blackburn

born 1948, Tasmania

Carol Greider

born 1961, United States

Nobel Prize for Medicine in 2009 with Jack Szostak for work on telomeres (DNA structures located at the ends of chromosomes) and the enzyme telomerase that protects cells from ageing (thus sometimes known as the "enzyme of immortality"). Her research is a major advance in the understanding of cancer (and a possible door to new therapies) and of cell death (leading perhaps to ways of extending human life).

The daughter of doctors, from a very early age Elizabeth Blackburn was intent on following a scientific career. If the remarks of a teacher who thought it odd that such a pretty girl should bother with science shocked her, they also steeled her resolve. After secondary schooling in Tasmania and Melbourne, she obtained a science degree and then her master's in 1972. Continuing her studies in England, she gained a doctorate from Cambridge, graduating further in molecular and cellular biology at Yale in 1975 and 1977. By 1978 she was professor of molecular biology at Berkeley, California, before entering the Department of Microbiology and Immunology at the University of San Francisco, directing it from 1993 to 1999. She is currently Morris Herzstein Professor of Biology and Physiology at University of California, San Francisco (UCSF).

Carol Greider has been professor at the department of molecular biology and genetics at Johns Hopkins University School of Medicine, Baltimore, since 1997.

Her father was a physics teacher, while her mother died when she was only six. A pupil of Blackburn's, together they identified and named telomerase in 1985, receiving many prizes and awards prior to the Nobel (three of them jointly). Greider defends the cause of women in her field—a relatively small number faced with a close-knit and self-interested old-boy network—contending that motherhood and its responsibilities should not prove a stumbling-block to a successful scientific career.

Carol Greider.

Emmy Noether

1882–1935, Germany/United States

German mathematician whose work founded modern algebra. Emmy Amalie, as she was originally called, had to overcome much misogyny to be able to sit in on university lectures; she even needed an exemption to be permitted to enter the examinations. She managed to register at the University of Erlangen, her native city, and submit a thesis on algebraic invariants. Her work impressed the great mathematician, David Hilbert, and he invited her to the University of Göttingen, where she became his assistant. After 1917, she was permitted to teach, unpaid. As this brilliant researcher progressed by leaps and bounds, Hilbert tried to secure a lecturing position for her, but sexist prejudice got the better of his efforts. It was only in 1922 that she was permitted to sit for her Habilitation (allowing her to teach at university); her dissertation on the theory of ideals in ring domains broke fresh ground, but she was only appointed to a part-time lectureship with a meager stipend. After she was expelled by the Nazis due to her Jewish descent, she left to teach in the United States, initially at Bryn Mawr College, and then at the prestigious Institute of Advanced Study, Princeton.

Quitting traditional algebra, with its calculations and operations, Noether's universe is completely abstract and based on purely formal properties and

Emmy Noether c. 1930.

concepts (associativity, commutation). In spite of the abstruseness of her subject, her students, the so-called "Noether's boys," formed something like a school. Her name has passed into posterity in terms such as Noetherian rings and modules.

Irmgard Flügge-Lotz

1903–1974, Germany

German engineer, a specialist in aerodynamics and the inventor of the automatic pilot. Her father was a mathematician, but it was her mother who awakened her interest in technical matters. "I wanted a career in which I would always be happy, even unmarried," she recalled in 1969. In 1929, Flügge-Lotz obtained an engineering doctorate from the Technical University, Hanover. She was named head of the aerodynamics department at the University of Göttingen, where, in 1931, she developed the method of calculating the distribution of lift forces

on a plane wing that bears her name (Lotz method). Pooling their expertise, and in spite of their anti-Nazi sentiments, Flügge-Lotz and her husband (also an aerodynamics professor), were permitted to remain in Germany throughout the war, since aeronautical research was under the authority of Göring, who put technological know-how above ideological "purity." It was in this period that Flügge-Lotz started developing the principle of the automatic pilot as a replacement for manual control.

Moving to the United States with her husband shortly after the war, they were named professors at the University of Stanford, Irmgard Flügge-Lotz becoming the first full-time female member of staff in the engineering department. Professor emeritus in engineering mechanics and in aeronautics and astronautics at Stanford in 1968, she was elected to the American Institute of Aeronautics and Astronautics in 1970, receiving an achievement award from the Society of Women Engineers.

Grace Hopper.

Grace Hopper

1906–1992, United States

American mathematician and inventor of the COBOL language in 1957.

Graduating with a BSc (1928) in mathematics and physics from Vassar College, she taught there, continuing to study mathematics at Yale where she obtained a master's. Serving in the Navy during the Second World War, she worked on the first entirely automatic computer, the Harvard Mark I, and was the first to program it. Subsequently involved in the development of Harvard Marks II and III, her chief concern was that computing languages should not be the preserve of mathematicians alone. She invented an intermediate process, the compiler, before going on to creating COBOL in 1959, the first language to allow programming using everyday vocabulary. For twenty years COBOL remained the most widely used computer script in the world. In 1951, together with her team, she developed Univac, the first computer with a buffer memory. The word "bug" also stemmed from her work: one day she discovered an insect wedged in between two contacts, creating an operating fault. The term soon caught on to mean a programming error. In 1967, the Navy called upon her expertise once again to draw up standards for their computers. She ended her record with the rank of rear admiral and was decorated with a Defense Distinguished Service Medal.

Daisy Bates

1863–1951, Ireland

Irish anthropologist and explorer. After a childhood in a Dublin orphanage, she emigrated to Australia, quickly leaving the Christian community in the city and moving into the Nullarbor Desert, where she found naked black men armed with hunting sticks, having herself arrived dressed in a silk gown, carrying a sunshade and wearing a hat, veil, and gloves,

Bates was utterly transfixed by these indigenous people, and lived among them for some forty years. Tending them for the syphilis transmitted by white people, she gradually learned about their language and religion, their festivals and customs. First empathically and intuitively, she slowly embarked on a fully-fledged anthropological survey that concluded that these people had culture and civilization of their own. In 1914, at the conference of the British Association for the Advancement of Science, she gave a speech in which she appealed for help for what she called "her" people—as well as indicting those accused of raping and mistreating ten-year-old indigenous girls. Describing how vicious whites would set upon the indigenous people near the railway lines, she demonstrated how brutality and savagery came from the settlers' side, not from that of the "savages." Demonstrating rare sensitivity and intelligence, this original point of view prefigures the indigenous struggle of the twentieth century.

In 1934, she was awarded a CBE and was appointed as an adviser on Aboriginal affairs. However, a few months after her death, "her" people were being evicted from their sacred lands to make way for a nuclear test site.

Dorothy Garrod

1892–1968, Great Britain

English archaeologist and paleontologist; first woman to be appointed professor at the University of Cambridge (1939–52). After studying both at Newnham College, Cambridge, and at the University of Oxford, and then under the direction of Abbé Breuil in France, her doctorate centered on Paleolithic France. She headed many excavations, in Gibraltar (1925–26), Palestine (1928–31), Iraq (1931–34), and Bulgaria (1938). During her two years on Mount Carmel, Palestine (today in Israel; the city of Haifa stands at its foot), she discovered Neanderthal remains (300,000 BCE), first a skeleton of a female, followed by others of men, women, and children. This find was extraordinary in that no skeleton from the period had hitherto been unearthed outside Europe ("Neanderthal" comes from the name of a valley near Düsseldorf in Germany). At the same site, she also found no less than 92,000 stone tools. In 1948 she returned to her excavations in Europe—in particular in France and Vienna, finishing in Lebanon in 1958. Decorated with a CBE in 1965, this archaeological pioneer received a Gold Medal from the British Archaeological Association shortly before she died.

Margaret Mead

1901–1978, United States

American anthropologist. A full life included three husbands and three divorces, one miscarriage, one daughter, months spent among the Samoans, as much time in Manaus, and a curious sojourn among the Iatmul (a New Guinea group renowned as one of fiercest on the planet), as well as authorship of a whole shelf of books. *Coming of Age in Samoa* and *Growing Up in New Guinea* show how boys and girls, brought up in heterosexual and homosexual freedom, can grow up into carefree adults. Subsequent anthropologists have contested the scientific veracity of her conclusions, however, suspecting her of wanting above all to prove that American society, with its "Puritanism," would do well to learn from these "savages." It is indeed conceivable that her ideas on sexual freedom colored her views, but the researches of this intrepid explorer, her thousands of photographs (of Bali especially), her innumerable discussions with local populations, remain invaluable. And it is in this context that she still deserves the international reputation she earned with *Male and Female* (1949).

Margaret Mead studying the shrunken heads she had brought back from her travels in New Guinea, 1934.

Gloria Montenegro

DOB unknown, Chile

Chilean researcher and winner in 1998 of the Oréal-UNESCO award for women in science, for South America. She began a program to rehabilitate zones threatened by desertification, releasing bees to pollinate medicinal plants and produce honey, from which is extracted an antibacterial spray that protects carrots and potatoes from rot.

Dian Fossey

1932–1985, United States

American zoologist/ethologist. With an alcoholic and violent father and an odiously authoritarian father-in-law, she was at her least troubled during the eighteen years she spent hermit-like among the mountain gorillas of Rwanda. Fossey was determined to defend these peaceful if powerful vegetarians—fond of bark, leaves, and fruit, and communicating through a wide range of signals in sound and gesture—that are so close to human beings but severely threatened by them, too, through poaching, deforestation, and thoughtless tourism. There probably remain around three hundred in the mountains of Central Africa. The primatologist set up the Karisoke Research Center in the Virunga Mountains, Ruhengeri Province, Rwanda, a haven where these great apes that can stand two meters tall are cared for before being reintroduced into the wild. But, because she got in the way of illegal trafficking, Dian was murdered, leaving behind her a bestselling book *Gorillas in the Mist*, which was made into a movie. The zoologist, surrounded by her charges, alerts us to what happens when humanity fails to respect the biosphere.

Jane Goodall

born 1934, Great Britain

English primatologist. Initially assistant to paleontologist and primatologist Dr. Louis Leakey, she lived with wild chimpanzees in the Lake Tanganyika region of Tanzania, where she discovered how they use twigs to dig out termites and stones as hammers. The chimpanzee is one of the very rare species with this type of predictive intelligence. Jane Goodall was also the first to realize that chimpanzees are omnivorous. Defending them in their last redoubts, they are threatened with extinction through poaching and galloping deforestation: every minute in the tropical rainforest the equivalent of eighty football fields is cleared. More than half of the forest has been felled since 1945. To alert people to the danger, in 1977 Jane founded the Jane Goodall Institute. Made a Dame of the British Empire by Queen

Dian Fossey.

Jane Goodall in Tanzania in 1994.

Borneo jungle, Biruté has observed that, if males rank physically above females, the latter are clever enough to join forces to avoid being dominated. In spite of their arms that dangle down to their ankles, this seriously endangered anthropoid looks so like a human that the Malay call it "man of the jungle"—*orangutan* in their language.

Elizabeth II and a "peace envoy" by Secretary General Kofi Annan in 2002, she has received the Tanzania Kilimanjaro Award, the National Geographic Society Hubbard Medal, the Benjamin Franklin Medal in life science, the UNESCO medal, and the Gandhi/King Award for nonviolence.

Biruté Marija Filomena Galdikas

born 1946, Germany

Canadian primatologist of German extraction, recognized universally for her studies on orangutans. One of "Leakey's Angels" (named for paleontologist Dr. Louis Leakey who was to give her guidance) and a researcher at the Simon Fraser University in Canada, she is president of the International Orangutan Foundation, devoted to publicizing information about the plight of these creatures. Spending prolonged periods in the

Shirley Strum

born 1947, United States

American primatologist,. After studying biology and anthropology at the University of Berkeley, in 1972 she set out for Kenya with the intention of ascertaining the capacities of early man by comparing them with those of baboons. Captivated by these monkeys, she studied them for twenty-five years. In the National Park of Amboseli, she worked courageously among these animals, and gradually the baboons allowed her to join the group. She discovered a whole network of alliances and subtle uses of communication, deciphering a rule system of social reciprocity and interrelationships forged by regular interaction. It is not brute force that reigns, but a complex system of compromise in which the females always have a chance. In her book *Almost Human: a Journey into the World of the Baboons*, Strum convinces her readers that these monkeys are sensitive and astute. She steps in when she witnesses farmers trying to kill baboons, though these gentle animals plunder their crops and the men have to put up some kind of defense.

Game Changers

"The organization of a woman's Olympics would be impractical, uninteresting, unaesthetic, and improper."

(Pierre de Coubertin, creator of the modern Olympic Games)

For several years, South Africa was excluded from the Olympic Games because it practiced segregation against black people. In Barcelona, however, thirty-five national delegations were made up exclusively of men. The officials, like audiences all over the world, hardly seemed to blanch at what was clearly apartheid against women. In blatant infringement of the Olympic Charter (which prohibits "any form of discrimination for reasons of race, religion, politics, or gender"), the countries concerned argued that from an Islamic point of view "the simultaneous presence of male and female athletes in the same place" could lead to "corruption." To preserve "feminine decency," men who demand that "their" wives leave home clad in garments that conceal them totally have organized rival Olympics at which men are forbidden to take part thereby neatly enshrining male/female segregation. A kind of dumbed-down Olympics, it has taken place behind closed doors every four years since 1993 in Tehran, and features women competing clad decorously in chadors. At the Atlanta Games in 1996, there were also veiled sportswomen among the delegations of Iran and Egypt.

The Atlanta Plus Committee, created by **Linda Weil-Curiel**, asked that countries practicing gender apartheid be forbidden to participate. At the Games in June 2008, an Iranian woman in a taekwondo event asked to wear a scarf. In October 2008, Rakia al-Gassra, a sprinter from Bahrain, ran with an Islamic veil aerodynamically shaped "to reconcile sport and faith, competition and religion." The Ligue des Droits des Femmes (League of the Rights of Women), founded in France in 1983 by Simone de Beauvoir, rightly pointed out that the Olympic Charter "debars countries that exclude women," while the league's president, Annie Sugier, recalls that "the oppression of women is vehicled by the body and that the place of women in sport is a litmus test of their place in society in general."

At the Olympic Games in Atlanta, United States, on July 19, 1996, Lida Farima heads the delegation of her country, Iran, as it enters the Olympic stadium.

This backward step is all the more regrettable in that the history of female sports has followed—often even preceded—that of the emancipation of women, a process predicated on freedom of movement and therefore on changes in attire. **Virginia Hériot** tackled head-on the deeply held prejudice that having a woman on board ship brought bad luck. Dubbed "the sailor in petticoats," this pioneer of the sea sported tailored suits with a white skirt, jewelry, and sandals, as well as a manly-looking beret over a short hairstyle. Such dress seems to us today pretty constricting. Taking vestmental audacity to new levels, the Australian **Annette Kellermann**

(1887–1975), a specialist in water ballet, was the first to wear a swimsuit that did not cover the whole body from neck to knee but stopped at the buttocks.

In 1919, English athlete **Elaine Burton** broke another strong taboo by wearing shorts. A Franco-Belgian born in the nineteenth century, Hélène Dutrieu (the first woman to receive the Legion of Honor), was the champion cyclist of France, Great Britain, Italy, Europe, and the world when just nineteen. Her secret? She rode without a corset (a thing almost unimaginable at the time, but it greatly assisted her breathing), and in trousers (formerly just for men). She was also to try her hand at motorbikes, stunt driving, and, in 1910, won the Femina Cup for flying. Also born in the nineteenth century, tennis champion **Suzanne Lenglen** revolutionized female sporting dress with pleated skirts that sometimes let a knee peek out, while back in 1900 **Charlotte Cooper** had hardly risked exposing an ankle. American tennis player Helen Wills was the first to replace tights with bobby socks. These examples show that, although far from being the only precondition for progress, freedom of movement is inextricably linked with liberty and equality. In South America, Amerindian women climb through the Andes to participate in football matches at which they can win a couple of chickens, as well as their husbands' admiration, playing in thick layered skirts and shoed in tatty sandals.

Constraints in clothing have not been the only factors hampering women in sport: macho prejudice has done its best too. Playing sport was considered unnatural and dangerous for the feeble constitution of females. Thus, at the 1928 Amsterdam Games, after the German athlete **Radke-Batschauer** won the 800 meters and received her medal, the authorities decided that the race was unbecoming for ladies and promptly banned it. This distance for women only reappeared in 1960. When **Junko Tabei**, a Japanese mountaineer who has climbed the seven highest summits on the globe, sought financing for a further expedition, she was greeted with a cringing example of threadbare sexism: "Raise your children before 'raising' yourself!" A woman only needs a few goals in life—to be a wife and mother, and, most crucially, to remain in "her" place, at the bottom (of the mountain). As if women not only had, inevitably, to become mothers, but also that maternity and sporting excellence are necessarily incompatible. Junko Tabei, for instance, has chosen both: a mother at thirty-five, she was still climbing.

Windsurfer **Raphaëla Gouvelot** expresses strong views when asked a question so often addressed to women: How can you think of not being a mother? "Does every woman's life have inevitably to include motherhood? Is one a 'subwoman' because one hasn't produced kids?" She goes on to talk about the children of her village and the hopes and dreams she offers them. And yet when the proposal was tabled to send **Valentina Tereshkova** into space, one specialist, Sergei

Wimbledon, 1908.
Charlotte Cooper winning the Ladies' Singles.

Korolev, declared: "Space is no place for chicks," because they are too nervous and likely to become sterile. (Valentina had a daughter a few years after the mission).

For competitors in all sports, the body is a tool. Certain sportswomen, for instance, eliminate their periods by mechanical or chemical means. They are often advised to defer pregnancy, or it can simply be forbidden to them; and, if they ignore the received wisdom, it can spell the end of their career. Despite all this, the facts show that women can be breakneck aviators like **Jacqueline Auriol**, boxers like **Anne-Sophie Mathis**, dancers like **Carolyn Carlson**, mariners like **Karine Fauconnier**, gymnasts like Larissa Latynina (a mother at sixteen), athletes like **Wilma Rudolph** (mother at seventeen), explorers of the ice sheet like **Bettina Aller**; that they can take deadly risks, face the most extreme ordeals, exceed their physical limits, observe iron discipline in a search for self-enhancement or in the hope of ultimate victory—but none of this needs prevent them from being mothers. **Caroline Aigle**, the first woman fleet commander, the first woman sharpshooter, world and French armed forces champion in triathlon, and skydiving ace, was the mother of a two-year-old boy. After becoming pregnant once again, she learnt that she had a fatal cancer; asking for a Caesarean so she could see her child alive, she died a few days later. Proof, if proof were needed, that having children is not a burden or handicap, but, on the contrary, a strength. Trainers, in the Soviet Union especially, have understood this fact and even ask high-level sportswomen to get pregnant, aware that in the first months of their condition the body possesses greater vitality, since an increase in blood volume provides an enhanced oxygen supply to the muscles. But, in what is a gruesome instrumentalization of this specific trait of

With more than 1,600 flying hours on the clock, Caroline Aigle piloting a Mirage 2000. It is 1999, the year she received her fighter pilot's license, a matter of months before she died aged thirty-two.

female physiology, trainers sometimes force their "charges" to submit to an abortion.

In general, however, groundbreaking women in sport are not easily led by the nose. The same qualities characterize almost all of them: dauntless courage, reckless endeavor, an unbending will to get the better not only of their rivals but also of their entourage and the stumbling blocks of prejudice. For, if all those who play sport have to learn to master their body and constantly push it to its limits, throughout the twentieth century sportswomen have also had to swim against the tide of the traditional image of womanhood: motionless, smiling and calm, with gentle, measured gestures. To do sport is a conquest and entering competitions and exceeding their physical capacities before everybody's eyes has long been seen as provocative. Female champions are fully conscious that their exploits transgress the ground rules. "The sky is the only place there's no prejudice," said **Bessie Coleman**, the first African-American pilot. **Tabei** also found it easier to breathe on the peaks: "Compared with the everyday world, mountains treat men and women equally."

Some women think of sport as an arena in which they can take revenge on men. The boxer **Myriam Lamare** has been champing at the bit that men put on her since the beginning of her career by not recognizing the value of her sport, she simply hits harder—at them too (figuratively speaking). "It's a challenge that offers the dual advantage of fighting as a sportsperson and as a woman." Perhaps more women should take up boxing so the rest can throw off their shackles? In Kinshasa, though, poverty-stricken girls take to the ring to survive, winning a wrap or a can of milk. "I'm sacrificing my body," says one. It's a dead end. There, sport does not harbor the promise of freedom it ought to.

The feeling many pioneers give us, however, as role models, as pathfinders for upcoming generations, is one of gleeful freedom. **Amelia Earhart**, the trailblazing American aviator, fired the imagination of many girls who saw her as an example they could follow. She was perfectly aware of this role, as her last letter to her husband shows: "Please know that I am aware of the hazards. I want to do it because I want to do it. Women must try to do things as men have tried. When they fail, their failure must be a challenge to others." All women who have since taken to the skies do so in her slipstream.

But then there are those who sail the seven seas on the bridges of steamers or of container ships; long-haul solo mariners who brave the Roaring Forties in monohulls or catamarans; those who dash across the surface of the waters on a sailboard or in a rowing boat; those who traipse through endless blizzards; those who beat men at tennis, or run against them in races or ride against them on bikes, or even come to blows with them in the ring.... All different ways of grappling with the toughness, the brutality of nature,

of risking one's life, of overcoming, of winning, of seeking pride in one's achievements. All different ways of exploding the outworn but indestructible myth of female inferiority.

One particularly heartwarming example was given by **Samantha Davies** (Englishwoman born in 1974). Coming third in the Vendée Globe of 2009, she stood clad in a bathing suit aboard her boat dancing to "Girls Just Wanna Have Fun" at full blast. Davies is proud of her gender: "I like being a girl," she said with a smile. Catherine Delahaie, editor-in-chief of the feminist *Clara Magazine*, voices her admiration. Samantha Davies "wasn't talking about headwinds and sporting exploits anymore; she was talking about life. I could no longer see the sea or the sail. She seemed to contain all of humanity. This is what women can do when they take up a discipline. With simple gestures, they can question the universal."

Samantha Davies aboard the single-hulled Roxy. *She came in tenth in the eighth Jacques Vabre transatlantic "Le Havre-Salvador" race.*

Loïe Fuller

1862–1928, United States

Dancer, choreographer, and producer. Born Marie-Louise, Loïe Fuller was perhaps not technically the most accomplished dancer in the world. Yet she invented new forms of dance, using sticks attached to veils and nets. Her movements were amplified in an effect enhanced by powerful spotlights to surround her with a strange, luminous halo, creating a living, moving light show. Her *Dance of the Butterfly* and her *Fire Dance*, for example, were both studies in motion that attempted to capture space. The "Electric Fairy" was soon the toast of Paris—at the Folies-Bergères, at the Olympia, at the Châtelet theater, and in even in private houses such as Pierre and Marie Curie's.

Isadora Duncan

1878–1927, United States

Pioneer of modern dance. Raised single-handedly by her Irish mother, the little Isadora was soon putting on shows with her two brothers and sister. Trained in classical ballet, Isadora Duncan little by little freed herself from its constraints and started improvising. Dancing in bare feet with her hair loose, she wore a light tunic resembling a toga. Fascinated by Ancient Greece, Isadora started out performing in London then in Paris, Berlin, Florence, and Moscow.

She was praised for her fluid style of dancing performed to music not originally intended for choreography, such as Beethoven's Seventh Symphony, Chopin, or Gluck. A strong personality and a liberated woman, she went on lengthy tours through the USA, accompanied by a group of her pupils known as the "Isadorables," and gradually her modernity began to be appreciated in her native country. Her many lovers included director Gordon Craig, with whom she had a daughter, and the industrial magnate Paris Singer, who gave her a son. Her life was beset by tragedy: the accidental death of both her children; the suicide of the alcoholic Russian poet Sergei Esenin, whom she had married (in spite of her long refusal to "lower herself" to what she called "the degrading state" of matrimony) and from whom she separated. Strangled by her scarf caught in a car wheel, her death seems in keeping with her troubled existence.

Ruth Saint-Denis

1879–1968, United States

The mother of modern dance. Influenced by Isadora Duncan and Loïe Fuller, Saint-Denis broke with the codes of traditional ballet, in particular by dancing barefoot. In 1915, she and her husband, Ted Shawn, founded the Denishawn School in Los Angeles; they trained the best dancers in modern dance, inspired by Egyptian and Indian influences. Martha Graham owed her vocation to her, a debt she acknowledged when she said: "She was everything to me." Saint-Denis was also a choreographer, and among her finest works are *A Pageant of Egypt* and *Greece and India*. In 1931, the couple separated and the school closed down, but the dancer continued her stage career to the grand old age of eighty-three.

Mary Wigman

1886–1973, Germany

German dancer and choreographer. A pioneer of modern dance, Mary Wigman only began to train as a dancer at twenty-four, since her parents, bicycle-sellers in Hanover, did not move in artistic circles. The choreographer Rudolf von Laban was an excellent teacher who enabled her to develop her own style. She opened a school of "free dance" in Dresden in 1920, where she encouraged her pupils to improvise without losing their sense of structure. She taught her highly original technique in various countries, and especially in New York, after a triumphant tour through America in the 1930s. In 1936, she composed the choreography for the opening ceremony of the Berlin Olympics, although she opposed the Nazi regime. Her most famous solo piece was the *Witch's Dance* (*Hexentanz*). "It was so wonderful," she commented, "to abandon oneself to one's malevolent desires, to absorb the forces that dare peek out from beneath the veneer of our civilization." She performed in a sort of trance shattering the trammels of traditional dance and eliminating prettiness to the sound of brutal drumming.

Mary Wigman.

Martha Graham

1894–1991, United States

Graham was the most significant American choreographer and dancer of the twentieth century. She was a pupil of Ruth Saint-Denis, but soon split from her teacher because she wanted to draw inspiration from real life. In *Imperial Gesture* and *Every Soul Is a Circus*, she seemed to fly. It's not that she had sprung wings; it came from her understanding of how to breathe. Her famous "contraction release" is close to the breathing used by African dancers, yogis, and Taoists. For Graham "modern dance" had to be based on respiration, since life begins and ends with the breath. "The spinal column is the tree of life."

So as to "return to the source of the emotions," Martha visited and drew on the first American communities (Sioux "spirit dances," etc.), as well as on the Incas (Xochitl, a barbaric earth dance), Egyptians, and other *Primitive Mysteries* (choreographed in 1931).

She explores the darkest recesses of the soul, primeval truths, the unconscious. Graham, whose father was a psychiatrist, took her audiences back to the days of elementary, violent emotions embodied by women: *Medea (Cave of the Heart,* choreographed in 1946), Jocasta (in *Night Journey*, 1947), *Clytemnestra, Legend of Judith*. "Every woman is Medea. Every woman is Jocasta.... Clytemnestra is every woman when she kills." Her early ballets were for women only. "Move your vagina," she told them. Only later did she use male dancers, exploiting their virility to the full—among them, Merce Cunningham and Erick Hawkins. She was forty-four when she allowed the latter to rehearse with her and fifty-four when they married. She believed that Europeans needed American dance so as to be able to become "acrobats of God"; the United States was a new nation, free of the paraphernalia of traditional classical ballet (*pointes*, slippers, tutu, and the rest), and the body of American women was freer.

Her native land was to return the favor: made a member of the Municipal Art Society of New York in 1935, in 1937 she was invited to dance by Eleanor Roosevelt in the White House, where she was received with all due solemnity in 1976 and awarded the Medal of Freedom, the highest civil distinction in the United States.

Martha Graham and Bianca Jagger in 1983.

Philippine-born German dancer, choreographer, and ballet director, known as an "anarchist of dance." Her choreography, in which performers of both genders play out the battle of the sexes in twisted, tormented, yet paradoxically harmonious pieces, is uncompromising. Bausch exteriorizes to the point of disgust the brutality and madness of dominant males intent on degrading female bodies only too glad to serve their ends. Performed in 2005, *Rough Cut*, is one of her most important pieces—dance, theater, music, and happening all rolled into one.

With eerie cries and trenchant gestures, the dancers shake with pleasure (or pain?), diving through turbid waters or plunging into flowers, in manifest revolt against our bloodthirsty world. Shocked at the outset, dance institutions eventually recognized Bausch as a new force in theatrical art.

From 1973, she was director of the ballet of the Wuppertal Opera, the Tanztheater, a new concept she helped launch on the international scene. The French filmmaker Chantal Akerman (a pioneer of feminist cinema) made a documentary on Pina in 1983, while Fellini filmed her in *E la nave va* as did Almodóvar in *Talk to Her*. Determined to undermine the hackneyed seductiveness of dance, in *Kontakthof* she directed older nonprofessional actors; she also created works for horses.

In 2004, she received the Nijinsky Prize for best choreographer and, in 2007, the Kyoto Prize, the equivalent of a Nobel Prize for culture. At the Venice Biennial in the same year she was awarded the Golden Lion.

Pina Bausch

**1940–2009,
Philippines/Germany**

The Rite of Spring,
*staged by Pina Bausch at Sadler's
Wells, London, in 2008.*

Carolyn Carlson

born 1943, United States

American dancer and choreographer of Finnish extraction. Carolyn Carlson was to reinvent dance and popularize it in its modern guise. Her parents wanted their children to be artistic, and her father encouraged her to improvise. She won her first prize for dance when aged only seven before going on to study dance at the University of Utah and at the San Francisco Ballet.

As international as she is innovative, she danced with the Alwin Nikolais Danse Theater between 1964 and 1971, where she proved to be a virtuoso performer. After posts in Avignon, Hamburg, Milan, and Bordeaux, she was appointed "*étoile*-choreographer" (a position specially created for her) at the Paris Opera in 1974, where she also headed up a theatrical research group. In this way she made an immense contribution to the emergence of "New French Dance" in the 1970s and 1980s. In Paris, she put on several daring pieces, such as *Density 21.5* to a score by Varèse (1973), and a famous solo, *Blue Lady* (1983), in which she evoked the birth of her

son, Aleksis (born in 1981), calling it a "moment when one returns to the past."

Her remarkable career has seen her perform with many great names in dance in the most prestigious venues, including, from 1980 to 1984, La Fenice in Venice, where she set up the Teatro Danza. Something of a nomad, she lived in Venice for eight years, before residing in Finland from 1991 to 1992, where she created the ballet, *Mao*, a work of "visual poetry," to music by Kaija Saariaho. She then directed the Cullberg Ballet of Stockholm from 1992 to 1994. In 1999, Carolyn Carlson's company settled at La Cartoucherie in Vincennes. There the choreographer has established an advanced contemporary dance center for professionals, directed by world-renowned choreographers. She has also been named the artistic director of the dance section of the Venice Biennial. In 2000 and 2008, she reprised *Signes* at the Bastille Opera in Paris, a work created in 1997 for the marvelous Marie-Claude Pietragalla and for the principal Kader Belarbi. Since 2004 she has been artistic director of the Centre Chorégraphique National Roubaix, Nord-Pas de Calais. She often works with jazz musicians, in particular with her partner, the French composer René Aubry. She describes herself as a "bird-woman."

Carolyn Carlson was awarded the Golden Lion for contemporary dance at the Venice Biennial in 2006.

of mixing genres, she has sometimes flirted with hip-hop and with the circus, as in a piece for horses and dance with Eva Schakmundès, a rider with the Zingaro Equestrian Theater. Offered carte blanche at the Theater Festival in Avignon, and founding her own company, "Dansoir," she is present every-where—on the precinct in front of the Bibliothèque Nationale in Paris, at the Comédie-Française, or even in the Stanislavsky Theater in Moscow.

Meg Stuart

born 1965, United States

American choreographer, born in New Orleans (Louisiana). With her "Damaged Goods" troupe, Meg Stuart did much to revive choreography in the 1990s. Training in New York, she started out as a dancer and assistant choreographer with the Randy Warshaw Dance Company. She quickly sought to gain her independence, and it was in Brussels that she unveiled her earliest creations, such as *Disfigure Study* (1991) and *No One Is Watching* (1995).

Meg Stuart attracted notice with conceptual dance pieces featuring violence, ugliness, and physical deformity, imposing her trademark style throughout Europe. A dance of devastation, shock, and injury, a piece like *Blessed*, staged in 2007 in Paris, refers symbolically to natural catastrophes, in an echo of hurricane Katrina, which devastated her birthplace. With *Do Animals Cry*, created in 2009, she turned to the world of the family, exploring once again the language of a body confronted with existential aggression. Collaborating frequently with artists from diverse backgrounds, such as the American visual artist Ann Hamilton, filmmaker Gary Hill, and musician Hahn Rowe, Meg Stuart is a central figure on the contemporary creative scene.

Karine Saporta

born 1950, France

Choreographer and multitalented artist. She combined studies of classical ballet with philosophy and sociology at the University of Paris X, followed by video, television, photography, and choreography in the United States. This education has made her not only an innovative choreographer, but also a photographer (as at the exhibition *Hurlante et douce Antigua*), filmmaker (*Les Larmes de Nora*), theater director (see her adaptation of Colette's *L'envers du music-hall* [*Music-hall Sidelights*]), a singer, a teacher at the universities of Paris X, Caen, and then at Évry, and finally a director of the Centre Chorégraphique National (Caen/Basse-Normandie). Coalescing into staccato, self-aware worlds, her choreographies take place against flamboyant, futuristic backdrops. Fond

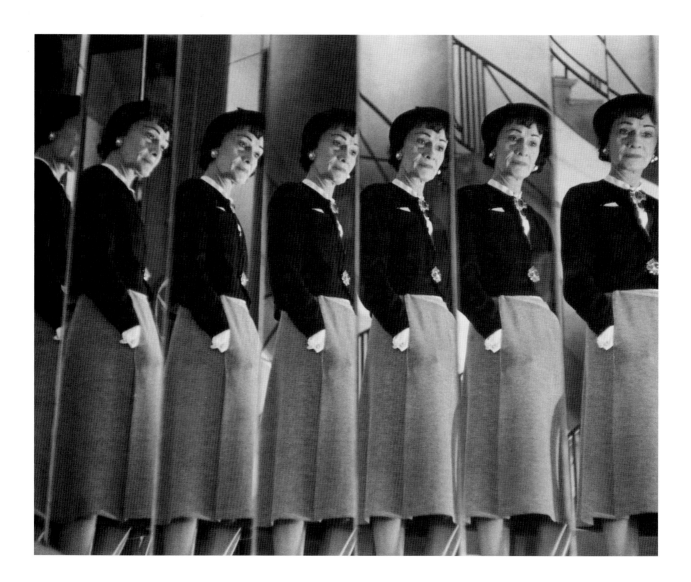

Gabrielle Chanel, known as Coco

1883–1971, France

French fashion designer, pioneer of the modern look for women. Orphaned at seven and destitute, she made her way to Paris where she succeeded, thanks to some well-heeled lovers, in opening a couture house on rue Cambon. In 1917, she was one of the first to cut her hair short and raise hemlines. She revolutionized fashions which until then had constrained the female body and covered it in haberdashery. For her, femininity can be conveyed in simple, comfortable attire, in dresses in which—as she said herself—a woman is able to ride a horse.

She chose fabrics that were easy to wear, such as tweed, jersey, and woollens, so that women could move freely without losing anything of their elegance. She even went on to launch the fashion for super comfortable travel coats and sailors' trousers. Black, a color hitherto reserved for mourning, was to become chic in any circumstance and for all echelons of society. Her suits for women, her fragrances (Chanel No. 5, created in 1924), her jewelry lines (the elaborate Tsarina model became an unpretentious necklace) were no longer to be the exclusive preserve of a tiny wealthy elite. She meanwhile became immensely rich and, disinclined to wed even the

Coco Chanel at home in rue Chambon, Paris, in 1954.

Duke of Westminster, one of the wealthiest and most refined men in England, received artists in her sumptuous private mansion, often offering them patronage.

The "Grande Demoiselle" shut up shop throughout WWII, which she spent at the Ritz in the company of a German officer. Regaining her position at the forefront of fashion proved a struggle, but in the end she succeeded once again in imposing her hallmarks of elegance and simplicity. The much-vaunted "Chanel suit," neat and black with a touch of color in the braiding and worn over a silk blouse, was a favourite with the Duchess of Windsor and Greta Garbo, as well as Jackie Kennedy, and was imitated by working women all over the world. This pleased her immensely, since, as she said, her "fashions were intended for every woman." She was buried in a suit by ... Chanel.

Gertrude Bell

1868–1926, Great Britain

English explorer, archaeologist, and spy. After leaving Oxford, she conquered several Alpine summits, before traveling from Jerusalem via Damascus to Baghdad and falling in love with the Middle East. She learnt to speak Arabic, spent entire days on horse- or camelback, and forged friendships with the Bedouins, so that, when the First World War began, she was able to pass on valuable information to the Intelligence services. But she went further and influenced diplomatic policy: for instance, so forcefully did she back Faisal ibn Hussein, son of the sheriff of Mecca, that the British Empire was persuaded to offer him the title of king of a new country called Iraq. She can only be compared to Lawrence of Arabia—though it was perhaps even harder for a woman to play a role as a "kingmaker" (indeed her protégés showed her scant gratitude). Alone in Baghdad, she was determined not to leave, eventually committing suicide.

Alexandra David-Néel in Tibetan clothes in 1929.

Alexandra David-Néel

1868–1969, Belgium/France

Franco-Belgian explorer and orientalist. Aged fifty-five, David-Néel marched for a whole month, with only Aphur (a Tibetan servant-boy she later adopted) for company, her face blackened with soot, pretending to be a beggar and eating nothing but scraps, sleeping in a tiny tent in intense cold and encountering hostile locals. On December 24, 1923, after falling into chasms and braving rain-, snow-, and sandstorms, she and Aphur had to boil bits of old boot leather to stave off hunger. They finally succeeded in reaching the capital of Tibet, a city then prohibited to outsiders. In 1926, on publishing her *My Journey to Lhasa*, "the woman on the roof of the world" became an international celebrity.

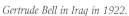

Gertrude Bell in Iraq in 1922.

After a dreary childhood in Belgium, as a young woman she had been a soprano and worked as a casino manager, living unmarried with a composer. "Live alone, remain free and proud and a virgin," she advised her fellow women. In 1904 she did marry Philippe Néel, but quickly bored of the wifely role and, shamelessly exploiting her husband's money and kindness, she left him (for just eighteen months, she claimed) and for the next fourteen years was an intrepid solo traveler and explorer of Asia.

Becoming a Buddhist and learning Sanskrit, her chief motivation was to get to know the land of the great teacher. She went to Colombo with various contraptions, including a zinc pipe, then on to Calcutta, where she draped herself in the orange scarf of a monk who has renounced the world, before donning an ocher-colored robe. In Sikkim, a tiny land then almost unknown to Europeans, and in Darjeeling, she was received by the son of the maharajah, who became a good friend, and then by the Dalai Lama (whom she found "not scholarly enough"). She rode on yaks, went over passes in the High Himalayas at 17,700 feet/5,400 meters (it was 19°F/-7°C inside her tent), repelling a tiger attack by the power of meditation, and traveled on to Nepal, Japan, Korea, and Peking. She received the title of "lady-lama" and was nicknamed the "lamp of wisdom."

In the midst of a civil war, and armed with little more than a revolver and a rosary of 108 pieces of human skull, nothing could hold her back—neither highway brigands, nor armed soldiers who barred her passage and whom she beat off with a walking stick, to the immense delight of her little servant-boy: "Oh! most revered lady, how well you beat them! Your stick has snapped in two."

On returning to France in 1924, she was received as a national heroine, a "superwoman." She bought a property in Digne that she called Samten Dzong, turning it into a haven of meditation. But she was unable to stay meditating in one place for long: aged sixty-eight, she once again set out for China, and aged eighty she was still setting up camp at more than 6,500 feet (2,000 meters). At the age of 100, David-Néel applied for a new passport.

Potala Palace, Lhassa.

Anita Conti

1899–1997, France

French marine explorer. First female oceanographer. A documentary photographer of humanist ideals employed by the French Scientific and Technical Office for Maritime Fisheries and later by the French Ministry for the Colonies. She worked in mine-clearance and journalism, as a researcher at the Oceanographic Museum in Monaco and as an ecologist.

Everyone has heard of Jacques Cousteau, and yet the figure of Anita Conti is much less well known, though both worked tirelessly to publicize the sea, its fragility, and its many treasures. Conti, an unassuming woman, indeed probably had the harder job, since she shared the life and work of fishermen. She had to gain acceptance in the savage world of the Newfoundland fishing-grounds, where a woman is traditionally regarded as little more than a distraction. She learnt to suffer, to go hungry and thirsty, and to take the lack of hygiene, the cold, the roughness and filth of the berths in her stride. And yet Conti felt real empathy for these "men, harried, with their backs hunched with exhaustion." She also had to fend for herself on trawlers loaded with thousands of kilos of stinking cod and manned by sixty sailors on the `Bois Ros`or in African dugouts fishing for shark—from Newfoundland to Dakar, from Conakry to Saint-Pierre, from Iceland to Gambia.

Her parents taught her the virtues of sport and the great outdoors from the cradle, throwing her into the sea a few days after her birth. This bracing start in life acted like a magic potion; she could swim like a fish, and she pursued her vocation relentlessly. A woman of indomitable spirit, it was her burning ambition to sail the seven seas.

Though unimpressed by school, she became a fully fledged scientist, taking water samples, calculating salinity, drawing fisheries' charts, analyzing food species and protecting their breeding grounds.

During the war, her exceptional knowledge of swells and currents gave her a special talent for mine-clearance, making her the first woman to earn the right to board military vessels. She later became the first woman to descend (to 920 feet/280 meters) in a bathyscaphe.

"Tough enough on my weatherside," as she said herself, Anita Conti was bold and adventurous, as she trembled with excitement on a sharking expedition ("a weird job for a woman," Cocteau opined) or laughing when "fishing" for mines. She combined the rigor of a scholar, when identifying unknown species or revealing the vitamin properties of shark liver, with the commitment of an ecologist when reminding us of our obligations to protect sea life, alerting the public to the dangers of by-catches that exhaust the oceans and prevent replenishment. Yet she also had the humanity to defend her fishermen, those "lords of a rough and ready trade," who, in the end, dubbed her "the first lady of the sea."

French yachtswoman. In 1928, she became the first female mariner to beat male competitors at the Olympic Games. Heiress to an immense fortune and married to a viscount (who gave her a yacht as a wedding present), she had a genuine passion for the sea, and commissioned some of the finest vessels in Europe, including the 33-foot (10-meter) *Aile*. "On the sea I glow," she would say. She lived in luxury on her 148-foot (45-meter), 400 metric ton schooner *Metéor II*, which boasted a sail area of more than 10,760 square feet (1,000 square meters). With a crew of twenty, Hériot crisscrossed the globe, covering around 150,000 nautical miles.

An excellent skipper, she won many yachting cups: in Spain in 1924, in Italy, England, France, Denmark, Finland in 1925 (with *Aile VI*), becoming Olympic champion in Amsterdam, a competition in which all the other boats were helmed by men. In 1929, the English dubbed her the foremost yachtswoman in the world. She strove to turn the sea into "a bridge between people who aim for the same ideals of prosperity, security, and mutual aid." Decorated with the Legion of Honor and Maritime Merit, this queen of the sea died, like the captain she was, aboard her yacht in the Arcachon Basin.

Virginie Hériot
1890–1932, France

Above
Virginie Hériot on the 8-meter (26-foot) craft she was to attempt to sail from Le Havre to Los Angeles in the 1930s.

Left
In Italy some time between 1929 and 1932. Virginie Hériot at the tiller of her 8-meter (26-foot) class sailing-boat AILE VI, when leading the San Remo regatta.

Sharon Adams

born 1930, United States

The first woman to sail solo across the Pacific. She sailed from California to the Hawaiian Islands, some 3,000 miles (5,000 kilometers), alone on a 25-foot sloop, a crossing that took just thirty-nine days. Upping the ante, she then sailed from Japan to California—7,400 miles (11,920 kilometers)—on board a 31-foot ketch, in just seventy-five days. In the midst of storms, with 40-foot waves, her boat capsized, her radio broke, and—unable to transmit news of her whereabouts for several weeks—she was presumed dead. She did, however, eventually arrive at port, proud of her record and yet calm.

Krystina Chojnowska Liskiewicz

born 1944, Poland

In 1976, she became the first woman to sail solo round the world. A graduate of the Polytechnic School in Gdansk, and a shipbuilding engineer, in 1975 this one-time captain of an ocean-going merchant ship obtained funds for a round-the-world trip from the Union of Polish Seamen. Having undertaken the construction of a splendid 36-foot (11-meter) vessel, *Mazurek*, she learnt of a condition to her contract: in what was a feminist-cum-publicity challenge, she had to be the first woman to sail round the world. In 1978, after towing her boat on a cargo liner from the icebound Baltic to the Canary Islands, a confident Liskiewicz set off, avoiding Cape Horn by passing through the Panama Canal. Then news came in that two other women had launched out on the same adventure.

The Australian Naomi James (born in 1950) confronted the Roaring Forties and an enormous storm in Tasmania, passed Cape Horn in freezing rain, and was forced to have her mast repaired in the Falkland Islands. She came into port on June 8. The Frenchwoman Brigitte Oudry (born in 1949) capsized in the middle of the Indian Ocean, sailed around Cape Horn in an icy wind and made it home on August 28. In the end, Liskiewicz had selected the best route: she arrived first on April 21.

Isabelle Autissier

born 1956, France

An engineer working in fisheries, Isabelle began her sailing career aboard a 21-foot (6.50-meter) steel-hulled craft, which she spent three years building. For a solo competition sponsored by *Le Figaro*, she set out on the *Écureuil Poitou-Charentes*, a very narrow vessel with a tapering hull. One night a "vicious wave with its pointed back splitting into a summit towering to five meters" crushed her boat, snapping the mast into several pieces. Nonetheless, Autissier came in seventh, becoming the first female to complete a solo, round-the-world race, in September 1991. In 1994 she set out for the Route de l'Or, 14,000 nautical miles (26,000 kilometers) against the prevailing winds.

Arrival of the Vendée Globe in 1997.

Near the Fifties, close to the Kerguelens, a snapped turnbuckle caused the mast to come crashing onto the bridge. A few days later the whole vessel capsized and Isabelle was stranded for three days before help arrived. This heroine of the high seas became a radio journalist and writer. In 2009, she chaired one of four marine research groups appointed by the French minister for the environment.

Florence Arthaud at the tiller of her boat in 1988.

Florence Arthaud

born 1958, France

In 1990 she broke the record for a solo crossing of the Atlantic and recorded the first victory by a woman in the Route du Rhum transatlantic race.

Arthaud has had to face her fair share of bad luck. In 1978, during her first transatlantic race on her X. Perimental, below decks filled up with water, a boom broke, stays snapped, ropes gave way, the top of her mast collapsed and was left hanging upside-down swaying from a cable, but she still came in eleventh, at just 21 years old. For the 1990 Route du Rhum, she set sail aboard a trimaran, Pierre I, handicapped by a medical collar after slipping a disc. She also suffered a violent hemorrhage. Despite all these setbacks, Arthaud won, making her triumphant entrance into Pointe-à-Pitre after 14 days and 10 hours.

Raphaëla Le Gouvello

born 1960, France

French windsurfer, the first to cross the Atlantic in 2000, the Mediterranean in 2002, the Pacific in 2003, and the Indian Ocean in 2006. The risks involved are hair-raising: drowning, shark attacks (though she wears leggings that emit electromagnetic waves), braving the vagaries of the weather practically defenseless (even if she did benefit from a system of airbags). But she was not just daring, she wanted to show us the beauty of the ocean and draw attention to the stupidity of using its waters as a dump for human refuse. A specialist in aquiculture, she started working in a pharmaceutical laboratory, before heading up a company dealing in hygiene and health for fish farms. Her social conscience was particularly stirred by the oil slick caused by the notorious stricken supertanker, *The Torrey Canyon*. Since then she has been tireless in alerting the public to water pollution, a significant threat to world survival. As she neatly puts it: "I windsurf for the planet."

Catherine Chabaud

born 1962, France

First woman to finish a solo round-the-world sailing race, the 1996/1997 Vendée Globe. Her other performances include the Route du Rhum in 1998, the Europe Race in 1999, and the Vendée Globe in 2000. She also worked as a writer and journalist, consultant for the radio station Europe 2, editor-in-chief of the review, *Thalassa*, administrator for the Musée de la Marine, and member of the French Yachting and Boating Council. But in whatever sphere she is active, she is always fighting to safeguard the maritime environment.

Victoria Murden

born 1963, United States

The first to row across the Atlantic, arriving at Pointe-à-Pitre in December 1999. She always had a taste for challenges. On board the American Pearl, she set out from the Canary Islands, rowing an average of ten hours a day and making landfall on Guadeloupe twelve weeks later. This triumph was all the more deserved since she had to brave Cyclone Lenny. In 2000, "Tori" received the Peter Bird Trophy. The Frenchwoman Peggy Bouchet (who had already made the transatlantic attempt in 1997 with a boat weighing 1,540 pounds (700 kilos) that overturned beneath a 20-foot (6-meter) wave, wedging her underneath) learnt of Murden's departure when she was already at the oars, being thrown about by heaving rollers, as if "locked up in the spinning drum of a washing machine." Bouchet succeeded in getting to Martinique on January 5, 2000, one month after Murden.

Elisabeta Lipa-Oleniuc

born 1964, Romania

The rower with the most major titles: seven Olympic medals, world rowing champion in 1981 and 1989, and the first woman to be named general in the army in her country for sporting endeavor.

She first triumphed at the 1984 Los Angeles Olympic Games, winning gold in double sculls, rewarding the young Elisabeta Oleniuc's (as she was) years of training in the frozen wastes of a native land that she is proud to represent. The biggest Romanian club, Dinamo Bucharest, recruited her, and she married Cornel Lipa—two factors that have encouraged and supported her in her sporting career. After a fifth victory at the Olympic Games (she won in 1984;

single sculls in 1992, and in the coxed eight in 1996), she took time off to look after her son, Dragos (born 1997), only to go one better after her break: with a very good Romanian team, she made off with gold in the coxed eights in Sydney in 2000 and then again in the same event in Athens in 2004. A national treasure, she has appeared on three series of postage stamps.

Karine Fauconnier

born 1972, France

French yachtswoman, and one of very few to skipper a 60-foot (18-meter) trimaran. While still young, she plied the oceans on one of the fastest boats in the world, a 60-foot multihull, and won as many medals as a top male yachtsman. She has even headed a crew of six men in a multihull regatta. In 2004, she won the Quebec-Saint-Malo transatlantic race, and in 2005 received the Golden Woman Trophy. Eighteen months after giving birth to a daughter, she returned to the waves, winning the Jacques Vabre transatlantic race in November 2007. She refuses to see any contradiction between being a "young mom and an adventurer."

Ellen MacArthur

born 1976, Great Britain

In 2005, Ellen MacArthur beat the record for sailing round the world solo and nonstop in a multihull: seventy-one days. People with such determination and such an early vocation are few and far between: when just eleven, she would go without her school lunch to save money to buy a boat.

An easy-going sort, MacArthur nonetheless knows what she wants and how to get it: through

Ellen MacArthur arrives after sailing round the world in 71 days, 14 hours, 18 minutes, and 33 seconds.

method, hard work, and a total lack of fear. Crowned "Young Sailor of the Year" aged seventeen for circumnavigating the British Isles aboard a tiny dinghy, she departed on the Mini-Transat from Brest in 1997, the only girl against fifty boys, capable of climbing the 100-foot (30-meter) mast. The result was a relatively modest seventeenth place. But it would take more to discourage MacArthur, who then learnt the trade in which she was to excel: solo long-distance sailing.

In 2000, she became the first woman and the youngest skipper to win the British Transatlantic race. In 2003, becoming the first woman to win the Vendée Globe made her a celebrity. She then set out on board the *Castorama* to circumnavigate the world. Facing terrifying storms and frustrating dog days, she battled on, determined, toiling ceaselessly, injured and unable to sleep more than two hours a night. And yet, aged twenty-eight, she managed to become the fastest solo round-the-world sailor, outstripping her chief competitor, Francis Joyon, by one day and eight hours. In 2008, the Frenchman went on to smash Ellen MacArthur's record, crossing the Indian Ocean solo and beating her record by fourteen days. A good loser, MacArthur

declared, in fluent French, that she is happy for him and that he deserves his victory. Not, that she won't try to beat him one day.

Maud Fontenoy

born 1977, France

From earliest childhood, Maud has had a passion for the ocean. On June 13, 2003 she started out on the frightening ordeal of rowing west to east across the Atlantic Ocean. With her back screaming in pain, with bruises all over her body, she was terrified at the idea of being crushed by the rolling waves and wary of whales, sharks, and cargo ships. Spending entire days in thick fog or icy rain, she barely got ten minutes rest during the sleepless nights and was often forced to cling on to avoid being slammed against the sides of her tiny cockpit. Leaving from Saint-Pierre-et-Miquelon, she arrived in La Coruña, Spain, on October 10, the first woman ever to have succeeded in this exploit. In 2005, she became the first woman to cross the Pacific Ocean. In 2007, she received the award of the Chevalier National du Mérite. Giving birth to a son in 2008, at present she anchors a program on Europe 1.

Maud Fontenoy in 2009, preparing to set sail around the world, solo and against the clock.

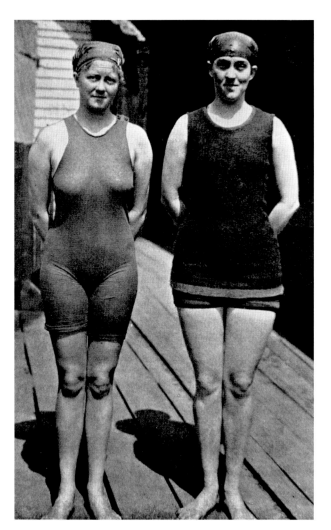

Fanny Durack (right) with another Australian swimmer, Mina Wylie.

Gertrude Ederle

1906–2003, United States

American swimmer and the first woman to cross the English Channel in 1926. Suffering from total deafness from the age of six, Gertrude Ederle possessed a will of iron. At fifteen, she swam across the Bay of New York, more than 18 miles (30 kilometers), in less than seven hours: faster than the men who preceded her. In 1923 and 1924, she beat the records for the 100-meter, 200-meter, and 400-meter freestyle. Her next idea was to swim across the English Channel: in pelting rain, "Trudy" rubbed her body with lanolin to fight the chill and plugged her goggles with rubber and wax to protect her eyes against the salty waves. She then swam across two hours faster than previous crossings, and in doing so entered the annals of American history. She was received at the White House, and paraded in triumph through the streets of New York.

Fanny Durack

1889–1956, Australia

Australian swimmer, she became the first female Olympic 100-meter freestyle champion in history in 1912. Her problem was whether she would be able to compete at all: the fact that men would see her swimming was seen as scandalous at the time. Needing a special dispensation to take part in the Games in Stockholm, she had none of the benefits enjoyed by her male counterparts—like an advance on expenses, for example. In her, however, Australia gained its first Olympic champion, and she went on to beat eleven world records from 1912 to 1918.

Gertrude Ederle.

Dawn Fraser

born 1937, Australia

Australian swimmer. In 1956, she earned gold in the 100-meter freestyle at the Melbourne Olympics, a feat she was to repeat at the Rome Olympics in 1960. She was the first woman to swim 100 meters in less than a minute, in 1962 in Melbourne. She was once again Olympic champion in 1964, in Tokyo, lowering her old record by a second in front of a fifteen-year-old American girl, Sharon Stander. Dawn was something of a rebel, refusing to wear the official uniform at medal ceremonies, and even once stealing an Olympic flag. The Australian Federation enforced its rules and suspended her three times, sabotaging the latter part of her career.

Lynne Cox.

Lynne Cox

born 1957, United States

American long-distance swimmer. First person to swim across the Magellan Straits in 1976 and then the Bering Strait in 1987. Cox began her swimming career with the Manchester Swim Team in New Hampshire. When only twelve, after her family had moved to Los Alamitos, California, she paired up with Don Gambril, coach of four US Olympic swim teams. So began her extraordinary record-breaking feats. At fourteen, with a group of teenagers, Cox swam across the Catalina Island Channel (down the Californian coast), a distance of 27 miles (43 kilometers), in 12 hours and 36 minutes. In 1972, at the age of fifteen, she swam the English Channel in 9 hours and 57 minutes, shattering both male and female world records for the distance. In 1975, she became the first woman to swim across the Cook Strait between New Zealand's North and South Islands, in a record 12 hours and 2 minutes. Her many other best times are just too numerous to mention. In 1985 she swam "Around the World in 80 Days," across twelve very demanding waterways.

Dawn Fraser.

Fanny Bullock Workman

1859–1925, United States

American explorer. She was the first woman to climb above 20,000 feet (6,000 meters), becoming "the highest woman in the world." Aged forty she struck out for the summits of the Himalayas wearing just a skirt. She claimed she would rewrite the maps, but she sometimes made mistakes of her own. In 1903, however, she embarked on a successful exploration of the Chogo Lungma. In 1906, she announced she had reached the summit of the Nun-Kun (26,982 feet/7,085 meters), though it is probable that she had actually ascended Pinnacle Peak (22,802 feet/6,950 meters) (another woman, Claude Kogan, became the first to climb the Nun in 1953). After many physical exertions and the most perilous adventures (crossing white-water rivers, falling into a deep crevasse), in 1912 on the Siachen glacier she still found the time to be photographed holding a sign emblazoned "Votes for women."

Junko Tabei

born 1939, Japan

This Japanese climber was the first to reach the summit of Mount Everest, taking the southern face route in 1975. In 1992, at the age of fifty-two, she became the first woman to climb the planet's seven highest peaks: Everest (Himalayas, 29,028 feet/8,848 meters); Aconcagua (South America, 22,841 feet/6,962 meters); Mount McKinley (North America, 20,320 feet/6,194 meters); Kilimanjaro (Africa, 19,341 feet/5,895 meters); Mount Elbrus (the Caucasus, 18,510 feet/5,642 meters); Vinson (Antarctic, 16,050 feet/4,892 meters), and Kosciusko (Australia, 7,310 feet/2,228 meters).

She first climbed Mount Nasu with her teacher when aged just ten. She graduated from the Women's University in Showa, and, in 1969, set up a mountaineering club for women. She conquered Mount Fuji (the famous 12,388-feet/3,776-meter high volcano in the center of Japan) and then the Matterhorn in the Swiss Alps (14,691 feet/4,478 meters), followed by Annapurna (a summit in the Himalayas towering to 26,504 feet/8,078 meters). At the age of thirty-six, she decided to tackle the highest peak in the world. An expedition was formed with fifteen Japanese women who set out from Kathmandu. But in their bivouac at 20,670 feet (6,300 meters), they were hit by an avalanche and had to be dug out. Tabei herself was injured and tended to by Nepalese Sherpas, but she nevertheless started her ascent once again with a solitary guide. In extreme pain, she said her heart was "in her mouth every five yards." Twelve days after the avalanche, on May 16, 1975, she planted the Japanese flag at the summit. (Eleven days later, Phantog, a Tibetan, was to become the second woman to climb Everest.) When the media learnt of Tabei's exploit, the headlines ran: "Japanese housewife climbs Everest."

Junko Tabei (left) with Christine Janin, the first woman ever to reach the North Pole, in 1997.

Catherine Destivelle on the Mont Blanc massif in 1993.

Catherine Destivelle

born 1960, Algeria

Mountaineer Destivelle, who grew up in Paris, was the first woman to conquer the dangerous north face of the Eiger (13,025 feet/3,970 meters) solo, in 1992, and to climb the Matterhorn solo in winter, in 1994.

In 1991, she had already blazed a path through the Drus, discovering a new route on the west face. A genuine trailblazer, she is only interested in "taking on hard climbs that have never been attempted." A "tamer of the slopes," in 1999 she ascended the north face of Cima Grande di Lavaredo, a friable, sheer cliff-face in the Italian Dolomites. In unbearable cold, she climbed for two days to become the first solo woman to succeed in the climb. Later, she tackled the north face of Ben Nevis, in Scotland, which is peppered with icy chimneys. Driven by the will to overcome, to win, and to prove herself better than all the others, she recounts how she "sped like a rocket past those splendid fellows, the guides, hard men of the mountains and proud of it, throwing them a beaming smile." Nowadays, she climbs more calmly, assured, but remains modest: "When I climb, I think only of the rock. I form a single body with it."

Oh Eun Sun

born 1966, South Korea

She is the first woman mountaineer to have conquered all fourteen summits above 26,000 feet (8,000 meters): on the planet. She started out "gently" in 1997, climbing just one peak, with another in 2004 (Everest), and one more in 2006. In 2007, she climbed two and in 2008 four. By 2009, she had already reached four summits, including the awesome Gasherbrum. Nothing seems to frighten her, not even the death of her compatriot Gi Mi Sun, who descended its 26,660 feet (8,126 meters) in July 2009. In April 2010, Oh Eun Sun reached the summit of Annapurna, completing the allotted fourteen. Hard on her heels are two women who have climbed twelve "eight-thousanders": Edurne Pasaban from Spain and the Austrian Gerlinde Kaltenbrunner, who failed in her attempt to scale K2 (28,250 feet/ 8,611 meters). All three female "summiteers" climb without a breathing apparatus. The Italian Nives Meroi was the first to climb ten "eight-thousanders." Women at the top!

Laurence de la Ferrière

born 1957, Morocco

"The Woman of the Antarctic," the first person to reach the South Pole on skis, solo, in 1997.

When starting off on her crossing from the western edge of the Antarctic continent to the South Pole, de la Ferrière was all too aware of the problems, since she had already unsuccessfully attempted this challenge with a team five times. On this occasion, without dogs for warmth or to pull her sledge, she traipsed off alone, slinging on her harness and dragging the 290 pounds (130 kilos) herself, food included, because she could only be supplied once during the whole 812 miles (1,300 kilometers).

For fifty-seven days, she staggered on in temperatures of -40°F (-40°C), whipped by blizzards, without stopping for fear of freezing, yet never slackening pace. She could feel nothing but the pain: cramp, aches, cracked lips, tendinitis, burns, pangs of hunger.

And the icecap has some nasty tricks up its sleeve: enormous crevasses that "shift about, that one feels are ready to break, that crack."

So why all this pain? For science? De la Ferrière takes samples of the snow for the national French research institute, the CNRS. She takes photographs and brings meteorite samples back to the French Institute for Polar Research and Technology. For the untold beauty of the landscape? Yes, the shimmering dawn that verges on azure: "It's one great chunk of opal." But beyond all this, what means so much to her is the feeling that she has managed to survive against all the odds; that what seemed beyond her was possible; that she put her life on the line and yet lives to tell the tale. An intense joy in keeping with the magnitude of her ordeal. To have gone to the limit of her potential and to have returned. She set out again in 1999: this time for 1,875 miles (3,000 kilometers), from the South Pole to the Adélie Coast becoming the first woman to cross the Antarctic in its entirety.

Shan Zhang

born 1968, China

At the Barcelona Olympics in 1992, this Chinese sports shooter beat all her male competitors, leaving supposedly superior male guns trailing in her wake. Unflappable and concentrated, yet fast, with her favorite twelve-bore rifle she achieved a 100 percent success rate: 150 clay pigeons were pulled and Shan Zhang hit every single one. Instead of admiring her success, however, the heads of IOC moved the goalposts: the skeet event was reserved exclusively for men for the following Olympic Games. However, in 2000, in Sydney, a women's skeet event was re-endorsed, running separately from the men's competition.

Shan Zhang in 1992 at the Barcelona Games carried aloft by the silver medal winner Juan Giha Yarur (left) and the bronze Bruno Rossetti (right).

Bettina Aller

born 1964, Denmark

This Danish explorer was the first woman to cross the Arctic on foot and skis, in 2006, with Jean Gabriel Leynaud. She acheived it in ninety-nine days, with temperatures plummeting to -40°F (-40°C), over 1,250 miles (2,000 kilometers) of frozen waste, complete with crevasses, shifting water holes, cracks in the ice-sheet, encounters with polar bears, and with one eye completely frozen over. When not tramping across the icecap, Bettina has two young children to deal with and runs a major publishing firm.

Ruth Law.

Ruth Law

1887–1970, United States

American pilot. Aged twenty-five, Ruth joined the aviation school at Burgess, very quickly obtaining a pilot's license and soon purchasing her first plane. By 1915, Law was performing aerobatics and founding "Ruth Law's Flying Circus." With two further airplanes, she performed pirouettes in the sky, surprising and delighting huge crowds.

She was the first woman to "loop the loop," and performed other dangerous acrobatics successfully; she was afraid of nothing, least of all her male rivals. After beating three records during a race between Chicago and New York, she beat all her male competitors in the same race in 1917, thus establishing a record of 590 miles (950 kilometers) nonstop. Her goal was to put an end to male supremacy, patent in her area of sport—and she succeeded. In 1917, again, she became the first woman to wear a military uniform, yet, as a female, she was not permitted to join the United States Air Force. A pioneer in many fields, in a further feat of daring, in 1915 she also beat the altitude record: 2 miles (3,300 meters).

Bessie Coleman

1893–1926, United States

First African-American female pilot, in 1921. Coleman's mother, who raised her five children alone, encouraged her children to study, despite knowing neither how to read nor write herself. Bessie finished high school and enrolled at university, but stayed for only six months, since by then the money her mother had managed to put aside had ran out. To survive, she worked as a manicurist in a barber's shop, all the while dreaming of becoming a pilot.

Her ambitions were encouraged by a journalist on the *Chicago Defender*, who became a kind of agent for her. He thought she should go and train in France, where racial prejudice was less constricting. She returned to her native country in 1921 with a pilot's license in her pocket, and she soon obtained an international flying license. She wanted to become a stuntwoman and met with success, making her first appearance in 1922, during a public event in Curtiss Field near New York. Her talent impressed David L. Behncke, founder and president of the International

Bessie Coleman.

Airline Pilots' Association, who was to become her official manager. Performing throughout the nation, at each venue her exploits attracted crowds of thousands, who dubbed her "Brave Bessie." Aged just thirty-four, she was rehearsing a stunt in Jacksonville, Florida, when the controls of the plane malfunctioned. She was ejected from the aircraft and died on impact with the ground.

Adrienne Bolland on April 1, 1921 in Santiago aboard her Caudron G.3.

Adrienne Bolland

1895–1975, France

French pilot and the first, in 1921, to cross the Cordillera of the Andes in her plane, a Caudron G.3. Her arrival in Le Bourget was a triumph.

In 1925, the International Committee for Air Navigation ordained that it would not grant a pilot's license to a woman for public transport aircraft. "Adrienne Bolland, the conqueror of the Andes, will thus see hers withdrawn," the French representative on the committee announced indignantly. She did however carry on beating records and performing tricks, especially her famous loops, much admired by crowd at air meets.

Amelia Earhart

1897–1937, United States

American airwoman, Amelia Earhart was the first woman pilot to fly across the Atlantic solo. In 1922, she established the world altitude record for a woman. Then, in 1932, having taken off from the United States, she landed in Ireland, with a speed record of 13 hours 30 minutes, thus repeating Lindbergh's exploit of five years previously. In 1935, she succeeded on the first solo crossing of the Pacific, from Hawaii to Oakland, bringing her worldwide fame. In 1935, she was again the first woman to fly from Mexico City to New York in a record time of 14 hours and 19 minutes. Finally, Earhart was the first woman to receive the Distinguished Flying Cross and the gold medal of the National Geographic Society. The public greeted news of her disappearance at sea with intense sadness.

Amelia Earhart.

Maryse Bastié (left) and Lilly Dillens, in Paris, 1936.

Jacqueline Cochran.

Maryse Bastié

1898–1952, France

French aviator who crossed the South Atlantic in less than twelve hours in 1936. Working in a shoe factory, with a child from an early marriage, she struggled to make ends meet. Later she married the pilot Louis Bastié and discovered the joys of flying. In 1925, she bet that she could fly beneath the transporter bridge in Bordeaux, and she pulled it off. In 1926 her husband died in an aviation accident, but she continued to fly.

Bastié specialized in distance records, flying 661 ¼ miles (1,058 kilometers) between Le Bourget and Treptow. In 1930, she beat the world duration record for a fixed circular route: 38 hours, solo, nonstop. "Alone in the night, as soon as I moved a leg, I would cry out in distress. My eyes would close several times a minute, but to sleep is to die. I have to say that I wanted to: I felt at the end of the powers of human endurance. I squirted eau de cologne into my pupils: a red-hot iron. I had the impression I had become a machine, a suffering, active machine that nothing would stop attaining its ultimate goal." Encouraged by the aviator Jean Mermoz, who acknowledged her as a dyed-in-the-wool pilot, she became a national celebrity, an image of modern womanhood that the government dispatched to South America to show off her talents. However, when she wanted to become a fighter pilot, the Air Ministry refused her application. A lieutenant in the Resistance, and the first woman to be named commander of the Legion of Honor for purely military endeavors, she had to confine her skills to the Infirmary and Supply Corps. She was killed flying a prototype.

Jacqueline Cochran

1907–1980, United States

First woman to break the sound barrier in 1953. Cochran learnt to fly around her twentieth birthday. A record-breaking record-breaker, at one point she held more than 200. In 1934, she performed the novel exploit of flying a plane with cloth wings to an altitude of 32,810 feet (10,000 meters). She was also the pace-setter in the Bendix-Transcontinental Trophy race in 1938, where she beat the greatest male aviators. She was in competition with the French pilot, Jacqueline Auriol, breaking the sound barrier shortly before her in 1953. Though the Press liked to call their rivalry the "duel of the two Jacquelines," they had the greatest respect for one another. Cochran was the first to pilot a bomber over the Atlantic. During the Second World War, she commanded the Woman's Airforce Service Pilots (WASPS), a program that trained more than 1,200 women pilots. In acknowledgement, she received the Legion of Honor and the Distinguished Service Medal.

Hélène Boucher

1908–1934, France

Having obtained her pilot's license in 1931, she set a world groundspeed record of more than 276.5 miles per hour (445 kilometers per hour), on August 10, 1934. Boucher enjoyed being an innovator; she was fearless, but not boastful. Early on in her career, she flew round France at the controls of a two-seater Gipsy Moth. During the Caen–Deauville rally, her plane got wedged in between the branches of two trees. She had to abandon the Paris–Saigon rally somewhere near Baghdad, though none of this prevented her from setting seven world records. She was nicknamed the "little fiancée of the air." In July 1933, she was second in the Le Mans twelve-hour race. In Villacoublay, she and the German Vera von Bissing performed an acrobatic duel, complete with full rolls, snap rolls, loops, and flips. She beat the world speed record for all categories over 625 miles (1,000 kilometers) in 1934. She was killed the same year in the cockpit of a Caudron "Rafale" during a routine test flight at an air show: her plane overturned and came down nose first. The death of this young woman was met with shock throughout France. For the first time a woman was honored at the French shrine in Saint-Louis des Invalides. A chevalier of the Legion of Honor, she was a national hero, and high schools, colleges, stadiums, streets, and a public garden in Paris all bear her name.

Sabiha Gökçen

1913–2001, Turkey

Turkish aviator and the world's first female fighter pilot. Born into a family of six, she lost her parents at an early age. In 1925, Kemal Atatürk passed through Bursa, the city where she was living, and adopted her, taking her with him to Ankara. When an air school opened in 1935, Sabiha was the first pupil to join before leaving for the USSR. In 1936, she trained as a fighter pilot in a military aviation school and obtained her diploma. She knew how to fly twenty-two different types of planes. From 1938 to 1954, she taught in a civil aviation school.

Jacqueline Auriol

1917–2000, France

French aviator and the first female test pilot in the world. Her speed record, set in 1963 in a Dassault Mirage IIIR, was 1,257.47 miles per hour (2,023.7 kilometers/hour) over 100 kilometers. She seemed to have several lives. Daughter-in-law of the first president of the Fourth Republic, Vincent Auriol, she was a favorite in fashionable high society; the Press adored her fine, couture clothes and her intense, bright blue eyes. Her husband, Paul Auriol, had been admired for his courage during the Second World War; she too had helped the French Resistance movement during the war.

In 1947, she began flying and as soon as she sat at the controls of her first plane, she felt born to fly. Things began very badly, however, with a seaplane accident, which ruined her looks, smashed an eye socket, and fractured her jaw. She underwent more than twenty operations and years of rehabilitation in the fight against pain and disfigurement

(catching sight of her face would make her cry out in disgust). Once recovered, she embarked on a triumphant orgy of breakneck record-breaking, dominating both the machine and her own fear, enjoying the fabulous sensation of power that flying gave her. Cutting her teeth in a Stampe, she obtained a pilot's license, followed by the far more demanding test pilot's license. She tested *Mystère II*, in which she put the "artificial horizon" through its paces, necessitating several full rolls and loops. Gripped by "an extraordinary joy, a kind of marvelous excitement," she ascended "dead straight into the sky," up to 45,000 feet (15,000 meters) and broke the sound barrier as barely ten pilots had done so before her. Dangerous? It was all part of the pleasure. She described the feeling as, "plummeting to the earth." One day, she saw "the ground rushing up towards her at hair-raising speed," and thought: "This is the instant of your death and it's

Jacqueline Auriol, leaving her Mirage (IIIR) aircraft after a trial run in Marseilles.

the most amazing moment of your life." She was awarded the Legion of Honor in 1963 and published her memoirs, *I Love to Fly*, in 1970.

Valentina Tereshkova

born 1937, Russia

Soviet cosmonaut and the first woman in space, on June 16, 1963. Aged twenty-six, this young textile worker had become an intrepid parachutist and secretary to the committee of Communist Youth, in perfect accordance with the ideal image of Soviet womanhood. Yuri Gagarin, the hero of the first manned flight in 1961, hailed her "astonishing abilities" and saw in her "a true Russian woman."

Admitted to the cosmonaut school in 1962 with the rank of second lieutenant, she succeeded brilliantly in all the tests, including the most grueling, the centrifuge. If there were scientists opposed to a woman in space (she might lose her cool or not have the stamina of a man or even become sterile), the "Gull" nonetheless finally won the day, taking off aboard Vostok 6 and orbiting the earth forty-eight times in little more than seventy hours. After her triumphant touchdown, she announced defiantly: "You thought that only you, the men, could bear that diabolical round-dance? Well, we women can do something too."

Acclaimed as a heroine at the 1963 International Women's Congress in Moscow, Valentina was promoted to the rank of lieutenant-colonel in the Soviet Army. Married and with a daughter, she became president of the Committee of Soviet Women in 1977, and then a member of the Central Committee of the Party and the Presidium of the Supreme Soviet in 1987. Pioneering female space travel was above all a question of symbolism. For the Russians, it offered proof that they were more

Valentina Tereshkova.

powerful than the Americans—the first American woman, Sally Ride, traveled into space twenty years later, after another Soviet, Svetlana Yevgenyevna Savitskaya, completed the first spacewalk. For feminists, Tereshkova, the "first Eve in space" "brought sexual equality to the skies."

So-yeon Yi

born 1978, South Korea

The first South Korean astronaut. In April 2008, she took off from Baikonur in Kazakhstan aboard a Soyuz rocket on a journey to the International Space Station (ISS). In Seoul, 3,000 people watched the launch on a giant screen.

Charlotte Cooper.

Charlotte Cooper

1870–1966, Great Britain

Tennis player and the first Olympic female champion at the 1900 Paris Games. With long skirts reaching down to her feet, and her hair tied up in a bun, the crowds watched safe in the knowledge that this queen of the grass was well and truly "feminine." She was even a wife (of another tennis champion) and mother (of a daughter, Gwen). All the same, faced with victories unique in the history of the sport and a dazzling style of play, she could only be characterized with the words: "Chattie plays like a man." This was intended as a compliment, since no woman had played at Olympic level before her, though in 1884 Maud Watson from Britain had won the first ladies' tournament at Wimbledon.

Suzanne Lenglen

1899–1938, France

French tennis champion who put women's tennis on the map. Six times world champion: the first time in 1914, in Saint-Cloud, on clay, at the age of sixteen. She won at Roland-Garros from 1920 to 1923, and then in 1925 and 1926. She triumphed at Wimbledon from 1919 to 1923, and again in 1925. Her game was crisp and rapid, while her volley and smash, taught by her father who had her play against men, were almost unreturnable. She loved to win, even if this meant having a little snifter before a big match to calm her nerves. The public had never seen a sportswoman, or a sportsman for that matter, jumping and leaping to the net like she did.

She dared to wear unusual—even shocking—garb, especially pleated skirts that *almost* showed the knee; in fact, she created modern women's tennis dress. A symbol of a contemporary, emancipated womanhood, she was the first professional female player to be paid money like the men. She made 50,000 dollars touring Canada, Cuba, Mexico and the United States, where she was adored. Dying of leukemia while still young, an entrance and an avenue in Roland-Garros Stadium in Paris have been named after her.

Suzanne Lenglen.

In the same era, the great American champion, Helen Wills (1905–1998), was assembling the most brilliant prize list in the history of world tennis.

Althea Gibson

1927–2003, United States

The first black tennis champion. Born in South Carolina in the era of segregation, Gibson spent a poverty-stricken childhood in the Harlem ghetto. But she had a gift for tennis and played with frightening precision and deft elegance. After being confined to championships reserved exclusively for black people, generally of a low level, the white tennis authorities decreed that she could be admitted to the Forest Hills West Side Tennis event in 1950.

In 1956, Althea Gibson won the ladies' singles and doubles at Roland-Garros, followed by the Wimbledon ladies' singles and doubles, the US ladies' singles and doubles, and finally the Australian Open. In celebration, she was driven in triumph down New York's Fifth Avenue in a convertible.

Maureen Connolly-Brinker

1934–1969, United States

The first woman to hold the Grand Slam (the four major titles: British, US, French and Australian) in the same year, 1953. The second was the Australian Margaret Court, and the third the German Steffi Graf.

At twenty, Maureen suffered a riding accident that put an end to a brilliant career. By this time, however, she had already accumulated an astonishing series of victories: between the ages of seventeen and twenty, she was United States champion no less than fives times, French champion twice, Australia champion once, and triumphed at Wimbledon three times.

Althea Gibson.

Maureen Connolly-Brinker.

Billie Jean King

born 1943, United States

American tennis player, née Moffitt. The first woman to beat a male tennis star in 1973 and the first to head a professional team of men. Although she entered her debut tournament when only eleven and was the best athlete on campus at the University of Los Angeles (where she studied history), as a female Billie Jean was not entitled to a sports' grant. Aged seventeen, she played at Wimbledon for the first time, before winning the tournament aged twenty-two. On that occasion she noted that the prize money for women was considerably lower than for men. At that time the media was much less interested in women's tennis, often ignoring it entirely. When she heard that the champion Bobby Riggs was forever trumpeting male superiority in the sport, Billie challenged him to a match. To huge media fanfare, and watched by 50 million TV viewers, the "Battle of the Sexes" match was held on September 20, 1973, with Billie winning in three sets. Her victory gave a fillip to the promotion of women's tennis and demands for equal prize money. King was the first female tennis player to earn more than 100,000 dollars in a single year. She won twenty-two titles at Wimbledon alone—more than any other player—and thirty-nine Grand Slam tournaments.

After finishing her playing career, King organized the first tournament reserved exclusively for women. To defend the rights of women players and earn them fair treatment, she founded the Women's Tennis Association and helped launch the magazine *Women's Sports*. She also set up the *Women's Sports Foundation* to encourage future generations of sportswomen. Finally, Billie became the head of the Philadelphia Freedoms TeamTennis, a coed squad of professional men and women who play together. She has been open about her homosexuality and is active in the fight against AIDS.

Billie Jean King at the Wimbledon Ladies' Final in 1973.

Sania Mirza

born 1987, India

The first Indian woman player to be ranked among the fifty best in world tennis. Winning the junior circuit in Wimbledon in 2003, in 2005 she became the first Indian woman to go through three rounds of a Grand Slam tournament and so gain international recognition in the sport. Sunnite clerics took a dim view of her success and lambasted her for wearing revealing apparel that might "corrupt" Indian youth.

Throughout, she remained calm: "I play tennis and I wear what I do to be at ease when participating in my sport." In her native land, she became an icon of the successful woman and a role model for many young people. She has contributed to changing the

Sania Mirza.

status of woman in a society where the female is often regarded as a burden. Putting her celebrity to good use and furthering the cause of women, she poses, cap on head, wearing a short-sleeve shirt and holding a racket. The byline runs: "Your daughter could be the next champion."

Alice Milliat

1884–1957, France

Organizer and president of the French Federation of Women's Sport Clubs and then, from 1921, of the International Women's Sports Federation. Initially a teacher, she was a gymnast, and soon a footballer; like other pioneers, such as the accountant Suzanne Liébrad, the typist Jeanne Brûlé, the philosopher Germaine Delapierre, she belonged to the Fémina Sport club in Paris, founded in 1912.

Milliat promoted the beneficial effects of sport on female health, in particular of mothers-to-be. She thus countered the censure directed in particular at female football players, whose earliest teams date to 1917. Women were only allowed to participate in the Olympic Games in 1928. Each time she visited London, the hugely popular Alice Milliat would be welcomed with great fanfare.

Lily Parr

1905–1971, Great Britain

English professional football player and first woman to be inducted into the "Hall of Fame" of the National Football Museum, Preston, England. While still very young, living in a deprived area of northwest England, she was taken on to work in an ammunition factory, Dick, Kerr & Co., and drafted into their football team, known as the Dick, Kerr Ladies. She immediately displayed extraordinary talent as a striker—especially with a left foot that could send the ball flying harder than many a male counterpart. Preceded by this reputation, she became known and admired throughout the land. In 1920 in Preston, Dick, Kerr Ladies beat a French team 2-0, Parr and her teammates being cheered on by a crowd of some 25,000. Over the next year, 90,000 came to watch her play. The Football Association, however, prohibited women's teams from playing on its property, because they deemed the game "unsuitable" for women. The Football Association ban was not lifted until 1971. But Lily Parr continued scoring goals (900 in total) and living, unapologetically, as a homosexual.

Mia Hamm

born 1972, United States

An American soccer player who scored 158 goals. A club foot made it seem impossible she should ever do sport; nonetheless she won a gold medal at the Olympic Games in 1996 and in 2004, as well as the World Championships in 1991 and 1999. She was selected 276 times in seventeen years for the national team. A political science graduate, she set up the Mia Hamm Foundation for Bone Transplant and helps to promote sport among girls.

Karoline Radke-Batschauer

1909–1983, Germany

German athlete. The first woman to win an Olympic middle-distance race, in Amsterdam in 1928. Before this date her feat had been impossible because women were barred from entering. Ladies had been tentatively admitted to the 100-meters, high jump, and the 4 x 100-meter relay. But the 800-meters—two laps in one go? How would women cope?

One woman, however, Lucie Bréard, had already triumphed over this distance, in Monaco in 1921, and Radke-Batschauer herself had even been champion of Germany over 1,000 meters, so when "Lina" slashed the world record with a time of 2 minutes 16.8 seconds, almost caught at the line by Kinue Hitomi from Japan, the authorities handed over her much-deserved medal with some reluctance. Then they forbade women from competing over middle distances and rescinded her title. She was finally presented with the trophy in 1956.

Mildred Didrickson

1911–1956, Norway/United States

American golf champion, "the greatest woman athlete of the half-century" (a title awarded in 1949). Born in Texas to parents of Norwegian origin, she competed or held records in a whole raft of disciplines: baseball, basketball, javelin, running, hurdles, high jump, gymnastics, tennis, skiing, boxing, football, and golf. Aged seventeen, "Babe" was already winning women's events at the United States Athletics Championships; the world javelin title came in 1930; two gold medals and one silver at

the Los Angeles Olympic Games of 1932, for high jump and the 80-meter (as it was then) hurdles; in just one day, she took part in eight events, winning six, including three in world record marks.

She was excellent at soccer, shooting, cycling, swimming, and billiards. Taking up golf in 1935, after a few brief years she soared to be world number one. In 1938, she married George Zaharias, a top wrestler. In 1946, she won the US Open; a year later, she notched up seventeen victories out of eighteen tournaments entered. She won the World Championship for four straight years from 1948 to 1951. Suffering from cancer, she could still win championships, including one hardly a month after an operation. The Americans honor her memory; in 1981 they published a stamp with her face on it, and in 1999 the magazine *Sport Illustrated* chose her as the "female athlete of the century."

Alice Coachman

born 1923, United States

American athlete, the first African-American woman to win a gold medal at the London Olympics in 1948. During her youth, Coachman experienced poverty and the horrors of racism in her native Georgia, which was plagued by the Ku Klux Klan. Sports facilities were prohibited to people of color. At the Tuskegee Institute, Alabama, her monitors were flabbergasted by her perfectly relaxed jumping style and devastating raw speed, particularly given that she had not any formal training. By sixteen, she was high-jump champion. While pursuing her studies at Georgia State University and emerging with an Economics diploma in 1947, she also found the time to become a top sprinter and basketball player.

Alice Coachman at the old Wembley Stadium in 1948 setting a new Olympic high-jump record of 5ft. 6 in. (1.68 m).

The podium for the women's 4 x 100-meters relay at the Rome Olympic Games in 1960. Wilma Rudolph in the center.

From 1939 to 1948, she triumphed at the All-American high jump, and, on August 7, 1948, she leapt 5 ½ feet (1.68 meters) at the first attempt at the London Olympics. Coachman belongs to several prestigious organizations, including USA Track & Field, the International Women's Sports Federation, the Black Athletes Hall of Fame, Georgia State University Athletic Hall of Fame, and Bob Douglas Hall of Fame. She carried the Olympic Flame at the Atlanta Games in 1996. Every spring, Albany, her birthplace, puts on "Alice Coachman" races.

Wilma Rudolph

1940–1994, United States

American athlete, known as the "Black Gazelle," and the first woman to run the 100-meter dash in eleven seconds in 1961. Already at the Rome Games the previous year she had carried off three gold medals, for the 100- and 200-meters, and the 4 x 100-meters relay with some other first-rate Tennessee athletes, Barbara Jones, Lucinda Williams, and Martha Hudson. She was named United Press Athlete of the Year 1960, and won the prestigious Sullivan Award for the best athlete in 1961.

These feats were all the more remarkable as Wilma's beginnings in life had been an uphill struggle. Twentieth child in a family of twenty-two, she was afflicted with scarlet fever, double pneumonia, and polio, leaving her disabled between the ages of four and ten. A metal splint had to be inserted into her left leg and her mother or siblings massaged her for several hours a day. Wilma, though, was blessed with uncommon reserves of energy. Her triple victory made her the most admired athlete at the Games.

Joan Benoit

born 1957, United States

American marathon runner and first woman to be crowned Olympic champion in the discipline in 1984. With her short, neat stride but constant speed, in 1983 Benoit covered the Boston route in 2 hours, 22 minutes, and 43 seconds, a world-best time that left her competitors floundering in her wake. Her average of 11 ¼ miles per hour (18 kilometers per hour) is superior to that of male runners such as Zatopek and Mimoun. At the Los Angeles Olympic Games the following year she won gold, running the distance in 2 hours, 24 minutes, and 52 seconds, even though she had undergone a knee operation less than a month previously. In 1985 she beat her own personal best with a time of 2 hours, 21 minutes, and 21 seconds.

Nawal El Moutawakel, 2005.

Nawal El Moutawakel

born 1962, Morocco

Moroccan athlete and first female Olympic champion from the Maghreb in 1984. Coming from a country that often frowns upon sport and women, relatively short (5 ft. 2 in./ 1.59 m tall), it came as a great surprise at the Los Angeles Games to see Nawal win the 400-meter hurdles, even though she had already earned a gold medal at the Mediterranean Games in Casablanca in 1983. Her career was furthered on going to the University of Iowa, where she graduated. After her victory at the Olympics, King Hassan II received her in triumph in Casablanca, she was hailed by the Moroccan people, while King Faisal of Saudi Arabia, several sovereigns from the UAE and Colonel Kadhafi showered her with gifts.

A trainer since 1989, she sat on the executive of the IOC (International Olympic Committee) in 2008, and chairs the evaluation committee for the 2012 Games. In her own country, she was made Secretary of State for Youth and Sports in 1997; named vice-president of the Moroccan Royal Federation of Athletics in 2007, and was promoted to Minister for Youth and Sports in the same year. Mother of a daughter, Zineb (born in 1992) El Moutawakel is a true symbol of emancipation.

Hassida Boulmerka

born 1968, Algeria

First Algerian woman to become Olympic champion in 1992. In 1991, she dedicated her first major victory over 1,500 meters, at the World Athletics Championships in Tokyo, to "the women of Algeria." Hassida thus defied the Islamic Fundamentalists who accused her of "dishonoring authentic Muslim women by running with bare legs and arms." She returned to Algiers, where she was hailed by a jubilant crowd. At the Olympic Games in Barcelona, she won

Hassida Boulmerka in 2002 at the Barcelona Games.

gold, powering round the four laps in 3 minutes and 55.3 seconds. Hassiba dedicated her victory this time to the assassinated President Boudiaf, adding: "I run for an Algeria in peace and free, and without extremism."

Receiving the medal in 1995 at Gothenburg, she dedicated it to "all women in the world who suffer as I do and, especially, to the women of Algeria." This was too much for certain clerics. She has received threats but continues to act as a spokeswoman for the dignity and liberty of her people and of women. "I offer an example of will," she declares. "I will never give in to blackmail. I want to help women in my country because I'm sure it is them who will save Algeria."

Cathy Freeman

born 1976, Australia

The first Aboriginal Olympic athletics champion, in 2000. Born into an oppressed, scorned people driven from its native lands during colonization, Cathy Freeman has made a point of linking her sporting achievements to the revival in her people's pride. From early on, at the Commonwealth Games in

Canada in 1994, when she won the 400-meter sprint, she did not refuse to wave the Australian ensign, but it was joined by that of the Aboriginal community: a sun on a red and black background. It was only on February 13, 2008, that the Labor prime minister, Kevin Rudd, presented an official apology for the two centuries of injustice they had suffered.

World champion in 1997 in Athens and Seville in 1999, she felt she just had to win at the Games of the XXVII Olympiad in Sydney. Realizing her dream, she nonetheless did not forget to congratulate the American Marion Jones (winner of the 200-meters) with affection. She even had the honor of lighting the basin with the Olympic flame. In 2001, she received the Olympic Order from the IOC. Cathy has emerged from her roots, a person, as she puts it, in search of freedom, proud of her identity and who tries to run as fast as she can.

Cathy Freeman at the Atlanta Games in 1996.

Juanita Cruz

1917–1981, Spain

Spanish *matadora*. In 1932, she delivered her first coup de grâce to a young bull, turning professional the following year. Wearing culottes (much criticized by the menfolk), she killed more than one thousand bulls, battling just as much against misogynistic prejudice (certain male matadors [*toreros*] refused to take part in *corridas* with her) and sexist laws (for a long time, women did not have the right to fight bulls). When the Spanish prohibited Cruz from fighting, calling her "red" and an "enemy of Franco," she went into exile in South America.

Conchita Cintron in 1949.

Conchita Cintron

1922–2009, Peru

Peruvian *torera* of mixed-race background. With a Puerto Rican father and an Irish mother, Conchita was born in Chile. Her bullfighting teacher noticed her courage and skill when she was just ten. She became the first professional *torera*, initially as a *rejoneadora* (on horseback), and then as a true *matadora* (on foot). She was acclaimed at every appearance, her first major bullfight taking place in Lima in 1936. She was immensely popular in South America, in Mexico—where she was dubbed "the gold goddess"—as well as in Portugal and Spain. After slaughtering some four hundred bulls in her career, in 1991 she handed her sword over to the French *torera*, Marie Sara.

Conchita Cintron in Bordeaux in 1950.

Myriam Lamare

born 1975, France

Frenchwoman and first female boxing world champion. Raised in the Parisian suburbs, she is the granddaughter of an Algerian immigrant and daughter of a warehouse operative. She studied a bit but was only really interested in sport: athletics, tennis, sailing, and scuba diving, in which she became an instructress. But she soon gained a real passion for full-contact fighting: powerfully built, she hit hard and beat any opponent. She started out as a lightweight in French boxing in 1996, then, in 1999, took up English boxing, a new discipline in her native land.

Lamare became champion of France by 1999, champion of Europe in 2000 and, since 2004, she has been world professional boxing champion and is recognized by the WBA (World Boxing Association). In late 2005 she also beat the Englishwoman Jane Couch for the world belt of the WIBF (Women's International Boxing Federation). She has won all eleven of her professional fights. She is a member of the IOC.

Regina Halmich

born 1976, Germany

World boxing champion from 1997 to 2007. "I am proud that women's boxing has emerged from the shadows, thanks to me!" she proclaims (forgetting a number of earlier champions). Halmich was already recognized in 1992, though women's boxing was forbidden until 1994. Excelling in karate and kick-boxing, she became a world boxing champion at nineteen.

Wild and unruly—she once broke a TV presenter's nose—she is Beauty and the Beast (when she poses for *Playboy*, all the scars, bruises and bumps seem to have miraculously disappeared), rolled into one. At

thirty-one, she decided to hang up her gloves at the height of her fame after winning one last fight in her birthplace, Karlsruhe, in the presence of thousands of excited fans and watched by countless more on TV.

Lise Legrand

born 1976, France

French wrestler, world junior champion in 1993, and senior champion in 1995, 1997, 2000, 2001, and 2003. Women's wrestling was only recognized as a discipline by the French Federation shortly before she was born and, at international level, only in 1983. When she was a child, she was timid and frightened of "meeting people." She soon caught the wrestling bug and remains as "happy as a fish in water" when she fights. Lise is sure that "practiced by women, wrestling is lighter, more open." This doesn't prevent her having a huge will to win, hence a slew of titles, France first in 1991, and then the world.

When the sport entered the Olympic Games in Athens in 2004 for the first time, Legrand beat the Greek champion, Stavroula Zygouri, in less than three minutes, earning bronze, which, she says, was "worth gold." She was awarded the Order of Merit. She was beaten in Beijing, but in any event she had decided to retire and leave room for younger competitors (such as world champion, Audrey Prieto), and she also wanted to commit more time to raising a son born in 2005. "High-level sport brings with it too many sacrifices," she concluded. Moreover, she now enjoys less competitive pursuits, as a child welfare worker in the Maison de la Petite Enfance, as a representative for top athletes at the French Wrestling Federation, and as a patron of the European Leukodystrophy Association.

Lise Legrand after she defeated Stavroula Zygouri at the Olympic Games in Athens, August 23, 2004.

against Ana "Dynamite" Pascal from Panama, an unbeaten southpaw and holder of the UBC title. Watching her opponent in the ring, Mathis licked her lips: "She hooks big, with real power. It'll be hard! I really love getting to work on this kind of fighter." And, on March 8, she won. Initially not sure about taking on a woman, her trainer René Cordier is all admiration: "She's hungry, in all senses of the word, and craves recognition. Girls work more, are good listeners, and better able to question themselves."

Anne-Sophie Mathis in 2008.

Anne-Sophie Mathis

born 1977, France

French boxer, superlight WBA and WIBF world boxing champion (fifteen victories, one defeat). On June 29, 2007, in Marseille, she faced Myriam Lamare; they had already fought at the Bercy sports hall in Paris in December 2006. Anne-Sophie won on both occasions. Orphaned on her father's side, and mother of Lena (born 2001), she says that the boxing ring has helped her to find herself and give meaning to her existence, even if her daughter remains paramount.

Trained as a sports teacher, her dream was to land a "permanent job" and find somewhere nice to live. In Metz, in 2008, she put her title on the line

Lekha Kozhummel

born 1981, India

Indian boxer and world champion. Coming from a middle-class family, she says she has never encountered obstacles to her practicing a sport that hardly conforms to the traditional image of an Indian woman, though her parents think that now—aged twenty-five—it's high time she got married and retired. She does not consider boxing a risky sport, as it is so often described—no more than judo, in any case, where she picked up her "worst injury." With calm assurance, weighing 168 pounds (75 kilos) and with an impressive left hand, in November 2007 she scrapped to four gold medals at the World Women's Boxing Championships held in Delhi. She had to defeat Russians, Koreans, and the Chinese, usually considered the strongest fighters. Her only regret is that women's boxing is not an Olympic discipline and that, consequently, it suffers from a lack of investment.

Alfonsina Strada

1891–1959, Italy

Née Morini, she was the first women's cycling champion, gaining thirty-six victories over male cyclists. He parents were ashamed to see their daughter pedaling away on local roads, so she moved as far away as possible from the family residence, to the remote countryside in Emilia. To get her to change her mind, they told her to get married, but her husband gave her a splendid bicycle as a wedding present. In 1917, she entered the Tour of Lombardy, finishing thirty-second and twenty-first in 1918. Though far from the best, of course, the other competitors were men, and it is fairly remarkable that she dared to start and managed to finish the race at all. Strada, though, wanted more—she was up for the greatest challenge, for the Giro d'Italia, with its 2,187 ½ miles (3,500 kilometers) in twelve stages. In 1924, registered under the name "Alfonso," she slipped in the mud, snapping off her handlebars. She managed to repair them with a broom-handle, but failed to be classified as she finished outside the time limit. Even disqualified, she refused to give up. At every stage, onlookers waited to catch sight of the "devil in petticoats," egging her on, and her arrival in Milan was greeted by a vast cheering crowd. The Italians recognize in her a woman who was willing to defy the odds—a real *campionissima*. Aged forty-seven, she was still able to beat the women's hour record. She died enjoying a new favorite sport, crushed under her motorbike.

Jeannie Longo

born 1958, France

Road-racer with three victories on the Women's Tour de France, in 1987, 1988, and 1989. In 1979, she took part in her first official race, the only girl

Jeannie Longo in 2001.

among some younger boys. She won easily. In 1989, she took her first world championship, as well as a women's speed record (28 miles per hour/45 kilometers per hour).

After winning gold at the Atlanta Olympic Games in 1996, in Mexico City in 2000, she beat the world hour record, cycling more than 28 miles (45 kilometers). In 2004, she won the French road race championships and, with a total of 800 victories, was voted sportswoman of the century. In 2008, aged fifty, she became champion of France in racing and against the clock. She has also chosen to sit on the French national oversight committee for male and female equality.

Artists

"The woman of genius
does not exist;
when she exists, she is a man."

Octave Uzanne

If a notion seemingly dating from the dawn of time is to be believed, women are faced with the stark choice between creating and procreating. And so, since only women give birth to children, they cannot (or should not) produce works of art. This bizarre cleft stick not only panders to a male sense of superiority, it has also been internalized by certain women.

Singularly disinclined to recognize the talents of her woman colleagues, the writer **Marguerite Yourcenar**, for instance (the first woman to be admitted among the "Immortals" of the French Academy), has argued that "a great novel presupposes an independent view on life and a surfeit of creative power that hitherto has expressed itself fully solely in physiological maternity." Only one female writer, **Selma Lagerlöf**, comes up to Yourcenar's expectations having neither partners nor child. Even the great

Marguerite Duras surrounded by papers in a room typical of her.

photographer **Gisèle Freund** (briefly married, but childless) believed that, if there were so few women reporters, it is not because they lack the requisite open-mindedness, patience, health, "skill and courage faced with the most unexpected situations," it is because photojournalism is so hard to reconcile with normal family life. How then did Murasaki Shikibu manage, in Japan around 1000 CE, to be mother of a daughter and the author of the two-thousand-page *The Tale of Genji*, one asks?

Centuries later, the prejudice that says a woman cannot be an artist and mother at the same time was still going strong. At the end of the nineteenth century, the painter **Suzanne Valadon** was stigmatized as "insane," the "bad mother of Utrillo *le maudit*" (though it was she who taught him to paint). Shouldn't the essential criterion for judgment be the power of her work? As a critic for *L'Intransigeant* exclaimed after viewing pictures by Valadon: "Tomorrow, woman painters will be free and the equals of men."

For a long time, as if to compensate for the fact that some women had deserted "their" accustomed roles, men with an axe to grind stressed the "maternal" aspects of their work. Juries for the Nobel Prize have tended to entertain an image of womanhood close to that of the Virgin Mary—the Madonna of the Seven Sorrows, who saves humanity through gentleness and compassion for the downtrodden. Indeed, the first five female winners of the Nobel Prize for Literature exalt motherhood—real or symbolic—in works littered with suffering and anguish. Like **Nelly Sachs**, or **Gabriela Mistral**, who placed her pen in the service of the poor of her country and its children. Similarly, **Sigrid Undset**, who dreamed of a world regenerated by female gentleness and motherly devotion. And **Grazia Deledda**, rewarded "for her many talents, she who is a model wife and housewife,

Sculptures by Niki de Saint-Phalle, Stravinsky Fountain, Paris.

and a novelist of great merit." The curious manner of putting literary recognition after an appreciation of her qualities as a homemaker in fact chimes perfectly with the author's own ideology.

Many women seem to crave forgiveness for the effrontery at wanting to be creative. **Selma Lagerlöf** remarked that women bring love and compassion to the world, whereas men bring only destruction; to prevent war breaking out, one just has to listen to the voice of women. For her, their writings thus might serve the welfare of all humanity.

In 1929, in *A Room of One's Own*, **Virginia Woolf**, tells us how, to be free, to create, "a woman must have money and a room of her own." Financial independence and inner tranquility, then. German artist

Paula Modersohn-Becker opted instead for the safety net of matrimony. But when her quest for pictorial clarity led her to primordial, primitive forms, her husband, also a painter, opined: "She adores color—but with a roughness at odds with painting. She venerates primitive art, and that's really a pity." Her genuine originality undoubtedly lies in the manner in which she affirms her femininity, but without submitting to the presumptions of her gender. In *Self-portrait with an Amber Necklace* (1906), her hands are heavy, her shoulders sturdy, her face tough-looking; her husband saw this as "hands like spoons, noses like clubs, mouths like gaping wounds." In her diary, she wrote: "It is good to throw off modes of behavior that deprive us of heaven."

Today, the fact that sculptress **Niki de Saint-Phalle** once shared her life with fellow sculptor Jean Tinguely does not seem to have handicapped her work particularly: on the contrary, they often joined forces in works such as the Stravinsky fountain (on Place Beaubourg, Paris, where spouting water sculptures perform a free interpretation of *The Firebird*) and in the *Cyclops* (deliriously inventive pieces erected in the woods at Fontainebleau), creatures that allowed two different and complementary geniuses both to enjoy free rein.

The progress made since the early twentieth century is palpable. When two earlier geniuses, Rodin and **Camille Claudel**, lived and loved, one had to drown, and it had to be the woman. Camille was all the more pioneering in that she was prepared to carve—as well as some sublime and sensual nudes—the bodies of aged, terribly withered women. But female artists had a real struggle to acquire this freedom to treat the female body—their own, for example—as they saw fit. Such an act represented a genuine transgression, because, since the birth of art, it has been male artists, and them alone, who have wielded control over the depiction of the female body, just as men exert control over women's bodies in real life. Camille Claudel and Valadon even turned the tables and tackled the male nude.

In the end, though, it was every traditional hierarchy—man and woman, passive and active, object and subject—that was turned on its head. An enthralling if arduous campaign was then being waged by female artists to earn not only recognition but even status as genuine creators. Didn't Cézanne once say: "One paints with one's balls"? Picasso went one better: "Art is mental ability, plus balls." Meanwhile Albert Cohen stated baldly that there can be no women writers because females are inferior to males and that Yourcenar was too unattractive

Karen Blixen.

to be a decent writer? At this level of misogyny—and thus of negation of the other—one can safely say that all female musicians, engravers, novelists, sculptors, painters, poets, singers, actors, filmmakers, and choreographers are pioneers, in the sense that they had to overcome deeply entrenched prejudices so as to prove the artistic fertility of the female gender. "For most people, a woman sculptor amounts to an act of defiance. They just can't see how women carry in them a life-force superior to that in men," affirmed the sculptor **Germaine Richier**. To gain acceptance in the male worlds of literature, music, or art, women have often found it advantageous to dissemble a femininity liable to sabotage their efforts. Artist **Leonor Fini** denounces this approach: "I find that, in striving to be the equals of men, women are being overmodest, [and,] in wanting to imitate men, who, let us not forget, are encumbered by an out-of-date civilization, they do little more than pay them homage."

While the Franco-American artist **Louise Bourgeois** complains that art is a "world where men and women try to satisfy male power." When she was asked whether there is a style specific to women, she responded that there was not yet one; before that occurred, women would have to throw off their desire to comply with the structures of the male power.

Virginia Woolf for one had thought of that already: "Yet who shall say that even now 'the novel'…, who shall say that even this most pliable of all forms is rightly shaped for [a woman's] use? No doubt we shall find her knocking that into shape for herself when she has the free use of her limbs; and providing some new vehicle, not necessarily in verse, for the poetry in her." It is this new dawn that is now finally underway.

Marilyn Monroe. Tireless femininity.

Germaine Tailleferre

1892–1983, France

The only important female composer at the beginning of the twentieth century. Born Taillefesse, and belonging to the group of Les Six (with Darius Milhaud, Arthur Honneger, etc.), she composed concertos for violin, piano, guitar, and harp, as well as ballets, operettas, operas, and film scores. Though part of it was lost or mislaid, her oeuvre—in spite of the obstacles put in her path by her father and then by her husbands—is first rate.

Lili Boulanger

1893–1918, France

French composer, and first woman to win the Grand Prix de Rome for musical composition. Lili Boulanger, sister of Nadia Boulanger, took the prize in 1913 for her cantata *Faust and Hélène*. Her mother, a Russian countess called Michetskaia, was a professional singer, and her father taught at the Academy. At only six she was already able to sight-read, and "Fauré often came to have her play through his melodies, expressing amazement at the child's gifts."

She was aged nineteen when she was awarded the Grand Prix and a grant for the Villa Médicis. Lili wrote *Les Clairières dans le ciel* to poems by Francis James, symphonic poems, and many works for choir and orchestra, such as *Hymne au soleil* and *Psaume du fond de l'abîme*. On her deathbed (aged only twenty-five) she dictated her Pie Jesu to her sister Nadia. A mass in her memory is celebrated each year at the Church of the Trinity and a Paris square has been named after her.

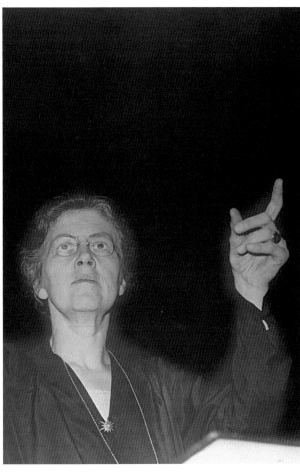

Nadia Boulanger.

Nadia Boulanger

1887–1979, France

Composer (*Rhapsody for Piano and Orchestra*), conductor, pianist, and organist. Nadia Boulanger was a major figure in musical life in France and abroad and had an immense influence on the younger generation. For seventy-five years she taught at the French National Conservatoire (in front of a bust of her sister, the composer Lili, whom she venerated), at the École Normale de Musique in Paris, at the American Conservatoire at Fontainebleau, and in Great Britain, the United States, and privately.

Alma Rosé

1906–1944, Austria

Conductor of the Mädchenorchester in Auschwitz. Musician Alma Rosé's mother was one of Gustav Mahler's sisters. A violinist, Alma had in fact been a member of the Viennese musical elite in the interwar period, but her meteoric career was cut short by the Nazis. After the Anschluss, the Rosé family went into exile in England. Alma's passion for music, however, proved her undoing; she agreed to give a concert in Holland and found herself trapped. Fleeing to Dijon in 1942, she was arrested by the Gestapo and deported to Auschwitz in July 1943. There she somehow managed to create an orchestra that she conducted in a terrifying atmosphere. "If we didn't play well, we'd have been gassed."

Anna Marly

1917–2006, Russia/France

Author of the famous "Song of the Partisans" that rallied the French Resistance. This song is generally ascribed to Joseph Kessel and Maurice Druon, but the truth is that these two well-known men—academicians and Gaullists—simply adapted the "Song of the Partisans," composed by Anna Marly in tribute to the heroic fight put up by the Russians against the Germans at Smolensk.

Née Betoulinski and of Russian origin, Anna was brought to France at the age of one, but went into exile in London to join up with the volunteers of Free France in 1941. She was to regularly whistle a version of the "Song of the Partisans" on the BBC.

Betsy Jolas.

Betsy Jolas

born 1926, France

The most highly regarded female composer on the contemporary music scene. Franco-American, a student of Olivier Messiaen's and a teacher at the American Academy in Fontainebleau, she has composed notably *Études campanaires*, *Lullaby*, *Signets*, and Caril*lons d'été*, for the Promenades Musicales in the Pays d'Auge. In 1970 she was the guest of honor at this festival, based around the theme of "female creative genius," with her piece, *Betsyades*.

On this occasion (with *Chemin des dames* by Geneviève Laurenceau and Lorène de Ratuld, *La vraie vie des divas* by Anna Destraël and Sylvie Lechevalier, and *Médée furieuse* by Stéphanie d'Oustrac), the undeniable importance of women in musical composition was made clear to all. Betsy Jolas paved the way for these young women, offering her help, for example, to Helena Winkelman, a highly promising Swiss violinist and composer.

Gertrude Pridgett (Ma) Rainey

1886–1939, United States

The first professional African-American woman singer of the blues. Christened Gertrude Pridgett in the First African Baptist church in Columbus (Georgia), both of her parents were singers.

Pridgett danced in *A Bunch of Blackberries* at the Springer Opera House in Columbus. She performed with "Pa" Rainey and they married in 1904. The couple worked in the dives and speakeasies of the Deep South; from 1914, they performed together under the name of Rainey and Rainey, Assassinators of the Blues.

Ma Rainey possessed a deep contralto voice, gravelly and sad, perfect for singing songs that delved into the extreme misery of the African-American condition: *Many days of sorrow, many nights of woe/An' a ball and chain, everywhere I go.* She thus became one of the earliest female exponents of "the blues."

Called "Ma," her title not only underlines her musical importance as "mother" of the blues, but also as a dependable, matriarchal figure; black women were so often the real mainstay in a family. A large, flamboyant figure, she wore jewels and sported a huge ostrich-feather fan, a necklace of gold coins, diamond earrings, and a pearl tiara—and even had gold teeth. She was also known for her generous nature.

She is alleged to have taught singing to the evergreen Bessie Smith, who covered her famous "Bo Weavil Blues."

The Raineys had an adoptive son, Danny, who worked with his parents in the 1920s, and Gertrude's sister, Malissa Nix, was also a singer. Still more famous after her death, Rainey left her tough and authentic mark on "classic" blues.

Ma Rainey.

Mamie Smith

1893–1946, United States

The first black singer to cut a record, on January 14, 1920. She began her career at the age of ten as a dancer, leaving her birthplace, Cincinnati (Ohio) to tour the Midwest and the East Coast with a group of African-American preachers. In New York, Mamie started a career as a cabaret dancer, singer, and pianist.

Perry Bradford, a black composer-songwriter, took her on for his musical show, *Made in Harlem*. He fought hard to get the white managers of Okeh Records, a small independent label, to record the voice of an African-American—particularly as she was a female as well. The challenge was far from insignificant: on the one side, as Bradford emphasized, millions of potential African-American purchasers; on the other, threats of a boycott that terrified the firm's directors.

But finally Mamie's voice, singing compositions by Bradford, was accepted, and she recorded with white musicians, "That Thing Called Love" and "You Can't Keep a Good Man Down." This was the first of the "race records." No boycott ensued. A few months later, Mamie Smith was heard singing "Crazy Blues" with black musicians, a number that became one of the greatest hits of the early 1920s, with nearly a million copies sold. The blues began to be transmitted not only orally but also mechanically, and so, potentially, to the whole world.

Bessie Smith

1894–1937, United States

African-American singer. Born in Tennessee into an extremely poor family, she was orphaned at nine. Elizabeth began as a street singer; Ma Rainey, struck by the girl's voice, soon became her mentor and took her on their tour. Pa Rainey then became her manager.

When she appeared in Chicago in 1924, a sublime beauty with the "allure of a queen, hour-glass figure, and with a personality like a high-voltage dynamo," she electrified the public and the critics alike with her traditional-style blues. Her interpretations of "Chicago Bound," "Nobody's Blues But Mine," and "St. Louis Blues" (with Louis Armstrong) provided conclusive evidence of her dramatic and vocal abilities. Her career took a vital turn in 1923 when she signed an exclusive contract with Columbia. Sometimes selling more than 100,000 disks a week, she soon earned enough money to buy a house in Philadelphia.

She performed 200 titles, some written by herself, accompanied by the best bands around. She was dubbed the Empress of the Blues, but she was also a heavy drinker, a man- and indeed woman-eater, and handy with her fists: she would lay into her husband's mistresses and once got the better of a member of the Ku Klux Klan. By the 1930s, her career was on the slide. When Columbia terminated her contract, Smith began touring the country again, appearing in various bars and clubs, as she had when she was young. By the end of the decade, she was attracting white audiences, who were becoming increasingly interested in the blues. She was killed in a car accident in Mississippi.

Alberta Hunter.

Alberta Hunter

1895–1984, United States

Winner of the Handy Award for the best blues singer in 1980 and for the best artist in New York in 1983. In the cabarets of the 1920s and 1930s, Hunter was a blues and jazz singer, passing effortlessly from one musical genre to the other, and was soon being accompanied by top musicians like Louis Armstrong and Sidney Bechet. She spent two decades in Europe where she was acclaimed, embarking on a world tour (Europe, Korea, India) during the Second World War. Singing to set the soul free, for her the blues was almost religious, like a spiritual.

By the 1950s, however, Hunter had left the world of music. She began studying to be a nurse, graduating from the Harlem Hospital School of Nursing in 1956 and continuing in the profession until her retirement. In 1977, Alberta took up music again and made a great impression on her comeback at Carnegie Hall aged eighty-two. After the American Press called her a "natural treasure," on December 3, 1978 came the crowning glory, when she sang for President Jimmy Carter at the White House.

Oum Kalsoum

1898 (or 1904)–1975, Egypt

Born Fatima Ibrahim, this Egyptian singer is one of the most famous Arab women of the twentieth century. As a child in her little village on the Nile Delta, she attended the Koranic school, since her father was an imam. Accompanying him at weddings, she started singing *suras*, acquiring the technical basics and a repertory. As her reputation grew, she was hailed as the "Nightingale of the Delta." Soon a rumor was heard around Cairo: the lute-player Zakaria Ahmed wanted her to come to the capital, where the great composer Aboul Ala Mohamud was soon giving her lessons. She also met the poet Ahmad Rami, who introduced her to Arabic literature and French poetry. In 1922, she sang for the first time for a paying public in Cairo to great applause. Seated, she could sing for five hours at a stretch, tirelessly waving her embroidered handkerchief, often closing her eyes to concentrate better. A single song could last for three hours, during which she languorously detailed the charms of her beloved's eyes and his seductive voice. "Set me free," she would beg or, still more fatalistically, "Love has condemned us." She is saved from melodrama by the beauty of her voice and the sincerity of the feelings she conveys to her ecstatic audience.

Releasing commercial recordings, she also sang on national Egyptian radio, The Voice of Cairo. An icon of musical, movie, and TV culture in Egypt, she campaigned for social justice and the self-determination of the Egyptian people, to which she donated some two million dollars. Her tours were always a triumph and, at the end of the 1960s, she was acting as a kind of ambassadress for her nation to all Arab countries. The princes, the great and the good, and showbiz stars alike couldn't get enough of her. As actor Omar Sharif said: "With every rising sun [she] comes back to life in the hearts of millions of Arabs and without her voice, the days would fade in the Orient." Her reputation has now far exceeded the borders of the Arab-Muslim world.

Josephine Baker

1906–1975, United States/France

Singer, dancer, chorus girl, and Resistant. Born in a very poor district of St. Louis (Missouri), by age thirteen she had to earn a living as a waitress. Managing to get into a theater company, she then joined the Folies Bergères, New York, at eighteen. But the racist American public at the time was hostile to "people of color." Paris was joyfully

discovering jazz at the time and, after touring with the Blackbirds, Josephine stayed on, triumphing in the "Revue Nègre" in the 1920s. The French dubbed her the "*négrillonne*," but also the "Ebony Venus." In a piping soprano voice, she would sing the famous "J'ai deux amours, mon pays et Paris" (I have two loves, my country and Paris, created at the Casino de Paris in 1930). Her success was beyond imagining—in spite (or because) of the scandal caused by her naked black skin. Formidably energetic, it was she who launched the vogue for the Charleston. She appeared in two films in 1930 (*Zouzou* and *Princesse Tam Tam*), which were hailed all over Europe; French nationality followed in 1937. During the Second World War, she engaged in the French Resistance, serving as an intelligence agent in Morocco with a courage that earned her the Military Cross, the Cross of Lorraine, and the Legion of Honor. She adopted children of all colors, orphans whom she would bring back from her world tours with her husband, bandleader Jo Bouillon, and housed them in the Château des Milandes. Acclaimed by Charles de Gaulle, Fidel Castro, Maurice Chevalier, and Grace Kelly, to name but a few, a Paris square bears her name.

Billie Holiday

1915–1959, United States

African-American blues and jazz singer whose life was no less touching than her voice. Born Eleanora Fagan, it is hard to imagine how she found the strength to become such a splendid vocalist after her terrible childhood, with a thirteen-year-old mother, an absent father, and experiencing an aggravated attempted rape when only ten—after which she was dispatched to a reformatory. First of all, she was faced with the problem of how to earn a living—by scrubbing the backyards of a white middle-class woman, or doing tricks as a call-girl. Jail, hospital, and her mother's sickness followed. One day, unable to pay the rent, they were on the brink of being thrown out, so Billie went into a dive bar, sang, and mother and daughter were not thrown into the street, and were even able to buy a whole chicken. This is how Billie tells it in her autobiography, *Lady Sings the Blues*. In 1933, she recorded with Benny Goodman and her dazzling

career was launched; she sold millions of records. "Lady Day" had a grave but sophisticated voice, at once voluptuous and searing, sometimes merry, often tragic, always moving. She had no truck with rehearsals, feeling her way by instinct. She sang songs that touched her, such as "Strange Fruit," which describes a lynching, charred bodies of black men hanging from the branches of a tree. Holiday certainly knew all about racism: when touring with white musicians, she would be refused service or made to lodge in a different hotel. "You can be up to your boobies in white satin, with gardenias in your hair and no sugar cane for miles, but you can still be working on a plantation," she observed. She took drugs: opium then heroin, and drank two to three bottles of gin a day.

Still wanting to sing, she began to be carried bodily onstage. But by now she was in a desperate state, and being dubbed "Lady Yesterday" by the public. After detox in a luxury private clinic, she was hunted by the police and charged with possession. Another bout of cold turkey, then prison and a hospital room guarded by policemen while she lay at death's door.

Édith Piaf

1915–1963, France

The best-known French singer of the twentieth century. It is said that she was rescued at birth in the early morning by a Parisian policeman who brought her in wrapped in his cape (she was actually born Giovanna Gassion in a maternity unit in the Tenon hospital). At three, she became blind, suddenly recovering her sight following a pilgrimage. Her mother, an Italian who sung in low-life bars, was penniless, and left her daughter in the "good" hands of her mother, who doped the feeding-bottle with wine. Her father, an alcoholic if understanding contortionist, in turn handed her over to his mother in her brothel in Normandy. At fifteen, she experienced her first love—and her first pregnancy, giving birth to an adored daughter, Marcelle, who died of meningitis when only two. By this time Édith was a street singer. Louis Leplée, the owner of a cabaret, struck by her powerful voice, took her on in 1935. He christened her Piaf—"sparrow" in Parisian slang—La Môme Piaf, the

"Sparrow Kid," and she sang songs such as "C'est lui que mon cœur a choisi" (He's the one my heart chose) and "Le fanion de la Légion" (The flag of the Legion). Becoming a stalwart of the rue Pigalle, it was for her that composer Marguerite Monnot set "Mon legionnaire" (My Legionnaire) and "Y a pas d'printemps" (There's no springtime) to music, assuring her success.

When Piaf bellowed in a raucous yet tender voice, utterly at one with the song and wringing every ounce of emotion out of it, the audience wept. Her great love, the one that got "under her skin", was boxer Marcel Cerdan, whom she met in the United States. She became an idol in America too, an amazing achievement for this Parisian for whom, when she sung in New York for the first time, the stage had to be raised so the audience could see her. Cerdan died in a plane crash in 1949. Addicted to drugs and at the end of her tether, before she died Piaf still had the courage to sing: "Non, je ne regrette rien" (No, I regret nothing). Two million people joined her funeral cortège to the Père-Lachaise cemetery in Paris.

scorching, almost raucous lows up to stratospheric top notes. "I am a dramatic coloratura," she said. Her voice was perhaps not as perfect as that of her greatest rival, Renata Tebaldi, but its harmonics were interesting and teemed with inexpressible emotions. A true virtuoso, the "La Divina" moved seamlessly from light lyric roles to the most dramatic, from the teasing gypsy of Carmen to Norma, the murderous mother.

Scarcely off the playbill, in five years Callas played eighteen different characters on 160 occasions. She even stood in for Tebaldi in Verdi's *Aida* at La Scala in Milan, an unforgiving venue where cognoscenti went wild with excitement at her performance. With a sublime Traviata (Verdi) and an impressive Norma (Bellini) at the Metropolitan Opera, New York, in 1956, and an overwhelming *Tosca* at Covent Garden in 1964, she attained the zenith of her glory. But she was not only a singer: she was a wonderful tragic actress. "This is the

Maria Callas

1923–1977, United States

Greek-American soprano. Her mother hated having a daughter and was always pushing her on to the stage to make money. Her father, a New York pharmacist, broke up with his wife, who returned to Athens. Maria was ungainly and short-sighted and her mother stuffed her with sweets in the belief that being fat would make her voice fuller. At fourteen the docile Maria entered the Academy, studying singing and piano before performing at the Athens Opera. In 1945, she played *La Gioconda* at the arena in Verona, kick-starting her career as a young diva. Endowed with an extraordinary range, Callas's voice went from

beauty of *bel canto*: it allows the public to read your thoughts before they hear the tune." Completely transformed physically, having lost forty kilos at the end of a Draconian diet (which also damaged her voice), she remained carried away by the music, overcome by the meaning of every phrase. *Vissi d'amore, vissi d'arte*.

But a passionate affair with Aristotle Onassis, a Greek shipping magnate, scuppered her career. To be at his side, she gave up singing and threw herself into high society. In 1965 at the Paris Opera, at the beginning of the second act of *Norma*, she could go on no more. Then the diva, who would have so loved to have been a mother, gave birth to a son who died at birth. Broken, in pain, she learnt that Onassis was to leave her to marry Jackie Kennedy. It was a double blow she never got over. Hiding away, alone, in an apartment in Paris, she died of pulmonary embolism. Or was it a suicide through her overuse of medicines?

Her ashes were scattered in the Aegean Sea, but the memory of this tragic actress, consumed by passion for her art and by an unhappy love story, still burns bright.

Miriam Makeba

1932–2008, South Africa

The first singer from the African continent to succeed internationally. South African-born little Zenzi was only a baby when her mother spent six months in prison (to make ends meet she had been selling beer) and was just five when her father died. Scarcely out of her teens, she worked as a child-minder and washed taxis. By the age of twenty she was an unmarried mother living in poverty.

Makeba was determined to take the fight to the apartheid system, doing so in magnificent songs. These are no sermons, but rhythmic powerhouses, foot-tapping songs such as "Pata, Pata," a record-breaking worldwide hit, written in 1956. But in 1959, she played in an antiracist film, *Come Back Africa*. Her punishment was an exile lasting thirty years. She was not even permitted to attend her mother's burial in her own land.

Taking refuge in the United States, she earned fame and fortune, rubbing shoulders with Marlon Brando, Duke Ellington, and especially with Harry Belafonte, with whom she won a Grammy in 1966, as well as with Marilyn Monroe; she sang with Monroe for Kennedy's birthday in Madison Square Garden.

But in 1969, she married Stokely Carmichael, a Black Power leader, so becoming persona non grata in the United States. Exiled to Guinea, she remained there until Nelson Mandela was released in 1990 and urged her to return. Ravishing in both gospel and jazz, as at ease in English as in Zulu, she paved the way for World Music. Nicknamed "Mama Africa," the lovely rebel died of a heart attack after a stage performance in support of a writer who had received death threats from the Camorra, the Naples Mafia. France made her an honorary citizen.

Tina Turner.

Tina Turner

born 1939, United States

American mixed-race singer, the "Queen of Rock and Roll." Née Annie Mae Bullock, of a black father and Native American mother, she would sing after the spirituals in her Baptist church, and she went on to perform with Ike Turner, who was to become her husband. Gaining success in 1959 with "Fool in Love," she also earned notoriety as a warm-up for The Rolling Stones. A triumphant couple then; but was she just an "Ikette"? In 1975, Tina made a breath-taking appearance in The Who's rock opera Tommy. And without Ike—who had mistreated and exploited her, even attempting to shoot her. At a low point in her own career, Tina Turner tried to commit suicide, but found the courage to publicly denounce her hellish marriage, and divorced him.

After a few years of uphill struggle, the "comeback queen" returned, all guns blazing, with the 1984 hit "What's Love Got to Do with It?", which sold 11 million copies. In 1988, in Mexico City, she played a concert before 180,000 delirious fans. She was no less in demand in the movies: in 1985, she played the female lead in *Mad Max*. Converted to Buddhism, she married a German singer and has four children.

Joan Baez

born 1941, United States

American folk singer with a profound commitment to human rights. One of the only women (the other was Janis Joplin) to take the stage at the legendary Woodstock rock festival in 1969.

Her father, of Mexican origin, and her mother who has Scottish roots, were both Quakers. Joan began by singing in their religious community, playing the guitar and maintaining "a strange relationship with God." She gave her first concert in 1958 at Club 47 in Cambridge, Massachusetts, and later performed at the Newport Folk Festival in 1959; the Press dubbed her the "barefoot Madonna." After a love affair with Bob Dylan, she wedded David Harris. Both militants against the Vietnam War, they encouraged desertion; boycotted by statewide TV, she was then imprisoned. Six months pregnant, at Woodstock she sang the number "Joe Hill"—a tribute to the executed labor activist—before a crowd of 400,000: more than just a gigantic concert, this event marked a turning point in social history. In 1963, in Washington DC, her friend Martin Luther King gave his keynote "I have a dream" speech: Baez intoned "We Shall Overcome" and 350,000 people of all colors took up the chorus.

In 1966, in the Mississippi, she offered her arm to King so he could get through the police cordon. Although she might have been afraid—police dogs attacked children and water-canons were deployed—she didn't give an inch. She was brave enough to go to Vietnam in Christmas 1972 under intense bombing from B52s and Phantom jets. Then came the immense success of *La ballata di Sacco e Vanzetti*, a story of two American anarchists condemned to death after a miscarriage of justice. Under the auspices of Amnesty International, Baez set up an association for the defense of human rights, Humanitas.

Aretha Franklin at the Nokia Theatre, New York, in December 2008.

Aretha Franklin at Caesar's Palace, Las Vegas, in June 1969.

Aretha Franklin

born 1942, United States

American singer and "Queen of Soul." Her father was Reverend Clarence L. Franklin, the most famous pastor in Detroit. The young Aretha started by singing in the New Baptist Church, displaying all the breadth, depth, and power of Gospel. At fourteen, she cut her first record; it became clear she had the finest voice since Billie Holiday and her reputation grew. In 1967, following an argument with her husband, Ted White (a musician and her manager), only one title was recorded instead of a complete album: "I Never Loved a Man the Way I Love You," which was a hit. The same year, she covered "Respect," a song demanding dignity for African Americans, composed by Otis Redding in 1965. She released "Young, Gifted and Black," one of her most splendid albums, tracks of which were also covered by Nina Simone. A feminist and black community leader, she played her part in the struggle for civil rights. In 1972, Aretha offered bail for the imprisoned Angela Davis. In 2009, she sang at the investiture of the first black president of United States, Barack Obama, in front of two million people.

Janis Joplin, 1966.

Janis Joplin

1943–1970, United States

American singer and the first female rock star. A rebellious young girl, she fled the family nest at an early age and joined the innovative and outlandish Beatniks. In 1966, at the pop festival at Monterey, with her group, Big Brother and the Holding Company, she unleashed a raucous, unhinged, electrifying voice, all howls and explosive runs that petered out into sensual murmurs. Her vocal power was not unlike that of Bessie Smith in the blues. In a miniskirt and fishnet stockings, or bellbottoms, gold kaftans and hippie jewels, Janis threw herself body and soul into the performance, vibrant, as if possessed by her sexually explicit songs.

At a time when girls tended to be groupies or sing in the background, she became a major rock star on the San Francisco scene and famous throughout the world. The album *Cheap Thrills* went gold. Forming a new group, the Kozmic Blues Band, she made an electric appearance at Woodstock. But, aged only twenty-seven, a drug overdose after years of alcohol abuse killed her. Yet it was Joplin who paved the way for so many female musicians after her, including Nina Hagen, Catherine Ringer of Les Rita Mitsoukos, Madonna, and Björk.

Jessie Norman, 2002.

Jessie Norman

born 1945, United States

An African-American soprano of international standing. Presented in 1997 with the Kennedy Center Honor, the highest US award for arts and letters. In a variety of styles, starting out with the Gospel tunes sung by her family in church, she has become a past master in German lieder and Italian arias alike; prepared to branch out into jazz and spirituals, she embraces the difficulties of Schoenberg and Berg. Ever popular, with a grandiose voice able to fill the most diverse venues, she made her reputation as a great dramatic soprano in crowd-pleasing operas traveling the world. Studying music in the United States, Norman debuted in 1968 at the Berlin Opera in *Tannhäuser* (she won the international music prize in Munich), becoming a magnificent interpreter of Wagner's Valkyrie and singing Mussorgsky in Moscow, before triumphing in Mahler's *Song of the Earth* with the Berlin Philharmonic in 1999. In Italy, she played Aida at La Scala in Milan in 1972, while at Covent Garden she was Cassandre in Berlioz's *Les Troyens*. She has won a London Gramophone Award and is also a laureate of the Grand Prix National du Disque Français.

In 1989 in Paris, Norman transfigured *La Marseillaise* at the celebrations for bicentenary of the French Revolution. In the United States, she sung at presidential investitures in both 1985 and 1997. In 1996, she dazzled crowds at the opening ceremony for the centenary Olympic Games in Atlanta.

Patti Smith

born 1946, United States

Cult rock star and punk muse, Patti has played a key role in the history of modern music. Though her mother was a jazz singer before becoming a waitress in a restaurant, Patricia started out working on the production line and then set out on her singing career armed with a searing voice and breathtaking vitality. She released her debut album, *Horses*, in 1975 featuring her androgynous body and face, rough voice, and inimitable blend of grace and violence. Painter and poet, she stopped touring for eight years to bring up her two children. Less rugged perhaps, her voice was even stronger and fuller, and she was more combative than ever. Refusing to bow to the demands of the market, she is a free and creative spirit as well as a dogged opponent of stupidity and injustice. A Commandeur des Arts et Lettres in France, she was inducted into the Rock and Roll Hall of Fame in 2007, and has been awarded an honorary doctorate from Rowan University.

Björk, 2007.

Björk

born 1965, Iceland

Offbeat electro-pop singer and the most famous living Icelander. Brought up on a hippie commune, a musician at five and a singer at twelve, in 1979 her debut band rejoiced in the provocative name of Spit & Snot. Her fame kicked off in London in 1993, as she oscillated between punk, pop, jazz, reggae, house, and medieval Icelandic music. A musical chameleon, to the accompaniment of violin and harp, tubas and trumpets, Japanese traditional instruments, or the choir of St. Paul's Cathedral London, she became a household name throughout the world. But it is the extraterrestrial sound of her voice that strikes one most forcefully, particularly in *Medùlla* (2004). This was a triumphant year, with her performance of *Oceania* at the opening ceremony of the Athens Olympics, wearing a dress with a train measuring 3,000 feet (900 meters) that rippled out like the sea.

She composed the soundtrack for and starred in *Drawing Restraint 9*, a film commemorating the Hiroshima atomic bomb made by her husband, Matthew Barney. Opposite Catherine Deneuve, she played the devastating leading role in *Dancer in the Dark* by Lars von Trier, which earned a Golden Palm in Cannes in 2000, and for which she won the Best Actress award.

Patti Smith, 1996.

Sarah Bernhardt in 1900 on the stage at the Théâtre de la Porte Saint Martin, Paris.

Sarah Bernhardt in Floria Tosca, *a drama by Victorien Sardou, in Paris in 1900.*

Sarah Bernhardt

1844–1923, France

Universally known French actress. Born out of wedlock, she escaped the traditional route of becoming either a prostitute or nun, and entered the theater. *Ruy-Blas* at the Comédie-Française, then *Phèdre*; Victor Hugo went into ecstasy over her "golden voice," while the playwright Rostand saw her as the "queen of pose and princess of gesture." Proust turned her into La Berma, Mucha designed posters for her, Nadar took superb photographs of her, poets like Théodore de Banville and writers like Jules Renard and Pierre Loti admired her, while playwright Victorien Sardou, artist Gustave Doré, and actor Lou Telleren (thirty years her junior) all became lovers. Having had a child by the Prince de Ligne, she married a down-at-heel, womanizing morphine addict from Greece. And yet "La Divine" remained a global triumph. In 1900, she appeared, dazzling and androgynous, in *L'Aiglon*, a role written especially for her by Rostand. A capricious super-star, surrounded by wild beasts, mastiffs, and croco-diles, the "Sphinx" made sure her photograph was taken in her coffin. Transforming the status of the actress, which had hitherto been indistinguishable from that of a "loose woman," she supported Zola in his defense of Colonel Dreyfus and, during the Great War, boosted the morale of the troops. The owner of the Théâtre de la Ville, in 1917 she was awarded the Legion of Honor. Aged seventy, by which time she had lost a leg, she continued to act in total symbiosis with her audience.

Alice Guy

1873–1968, France

The first woman filmmaker (in 1900) and the first director of a fiction film. A shorthand typist and then secretary to Léon Gaumont, she was present at the inauguration of the projector designed by the Lumière brothers for their documentary films. "From morn to night, I heard people talking about cinema. But the films showed workers leaving the factory, trains on the move, march-pasts.... It seemed to me that one could do something different." Alice was instead to invent stories, offering to write sketches for Gaumont and film them. Her superiors agreed, provided that this little fantasy took place outside working hours. She found the time to shoot a film entitled "The Cabbage Fairy" in the garden of a little house in Belleville with an amateur cameraman, acquaintances as actors, a real bawling infant, and a set comprised of a backcloth behind rows of wooden cabbages. She managed to make unsophisticated audiences laugh or cry with mystery films such as "The Alcoholic Mattress," comedies like "I have a cockchafer in my trousers," or grand historical films such as the "Life of Christ." Together with her team, she experimented, shooting from various distances, speeding up, slowing down, or running the film backwards (at a time when Méliès was inventing animation). She even realized the world's first attempt at a talkie.

When Gaumont set up a fully fledged studio, she would have preferred to hand over its management, but Alice, combative and supported by Eiffel, remained in charge until 1907. She made some 400 films, feature-length and shorts, some of which have experimental value. She went on to film in the United States (*The Shadows of the Moulin Rouge* and *The Sewers*, as well as westerns) for a company called Solax, a rival of Fox, established with a husband who turned out to be a thief and an adulterer. Alice returned to France with her children, finding herself

Alice Guy.

forgotten and all doors closed to the artist and author of *Autobiographie d'une pionnière du cinéma*. Late on, in 1955, she was awarded the Legion of Honor. Today, Alice is a real star in the United States and has had a retrospective at the prestigious Whitney Museum of American Art.

Lois Weber

1882–1939, United States

The first female film director in America, she made hundreds of films. In 1914, *Hypocrites* denounced corruption in political and religious circles countered by the "naked truth" in the guise of a completely nude woman. Despite falling foul of censorship by the mayor of Boston, who ordered that clothing be hand-painted on the image frame by frame, the movie was immensely successful.

Marlene Dietrich

1901–1992, Germany/United States

American actress and singer of German extraction. In her first major movie, *The Blue Angel*, she played a man-eater who pulls the wool over the eyes of a worthy professor; in her second, *Morocco*, she falls for a legionnaire and docilely follows him to the bitter end. Marlene managed to fuse these two apparently contradictory aspects into a figure of mythical womanhood. Devastating temptress in Sternberg's film, enveloped in a steamy, chiaroscuro atmosphere; in *The Scarlet Empress* she becomes a demanding lover; little girl lost in *Shanghai Express*; she brings a hint of scandal to Wilder's *Foreign Affair*; a lovely enchantress for René Clair, an angel for Lubitsch, and half-woman half-demon for George Marshall. She was above all a truly great actress who played opposite the most famous stars—Gary Cooper, John Wayne, Jean Gabin (a real-life lover). Lubitsch used her brilliantly on set, as a bewitching singer whose gravelly yet silky voice gives us the spine-tingling news that she's *Falling in Love Again*. A committed anti-Nazi, she succeeded in transforming the famous "Lili Marlene"—once a rallying song for Hitler's troops—into an anthem of joy and victory that gave courage to 150,000 soldiers. For her engagement on the Allied side, America awarded her the "Medal of Freedom" in 1947, while France presented her with the Legion of Honor in 1951. In 2002, she was posthumously made an honorary citizen of Berlin and a public square was named after her.

Jale Afife

1902–1941, Turkey

First Turkish actress. Hailing from Istanbul, she was a granddaughter of Sait Pasha. One day, she entered an acting contest to find a stand-in for an Armenian performer. Afife had the audacity to present herself at the theater of Kadikö; her performance was a triumph, but, as the first woman to tread the boards, there was inevitably a price to pay. In her father's eyes, Afife was no better than a prostitute and she had to leave the family home. On several occasions she was hauled off to the police station, where officers mistreated her, shouting: "You are betraying your religion and your country." In 1918, the Ministry of the Interior promulgated a circular prohibiting "Turkish Moslem women from playing onstage." She was thus expelled from the theater and found herself penniless and with nowhere to hide. Prone to terrible migraines, she treated them with morphine and became an addict. She died aged thirty-nine in a psychiatric hospital. Only four people attended her funeral. Since 1923, Turkish women have been allowed to go on stage and today Afife has become a respected figure in her homeland where the most prestigious acting award is called the Afife Prize.

Marilyn Monroe

1926–1962, United States

Born Norma Jeane Mortenson, the most famous American actress, known the world over. Her mother was a manic depressive, frequently interned, her father unknown. A little girl, starved of affection, she was sexually assaulted in a foster family. Though she reveled in displaying her sensuality and dazzling smile, Marilyn's life was one long search for security.

Married at sixteen, working in a parachute factory, she made the cover of the magazine *Mmmmm Girl*, appearing naked, her generous curves plain for all to see on a calendar.

Initial success came in *Love Happy* by the Marx Brothers, in Joseph Mankiewicz's *All About Eve*, and in John Huston's *The Asphalt Jungle*. These were followed by great movies and international celebrity: an impressive tragic actress in *Niagara*, and *The Seven Year Itch*; irresistible in *Gentlemen Prefer Blondes*, *How to Marry a Millionaire*, and *Some Like It Hot*; profound in *River of No Return*; touchingly pathetic in John Huston's *The Misfits*. "A career is wonderful, but you can't curl up with it on a cold night," she confessed. She sought warmth through marriages—Joe Di Maggio, a leading baseball player, who adored but beat her; Arthur Miller, who as a serious writer for a time brought her a measure of respectability—and a string of lovers: the son of Charlie Chaplin, Elia Kazan, Frank Sinatra, Yves Montand, John and Robert Kennedy. Her tragic end—found dead on August 5, 1962, aged just thirty-six—only reinforced the myth behind this idol of the modern age.

Marilyn Monroe in The Seven Year Itch, *1955.*

Agnès Varda

born 1928, France

French scriptwriter and committed feminist. Born in Belgium to a Greek father and French mother, and married to Jacques Demy, she now lives in Los Angeles. Without her film *One Sings, the Other Doesn't*, we would have but few visual traces of those turbulent years in which women were beginning to rebel against the dangers of backstreet terminations, joining forces to demand the right to abortion like the Dutch, and not afraid to sing songs on the subject. Agnès Varda has been vocal in her support for the cause of these women and—more broadly—in the struggle for life.

Brigitte Bardot

born 1934, France

French actress who, in the 1950s and 1960s created the "BB" icon. After *Manina*, she became famous thanks to her first husband, Roger Vadim, who made *And God Created Woman* in 1956. She appeared naked, superb, and provocative in a St-Tropez that was soon to become a hot-spot. "Have you no shame?" she was asked. "It wasn't dirty because it

was beautiful," came her famous reply. She played a tragic figure in Clouzot's *Truth* (1960), and again in Godard's 1963 *Contempt*, which propelled her into the New Wave. Memorable in Vadim's *Love on a Pillow*, Louis Malle gave her a more complex role in *A Very Private Affair*.

A sex symbol pursued by the paparazzi, an icon of French female sensuality, in 1967 she occasioned a riot at Cannes. Her initials B.B. (i.e. "baby") spawned the myth of the child-woman. She had several husbands, including Jacques Charrier, with whom she had a son; as many divorces and lovers, too (including crooner Sacha Distel and actor Jean-Louis Trintignant). At a time when it was regarded as sinful for a woman to divorce, BB didn't give a hoot; not though without tragic repercussions, including several suicide attempts. Even Britain's Queen Elizabeth received her, while General de Gaulle waxed tenderly over this "young woman of marvelous simplicity." Carved by Aslan in 1966, she is transformed into Marianne, the symbol of the French Republic. Since 1973, she has been an active defender of animal rights.

Ariane Mnouchkine

born 1939, France

French theater director with a popular and political edge. Her troupe, Le Théâtre du Soleil, founded in 1964, operates as a cooperative. Her *1789* at the Cartoucherie de Vincennes was an immense success. Her *Molière* was a triumph that ran for two years. A close friend of feminist writer Hélène Cixous, she has directed two of her plays: *L'histoire terrible mais inachevée de Norodom Sihanouk* (The Terrible but Unfinished Story of Norodom Sihanouk) and *L'Indiade*. She has been tireless in the fight against injustice.

Jane Campion

born 1954, New Zealand

New Zealand filmmaker, the first to receive the Golden Palm at the Cannes Film Festival in 1993. Born into an artistic family, she took courses at the Sydney College of Arts and at a film, television, and radio school in the same city. Her masterpiece is surely *The Piano*. In 1996, she shot *Portrait of a Lady* after Henry James's novel, and in 1999 *Holy Smoke*, whose sexual license shocked audiences. In 2009, she made *Bright Star*, the tale of John Keats's doomed romance with Fanny Brawne.

Hiam Abbass

born 1960, Israel

Palestinian actress of Israeli nationality. Born in Nazareth in an Islamic community, and brought up in Galilee, she studied and taught photography in Haifa before embarking on a career as a stage actress in the Palestinian arts center at Jerusalem. She played in the film *Wedding in Galilee*, directed by the Israeli director Michel Khleifi, in 1987, and then in 1996 in *Haifa*, which showed life in a Palestinian refugee camp. In France (where she lives), she played opposite Gerard Depardieu. In 2001 she appeared in *Red Satin* by the Tunisian Rajah Amari. Hiam also starred for Amos Gitai in *Free Zone*, for Spielberg in *Munich* and in *Paradise Now* by Hany Abu-Assad. In 2008, she featured in the superb film by Eran Rikilis, *Lemon Tree*. At the intersection of several cultures, Hiam Abbass, a passionate actress, is also an ambassadress for peace.

Naomi Kawase

born 1969, Japan

Japanese female filmmaker and the first to receive a Golden Camera at Cannes in 1997 (aged twenty-eight); the first woman to receive the Grand Prix in 2009. Almost all her films seem to stem from her traumatic childhood when she was abandoned by her parents. *Ni tsutsumarete* (Embracing, 1992) dramatizes her quest for her father. Having studied photography at the School for Visual Arts in Osaka, she films quiet close-ups, often of non-professional actors; using a hand-held camera, she dispenses with a large technical crew in order to capture a more human truth. The story of intense tenderness and terrible brutality of her great-aunt is told in *Birth/Mother* (2006), which opens and closes with a shot of a placenta; she spins a tale of death, with photographer Kazuo Ishii, in *Letter from a Yellow Cherry Blossom*. Her full-length fictional film, *Suzaku*, was given an award at Cannes.

Selma Lagerlöf.

Selma Lagerlöf

1858–1940, Sweden

Swedish novelist and winner of the Nobel Prize for Literature in 1909 (the first woman to receive the award); the first woman to be inducted into the Swedish Academy in 1914. She became lame at three, but wrote a great Nordic favorite with children, *Nils Holgersson's Wonderful Adventures through Sweden*, a bird's-eye view of humanity from the back of a wild goose. With some difficulty she managed to convince her father—a ruined alcoholic who lived in his dreams—to let her sit the teacher-training examination and become a primary school teacher. *Gösta Berling's Saga* was informed by aspects from her Protestant background (sin and redemption, suffering just and unjust) as well as Icelandic sagas and pagan sources. She gave a visionary speech at the Nobel Prize award ceremony in which she conversed with her dead father. Captivating in its strange lyricism, her work portrays human beings confronted by the violence of their passions—bankruptcy, infanticide, sexual anguish—as well as by trolls, fantastic beasts, and the uncontrollable elements (tumultuous storms or miraculously blossoming flowers).

Edith Wharton

1862–1937, United States

American writer, and the first woman to receive the Pulitzer Prize in 1920 for her book, *The Age of Innocence*. Born Newbold Jones, she was to describe her ignorant, petty, spiteful—if fabulously wealthy—middle-class family in *Old New York*. Although in love with Walter Berry, she married Edward Wharton, a well-heeled Boston businessman. The marriage was a fiasco and she divorced in 1913. In 1905, Edith became friends with Henry James (impressed by her indomitable character, he dubbed her the angel of devastation) and published her first elegantly savage masterpiece, *House of Mirth*, a pitiless account of the cruelty of New York high society. From 1906 on, Edith lived for the most part in France, continuing to write frenetically, throwing receptions and frequenting a circle in which she met poet Anna de Noailles, writer André Gide, and Jean Cocteau. When forty-five, she started a sexual liaison with Morton Fullerton, which proved to be the crucial passion of her life. The next was Walter Berry, whom she never forgot and who was to be buried in Versailles by her side. She was the first woman doctor honoris causa at Yale University.

Edith Wharton.

Grazia Deledda

1871–1936, Italy

A writer from Sardinia, and the second woman to receive the Nobel Prize for Literature in 1926. *Racconti sardi* (Sardinian Tales, 1894), *La Via del Male* (The Evil Way, 1896), *Cenere* (Ashes, 1904), and *Marianna Sirca* (1915), as with the majority of her thirty-five novels and four hundred short stories, are set in Sardinia, among shepherds, gangsters, fiancées faithful until death and aged countrywomen, in a sad, affecting world, unflinchingly described. Imbued with dark hints of guilt, with fate and angst, both pagan and Christian (especially in *La Madre* [The Mother]), the atmosphere, as D. H. Lawrence observed, is often reminiscent of *Wuthering Heights*.

In spite of the "curse" that was meant to afflict female writers, even they can marry and have sons. Indeed, Deledda went one step further: "Creativity finds its noblest expression in childbirth." She adhered to Mussolini's political line: "The goal of his struggle was always the same as mine when I write: the purity of family life, a love for one's native soil and the glebe, simple ways of life."

Colette.

Colette

1873–1954, France

Sidonie Gabrielle Colette, the greatest female French writer of the first half of the twentieth century; the first woman elevated to the position of Grand Officer of the Legion of Honor in 1953; member, then president of the Académie Goncourt; the first woman to be honored with a state funeral.

Her braids down to her ankles, as a girl she ran free through the woods under the watchful eye of Sido, her all-powerful and much-loved mother: "When I was twelve I was queen of the earth!" This feeling of returning to the maternal body in the joyous, milk-white dawn, the wisdom of the ceaseless cycles of Nature resurfaced in 1928 in *Break of Day*.

Aged twenty, she married Willy Gauthier-Villars, a man "worse than ripe" and a notorious figure in Paris high society: held captive, unashamedly betrayed by her husband, she had her hair cut short. At Willy's request, in 1900 she spiced up her memoirs and published *Claudine at School*, though it was her husband who signed all the Claudine books. In spite of this runaway success, Colette remained dependent, without money; she was even thrown out on the street by her errant spouse, though she only dared to speak of this period after Willy's death, in *My*

Apprenticeships. For six difficult years she engaged in a lengthy struggle for her independence as a woman, becoming the mime and variety artiste depicted in *The Vagabond* (1910). *Music Hall Sidelights* portrays for the first time, and through the eyes of a woman who lived with them, the real life of the "dancing girls" (as in Gribiche's fatal abortion). With Missy, Marquise de Belbeuf and a daughter of the Duc de Morny, a cross-dresser who scandalized the Moulin Rouge, she discovered the comforting, motherly pleasures of female homosexuality. In 1932, she railed against Proust's vision of lesbians as vicious and immoral in *Ces plaisirs qu'on dit à la légère physiques* (These Pleasures).

Becoming Baronne de Jouvenel des Ursins, Colette worked as literary editor at *Le Matin* and embarked on a career as a reporter. After the difficult birth at forty of a daughter, she forsook her child and took her son-in-law Bertrand de Jouvenel, a sixteen-year-old boy as beautiful as Apollo (she was then forty-seven), as her lover. Curiously enough, a little earlier she had published *Chéri*, which depicts the love between a young man and a mature woman. In 1923 the first book signed Colette appeared: *Le Blé en herbe* (The Ripening Seed). At fifty-four, then, she decided to choose a literary pseudonym, that of her father, Captain Colette. Even married to Maurice Goudeket (also many years her junior), she was still Colette, the celebrated woman author. For sixteen years, she lay immobilized on her "raft bed" in the Palais-Royal in Paris.

Colette exploded the traditional form of the novel, creating a poetic ferment of all the kingdoms of nature—plant, animal, human—as well as everyday objects and food. "And you, black roses, you fragrant jam." The great innovation though is that her writing is rooted in gender difference, daring to describe the female sex as a "deep trap, a smooth pit, a living corolla of the sea." Compared to this strange domain, male sexuality is characterized as "state of misery." Her descriptions of female pleasure harbored great promise for women's liberation.

Gertrude Stein

1874–1946, United States

American writer and art collector who ran a famous Parisian "salon." A wealthy Jewish heiress originally from Pennsylvania, and a lesbian, she choose to live in Paris with her partner, Alice B. Toklas. In her splendid mansion, she received F. Scott Fitzgerald, Ernest Hemingway, poet Max Jacob, Jean Cocteau, Braque, Matisse, Picasso, and many more luminaries of the day. Her innovative, fragmented style, always in the present tense and almost without punctuation, prefigures the French New Novel and evokes cubist pictorial techniques. With *Autobiography of Alice B. Toklas* (in fact an account of her own life), she was acknowledged as a consummate writer.

Gertrude Stein in Los Angeles, 1925.

Sigrid Undset

1882–1949, Norway

Norwegian novelist, winner of the Nobel Prize for Literature in 1928. An orphan at sixteen, she worked for an electricity firm but, after publishing her first books, was able to live from her writing. She met a painter, Anders, who was married, and he became her "lord and master." Marrying him in 1912, she gave him a further three children (two boys and a girl, who was disabled), and also cared for the three children from his first marriage (one of whom was also disabled), looking after them all until the couple divorced. Complex, contradictory even, Sigrid was capable of portraying a tough Viking in her novel *Gunnar's Daughter*, as well as publishing "From a woman's point of view" (1919), an anti-feminist tract that declares "it's wretched being a woman."

Depicting a world of sin, thunder and lightning, pilgrimages, and violence, and dreaming of a place regenerated by female gentleness and motherly devotion, she embarked on a veritable aesthetic and ethical edifice in her immense fresco, *Kristin Lavransdatter*. A second blockbuster, *Olav Audunssoen*, was set in thirteenth-century Norway. She was decorated with the Grand Cross of St. Olaf (Norwegian order of chivalry awarded for exceptional contributions).

Helen Keller

1880–1968, United States

Deaf, dumb and blind American woman who managed to become a university lecturer and writer. Unhinged, scarcely articulate, she lived in a world of total non-communicability until Anne Sullivan, a specialized teacher at the Perkins Institute of Boston, deployed all her patience and intelligence to make contact with the young patient. Once the penny dropped, Helen made astonishing strides, becoming able to read and write in English, French, German, Latin, and Greek. At twenty-four she graduated *magna cum lauda* from the University of Radcliffe.

The author of *Light in My Darkness* and *My Religion,* she was at one point a household name. A socialist, suffragette, and pacifist, according to Mark Twain she was simply "the greatest woman since Joan of Arc."

Virginia Woolf

1882–1941, Great Britain

English "feminist" authoress who placed the art of the novel on a modernist footing. "A woman must have some money and a room of her own if she wants to write fiction," Woolf had the good sense to recommend, though she herself had access to 300 rooms, in the parental country-house of her lover, Vita, daughter of Baron Sackville-West, as well as thousands of books belonging to her father, an eminent Victorian intellectual. In addition to these material comforts, Virginia was fortunate enough to marry author Leonard Woolf, a devoted husband who protected her from external difficulties and took care of her in what was a curious relationship.

Together they founded the Hogarth Press, an innovative publisher's that brought out stories by Katherine Mansfield, essays by Freud, and poems by T. S. Eliot. If the backdrop was all wealth and intellectualism, in the end there was much mental affliction. She had undergone psychological trauma in her childhood—including a sexual assault by her half-brother when only six, and the death of her mother when Virginia was just thirteen. She fell into a "pit of absolute despair," and it seemed that only writing could save her. Indeed, as she saw it, it was an ability to make the most of the horrors she endured that turned her into a writer, affording her pleasure and delight. This resulted in novels such as *To the Lighthouse*, *The Waves*, *Mrs. Dalloway*, and *The Years*, where "unrecorded gestures, those unsaid or half-said words ... form themselves, no more palpably than the shadows of moths on the ceiling, when women are alone, unlit by the capricious and coloured light of the other sex." With delicate, impressionistic touches, all the inner movements, all the subtle states of the soul unfurl at the limit of the subconscious; by nature shift and transition, all is in harmony with nature, in rhythm with the sea.

"It was as if the water floated off and set sailing thoughts that had grown stagnant on dry land and gave to their bodies even some sort of physical relief. First the pulse of colour flooded the gulf with blue and the heart expanded with it and the body swam." There is a joyous, lightheaded feeling of melting into the water, the element that bathes her whole oeuvre. After several phases of acute depression and two suicide attempts, however, it was in water that she took her life, weighed down by stones in her pockets.

Virginia Woolf's work infused modernity into literature, paving the way for the New Novel in France, in particular for Nathalie Sarraute's *Tropisms*. She also broke new ground in feminine writing, because, according to her, women have a creative capacity very different from that of men and therefore have no need to restrict themselves to imitating male writing. Her profession of faith was that, once they had earned sufficient freedom of action, women would change the nature of the novel.

Karen Blixen

1885–1962, Denmark

Danish authoress with a taste for adventure. Born Dinesen, her father—a writer and explorer—committed suicide when she was only ten years old; she wanted to emulate him. She wed the Swedish Baron Bror Blixen in Kenya, where they set up a coffee plantation. In love with this region of savanna, buffaloes, and lions, Karen found herself doing the hard work on the farm, while her husband slept around, infecting her with syphilis. Treated with mercury, the once beautiful and now ruined woman lost weight catastrophically and died of anorexia. In the magnificent *Out of Africa* published in 1937, she writes of her nostalgia for a world of heady fragrance, of the complex and ill-fated loves of a decadent aristocracy, of calculating men and captivating wild beasts, of the tangled relationship between the baroness and her staff. Its precedent, the very different *Seven Gothic Tales*, had been no less successful.

Karen Blixen.

Gabriela Mistral

1889–1957, Chile

Chilean poetess who won the Nobel Prize for Literature in 1945, awarded for the first time to a South American writer. Born Lucilia Godoy Alcayaga, her penname combines the words for the Archangel Gabriel and a violent wind—a force of nature in the Andes. This choice reflects her poetry, which is shot through with suffering and with a thirst for solace and tenderness. Her alcoholic father vanished when she was three, leaving her grandmother to bring her up religiously. She became a teacher, of children during the day and workers at night. Her tragic love affairs marked her forever, her

Gabriela Mistral.

first major collection being entitled *The Sonnets of Death*. Motherhood, too, which she was never to experience personally, was also a cause for suffering (*Poemas de la madre mas triste*). The writer and politician José Vasconcelos invited her to collaborate on a program of educational reform in Mexico. She spent two years there, writing *Lecturas para mujeres* (devoted to the education of girls), and founding schools and libraries. She became Chilean consul and worked as a journalist on *El Tiempo*.

Agatha Christie, 1924.

Agatha Christie

1890–1976, Great Britain

English writer of the most widely read detective novels in the world. She grew up in England but spent her adolescence in Paris so as to make a career in music. She married Colonel Christie, who soon went to the front, leaving her with a daughter, Rosalind. During the First World War, she worked as a nurse in a hospital, where she became acquainted with the properties of poisons. Her mother brought her up with the idea she would become a woman of letters, while her sister bet that she couldn't write a detective novel in which the mystery would only be solved at the end. Taking up the challenge, she penned *The Mysterious Affair at Styles* (1920), in which the celebrated Belgian detective Hercule Poirot made his first appearance. That book was refused by six publishers, but in 1926 *The Murder of Roger Ackroyd* made her famous. From then on, she turned out manuscripts at the rate of two a year, writing books like one "makes sausages," with a perfect mastery of the genre combined with relentless logic. Breaking new ground in the psychological detective novel, the crimes she imagines can all be explained by the past and the personality of the assassin. The clues that come to the aid of her two indefatigable detectives—Poirot and Miss Marple, an astute elderly spinster—are not physical but moral and psychological, the enigma being clarified through reasoned deduction. *Murder on the Orient Express*, which appeared in 1934, sold two million copies. The suspense is similar, if more disquieting, in *Ten Little Niggers* (now entitled *And Then There Were None*; 1939), a closed world in which everyone suspects everyone else. Christie delighted, not only in shaking up this cocktail of crimes, but also in attacking the middle-classes—the judges, doctors, and bigots that comprise "good society," all of whom she believed capable of the basest crimes and of a sadism that, she hints, is inherent in humankind.

Agatha Christie, 1950s.

Nelly Sachs

1891–1970, Germany/Sweden

Poetess, joint winner of the Nobel Prize for Literature in 1966. As anti-Semitism took hold in her country, Sachs refused for a long time to flee Germany, only doing so eventually for the sake of her mother; Selma Lagerlöf helped them to get to Stockholm in 1940. Yet she was forever to be haunted by the Shoah (Holocaust), as her poem collections testify: *In den Wohnungen des Todes* (In the dwelling-place of death, 1947); *Fahrt ins Staublose* (Journey to the beyond, 1961); and the play *Eli: Ein Mysterienspiel vom Leiden Israels* (Eli: A mystery play of the sufferings of Israel, 1950). Obsessed by the guilt of having survived, she slowly sank into persecution mania.

Pearl Buck

1892–1973, United States/China

American authoress, winner of the Nobel Prize for Literature in 1938. Her parents were missionaries in China. She felt an affinity with the local population, while her teacher, a Confucius scholar, taught her

Pearl Buck receiving the Nobel Prize for Literature in 1938.

writing and Chinese culture. Choosing China as her homeland (even though she studied successfully in the United States), she married the agronomist John Buck, with whom she had a daughter who suffered mental disabilities. Throughout her life, Pearl Buck was haunted by suffering, adopting a girl and then boys (when she remarried her publisher), setting up the Welcome House for infants born to American soldiers and Asian mothers, as well as a foundation for disabled children.

The Mother is a superb epic novel that details the burdens women carry: numerous children, bloody abortions, being badly treated and abandoned. Her first book published in 1930, *East Wind, West Wind*, describing the pain of a young wife whose husband unbinds her feet, met with worldwide success (almost two million copies sold). In 1932, she was awarded the Pulitzer Prize. She had to quit her beloved adoptive fatherland in 1927 after being almost killed by revolutionary troops.

Pearl Buck, 1959.

Anaïs Nin, 1974.

Anaïs Nin

**1903–1977,
France/United States**

American woman of letters. Her famous journal is a testimony to female emancipation in the twentieth century. Holding a US passport, Spanish by her father (who abandoned the family home when she was eleven), Danish by her mother, French by choice, for a long time living in Paris and at Louveciennes (where her house became a literary and artistic salon), Anaïs Nin was a cosmopolitan who started out in life as a model and dancer. Her first book, the poetic *House of Incest* (1936), is bathed in a surrealist atmosphere where dreams, symbols, and incantations exalt the feminine. Composed in 1940, *Delta of Venus*, was certainly written to order and paid a dollar a page, but its audacious sexual descriptions represent, as she said herself, the first effort by a woman to speak about things that had been hitherto left to men. The writer unveils the mysteries of female sensuality ("so different from that of a man"), including bisexuality. Considering male language "inadequate," for her, "only the united beat of heart and sex can attain ecstasy." The content is thought to derive from experiences in her own sexual life, if one judges by the many encounters she recorded in her journal, a literary monument running to several hundred notebooks which, according to author Henry Miller, Anaïs's adoring lover, is comparable to the confessions of St. Augustine, to Petronius, Abelard, Rousseau, and Proust.

Marguerite Yourcenar

1903–1987, Belgium/France

Née Crayencour, Franco-Belgian writer. In 1970, she was inducted into the Royal Academy of Belgium and became the first woman to enter the Académie Française in 1980. Truly her father's daughter, she identified with him to the point that he published her work under the name "Marg," while she signed a story written by him about his honeymoon. She had no mother, who had died giving birth to her daughter—an irrelevant fact, the authoress assures us. Her relationships with men proved painful, from a masochistic passion for André Fraigneau, (she wandered through Paris at night, shattered with pain, like an "exhausted beast") to the young tennis champion who beat her (she was seventy-seven at the time). Between the two, she lived for fifty years with a woman, her American partner, Grace Frick, in their house "Petite Plaisance" on the American coast of Maine. Grace served primarily as her assistant, an anchor in the maelstrom of travel and torment, a soothing presence that cosseted her creative genius.

Yourcenar was not afraid of following in the footsteps of great men. Her male characters—Alexis (published in French as *Le Traité du vain combat*, 1929), the Emperor Hadrian (in *The Memoirs of Hadrian*, 1951), Zeno Ligre—are all-powerful free spirits whose knowledge gives them a sense of superiority; then there are historical heroes such as Erasmus, the executed scholar Étienne Dolet, Leonardo da Vinci, Giordano Bruno, burned at the stake, Paracelsus, and Copernicus: all men who revolutionized the world, depicted in descriptions that seek to emulate these "immortals." Imaginary or real, it is these men who were her companions. Highly constructed, the works of Yourcenar, an authority on the Antique world, are like perfect jewels: they satisfy the mind, slake one's thirst for knowledge and reflection, but are entirely devoid of the warmth of the flesh, the warmth of the feminine—just like Zeno, philosophy, alchemist, physician, visionary scientific inventor, bleeding himself to death at the end of *The Abyss* (*L'Oeuvre au noir*; Prix Femina, 1968). Her works have now been issued in the prestigious La Pléiade collection. An avenue and a media library in Paris bear her name.

Marguerite Yourcenar, around 1981.

Marguerite Duras

1914–1996, France

Winner of the Prix Goncourt in 1984, French authoress and scriptwriter. If her life was punctuated by explicit violence, in her oeuvre it is understated or erotized. In the Cochinchina (southern Vietnam) of her childhood, her mother purchased a plot of non-arable land (flooded every year by the ocean), building a "barrage against the Pacific" (the French title of her first well-known book, *The Sea Wall*); it collapses and the whole harvest is ruined in a single night. Then came more extreme texts in which the feminine rules supreme, such as *The Ravishing of Lol. V. Stein* (1964), a story riddled with holes and omissions about Lol—"a figure for the wounded, exiled from things," as the great psychoanalyst Jacques Lacan put it. Writing serves to unveil what remains hidden, "from the deepest depths of my blind flesh, like a newborn baby on the first day," as the writer has declared.

Superb and impassioned, Duras could be unjust and felt driven to attack the male sex at every turn: "There's a GI in every guy. It's the phallic class." She always fought with those close to her: with Dionys Mascolo, "as beautiful as a god," and father of her child; she also developed, aged sixty-six, a savage, unhappy passion for the young homosexual Yan Andréa. Or else, as with Gérard Jarlot (*The Man Sitting in the Corridor*), she had a lover who beat her. But, for Duras, the great event was motherhood. In the women's review, *Sorcières*, in 1975, she related an extremely painful experience she had kept secret until then: a stillborn child in 1942.

In "la maison des femmes" (a center for women), where she made the movie *Nathalie Granger* with Jeanne Moreau, the brutality of childhood and the hidden lives of housewives resurface. For Duras, a woman should be a mother and that's that. Her body is a dwelling-place; in giving birth, she kills her child. Her own mother, meanwhile, used to beat her almost

Marguerite Duras in Saint-Germain-des-Prés, Paris, in 1955.

to death. Then, in the suffocating heat of Calcutta, a pregnant beggar, ravaged, swollen by misery, tries to sell her child, "into the same misfortune of existence" as *The Vice Consul* (1966), the creepy male virgin.

After these pot-boilers came the unbelievable success, when she was seventy years old, of *The Lover* (1984, two million copies sold), a wonderfully sparse book honored by the Prix Goncourt. After her engagement with communism, she supported Mitterrand's brand of socialism; after the women's struggle (she signed a proclamation with 343 other women that declared "I had an abortion"; at the time terminations were illegal), she embraced anti-feminism; after rejecting the world, she became a self-promoting superstar; after the love of life, she pursued self-destruction through alcohol.

Still, Duras revolutionized twentieth-century literature, evolving a completely innovative style, a "white" writing whose phrases are chopped about as if by the emotional violence they communicate to the reader. The storyline is blurred, the characters sketchy outlines. Only the flayed and flaying nerves remain; the suffering, the desire, mourning, and madness. Near to poetry, writing, for Duras, meant lending an ear to "the sound of the soul."

Doris Lessing

born 1919, Great Britain

Doris Lessing.

British writer and winner of the Nobel Prize for Literature in 2007. Lessing is the name of Doris May Tayler's second husband, though she is on record as saying that marriage is a state that does not agree with her. Gottfried Lessing and she have a son, with whom she came to live in London after the war, in 1949. She left her first two children with her former husband and expresses little regret as, in her opinion, they were better off with him. Her youth was spent in Southern Rhodesia (Zimbabwe) and Africa left an indelible mark on her. Her strong personality was further molded by a relatively tough start in life: after quitting school at a very young age, she worked as a governess and then as a telephonist.

Her first book, published in 1950, *The Grass Is Singing*, has as its backdrop a farm in Rhodesia and depicts the conflict between the white wife of the owner and her black servant. Is it autobiographical? Her ironic responses in the past to such questions are characteristic, and a feature of a writing style construed as if to ward off the pain of the world. Joining the Communist Party, she was to leave in 1959 after the invasion of Hungary by Soviet Bloc forces. Long committed to the anti-apartheid movement, she has ceased to support Robert Mugabe.

In 1976 the Prix Médicis (a prize for foreign fiction in France) was awarded to her for the famous *Golden Notebook* (it appeared in English in 1962). The novel—an investigation of the pleasure and despair of motherhood—is particularly admired by women readers. *The Children of Violence*, a five-volume saga (appearing between 1952 and 1969) retraces the life of a certain Martha Quest, her childhood, her *Proper Marriage*, and her ensuing life in postwar England. There then came a highly imaginative science-fiction universe with the *Canopus in Argos: Archives* series, published from 1981. In consecrating her oeuvre, the Swedish Academy saw itself as rewarding an "epicist of female experience, who, with skepticism, fire, and visionary power, has subjected a divided civilization to scrutiny."

Eileen Chang

1920–1995, China/United States

Chinese writer, one of the greatest in her country. She was born into a large if dysfunctional Shanghai family; her mother departed for England, leaving her five-year-old daughter (Zhang Ailing is her real Chinese name), while her father divided his time between his concubines and his opium pipe. The seeds for the disturbed and disturbing themes of her oeuvre were thus already sown and were compounded (after studies in England in 1938 and in Hong Kong) by the onset of war and a head-over-heels affair with the seductive Hu Lancheng, a collaborator. They were married in 1944, but he betrayed her and they divorced in 1947. Emigrating to Hong Kong in the 1950s, she worked at American Express, before moving to the United States. In 1956, she wed the writer and filmmaker Ferdinand Reyer, her senior by thirty years, who died the following year. The authoress with the sublime, imperturbable face ended her existence as a voluntary recluse. Her body was discovered in her Los Angeles apartment in 1995.

Her books include *Love in a Fallen City*, *Red Rose and White Rose*, *Eighteen Springs* (adapted for the screen by a woman, Ban Sheng Yuan), and the eloquently entitled *Traces of Love*. She was dubbed the "Chinese Jane Austen." She spent nearly twenty years writing *Lust, Caution*, comprised of four short stories: a tale of love, a dangerous game of torrid, tortured passion between a student and a collaborator during the occupation of China by Japan in the 1940s. A group of rebellious students plan an attack against the head of the secret police and adopt the "strategy of beauty"; the young Wong Chia Chi is given the responsibility of seducing him. Readers might expect a classic spy novel in which the heroine sacrifices herself for her homeland: with Eileen Chang they will be disappointed, as the story is sidelined and it is traditional morality that is put to the sword. For the tumult of war destroys families and undermines paternal authority, while the girls suffer the torments of untold desire. The narrative is all the more effective as it is conveyed in such an incisive and elegant style.

In 2008 Ang Lee adapted this masterpiece for the movies (having filmed *Sense and Sensibility* and Annie Proulx's *Brokeback Mountain*), obtaining a Golden Lion at the Venice Mostra in 2008. The erotic scenes in the film were cut by the Chinese censor. In the book, they are more suggestive than explicit and for that reason, perhaps, all the more intense. Ang Lee declared: "No writer has used the Chinese language with more cruelty than Eileen Chang."

But this language is awesomely resonant and rich. Even the title in translation, *Lust, Caution*, hardly does justice to *se jie*. *Se* connotes color, feminine charm and sexual desire (her translator explains in the foreword), whereas *jie* means abstinence, reserve, and prudence, but together the two terms imply a role on the stage, rings, and also to encircle or sound an alarm.

Nadine Gordimer

born 1923, South Africa

South African novelist and winner of the Nobel Prize for Literature in 1991. Her parents were supporters of apartheid, but she joined the fight in favor of the social aspirations of black people. Two of her novels, *A World of Strangers* and *The Late Bourgeois World* (1966), were banned by the censor for ten years. *The Conversationalist* won the British Booker Prize. She has explained her position in an essay, *South Africa Writing Today*, in 1967. In 1980, she was awarded the Central News Agency Prize, one of the chief literary honors in South Africa. When it comes to gender difference, she explains that she is just like Camus except that she does not play football, and that, when a girl, her only "genuine relation to the social life of the town was … through [her] femaleness." She leaves gender at the door to the study, however, because, "when it comes to their essential faculty as writers, all writers are androgynous beings."

In 2005 and over eighty, she brought out *Get a Life* that deals with ecology. Sensitive to environmental pollution on a worldwide scale, in particular to the dangers of nuclear power stations, she imagines a young militant afflicted by cancer caused by radiation that transforms him into a walking Chernobyl. Rejecting all Manichaeism, Gordimer carries with her the conflicts that lurk in every conscience. Evoking complex "states of life," she dreams that the immense and wild Okavango River, more enduring than humanity, will—if "left to itself"—regenerate forever.

Wislawa Szymborska

born 1923, Poland

Polish poetess and winner of the Nobel Prize for Literature in 1996 "for poetry that with ironic precision allows the historical and biological context to come to light in fragments of human reality." Her masterpiece, *Wszelki wypadek* (Could have), appeared in 1972, and established her literary reputation. In 1991, she won the Goethe Prize of the city of Frankfurt. She has been dubbed the "Mozart of poetry."

Janet Frame

1924–2004, New Zealand

New Zealand's greatest female writer. Prizewinner in 1980 for the Best New Zealand Novel; made Companion of the British Empire in 1983; awarded the New Zealand Book Award and the Sir James Wattie Prize. Interned for eight years in mental institutions, she underwent some two hundred sessions of electric-shock treatment. Why? Because she was not "malleable" enough, not deemed socially "acceptable." The staff asked her why she wouldn't conform and get a nice job, but she wanted to write, and write she did, and it was writing that saved her. Once her books were recognized, the press referred to the tragic, unbalanced power of her talent. Highly strung, introverted, afraid of everyone and every-

thing, as if skinned alive, she was like the *matagouri*, "a desert thorn-bush of ragged, stunted growth" that can suddenly burst into glory.

Toni Morrison

born 1931, United States

African-American novelist; the first African-American to hold a chair at Princeton; winner of the Pulitzer Prize in 1988 for the novel *Beloved* and the Nobel Prize for Literature in 1993. Born Chloé Anthony Wofford, her childhood during the Great Depression in the steel city of Lorain (Ohio) was tough. Her father was a building-site welder, while her mother was an activist, campaigning against evictions of African-American tenants unable to pay

Toni Morrison.

their rent. From 1949 to 1953 she studied at Howard University, an all African-American establishment, then earned a Master's in English at Cornell. On the staff of Texas and then at Howard (and today professor at Princeton), she married the Jamaican architect Harold Morrison, divorcing in 1964. She brought up her two sons alone, working as an editor at Random House, New York, advising Angela Davis on writing her memoirs.

Morrison combed the archives of African-American history to create a literary corpus in which black people address each other, being the driving force behind *The Black Book*, a history of the African-American people. Her first two novels (*The Bluest Eye* in 1969 and *Sula* in 1973) explore the difficulties faced by African-Americans in white society. *The Song of Solomon* in 1978 became a bestseller, but her unquestioned masterpiece is *Beloved*, the plot line for which she discovered in a news item of 1870: a fugitive slave-girl saws through her little daughter's throat to stop her falling into the hands of her white master. How can one live with most horrible of crimes—even one that was committed through love—forever lurking in the back of one's mind? At the beginning of the book, Sethe seems to have forgotten the event. Little by little, though, the memories branded into her flesh rise up like a wave: the marks of the whiplashes on her back in the shape of a tree; the way she was tortured by the son of the schoolmaster who would milk her like a cow; and "what courage it took to draw the teeth of that saw under that little chin." The lyrical handling, as rhythmical as a chain-gang chant, as broad as a spiritual, speaks volumes as to the ordeals and suffering undergone by African-Americans in their long emergence from slavery. The force of *Beloved* is that no reader comes out of it unscathed.

Françoise Sagan

1935–2004, France

Author of *Bonjour Tristesse* (1954), published when this atypical French writer was just nineteen years old. A huge *succès de scandale* (girls were advised against reading it; it was prohibited in Portugal), it sold like hot cakes (one million copies in the United States), and its authoress became a living symbol for the liberated young women of the 1950s. Its young heroine has the audacity to make love and to enjoy it—at a time when a Christian and patriarchal morality required that a girl be a virgin on her wedding day. Embarking on a host of liaisons and adventures with both men and women (Ava Gardner was one), wealthy and indolent, Sagan sped about in luxury sports cars, frittered away even more money than she earned, drank like a fish and took drugs with gusto. Though her name was rarely out of the headlines, the slick veneer concealed a consummate writer—even if the literary reference (the "Princesse de Sagan") to Proust raises a smile, since her books can be read in half an hour—and a committed woman who took up strong positions against the Algerian War and for freely available abortion.

Assia Djebar

born 1936, Algeria

The first Algerian woman writer to be elected to the Académie Française in 2005. Born Fatima-Zohra Imalayène, daughter of an Islamic teacher and a Berber mother, she studied at the French School, then at a Koranic school, learnt Greek, Latin, and English, dreamed of becoming a philosopher like Averroes, the "genius of Andalusia," and undertook research into female mysticism. In 1955, she became the first Algerian coed to enter the prestigious teacher-training school for women at Sèvres. When war ensued she was exiled with her husband to Tunis, where she worked as a journalist, then on to Rabat, where she taught modern history, finally returning to Algiers on Independence in 1962. But, from 1965 on she resided principally in France; between 1983 and 1989, she represented Algerian emigration at the Ministry of Social Affairs. During the war of Algerian liberation, she declared that women "carrying bombs" leave the harem only to shroud themselves beneath the veil: shortly after Independence, "the female body incarcerated from the age of ten between walls, at best under veils" is a "liberated eye," perceived by men as a threat because it is a "sign of the conquest of light."

In the French language she now adopted, but also in an adaptation of "popular Arabic, or feminine Arabic, that is to say of underground Arabic," she proclaims Algerian identity and its struggle to come to terms with the modern. In wonderful novels such as *Women of Algiers in Their Apartment* she records the "intoned, chanted, howled" words of those without a voice. Through her blood (as in her play, *Red the Dawn*) Djebar seeks, desperately but tirelessly, a *Happy Algeria* (poems). The pen name she chose has a dual aspect: Assia—consolation, she who gives solace by her presence; and Djebar—the intransigent, one of the ninety-nine names of the Prophet.

Assia Djebar the day she entered the Académie Française, June 22, 2006.

Elfriede Jelinek

born 1946, Austria

Austrian author, winner of the Nobel Prize for Literature in 2004. Highly subversive, she sees sexual (as well as parent/child) relationships in terms of class conflict: i.e. as relationships of domination. Thus are the laws of matrimony predicated on the laws of the market. When things go wrong, though, "there's always some wife or mother on whom one can take revenge, who can be told that her body increasingly resembles a hunk of rancid cheese." Virulent and obscene, she ironically dismembers every stereotype, denouncing the violence of pornography with a pornography of her own. Even the titles of her books make clear the ruinous drives at work in them: *Lust, Greed, Lovers*, with their attendant lesbians, whores, mothers, girls dreaming of prince charming, and women staff in a bra factory.

The Nobel jury justified their choice by stating that her "novels and plays ... with extraordinary linguistic zeal reveal the absurdity of society's clichés and their subjugating power." For her part, Jelinek wanted to make it clear that the prize was not to be viewed as a "flower in Austria's buttonhole." Ferociously opposed to the FPO (an extreme-right party), she deliberately drags Austria—with its Nazi background—through the mire.

Camille Claudel

1864–1943, France

French sculptress and symbol of the unfortunate woman artist. Gorgeous when young (she was twenty years old when Rodin took her on as a pupil and she went on to become his studio assistant), she was, though, possessed of "terrifying violence of character." She and Rodin had a passionate love affair; he adored her and never flagged in his belief in her creative strength: "Do something for this woman of genius (the word is not too strong) whom I love so much. For her art," he wrote to a critic.

Camille wanted it all, however, without help and immediately. She refused to share her love with Rodin's models or with Rose Beuret, his official concubine, with whom he had been living for almost twenty years. In her work, she attacked the marble straight off ("direct carving"), a very delicate enterprise that not even Rodin often risked. Camille even used onyx, a still more fragile material whose translucence gives her works their carnal radiance and delicacy.

Camille's desire for overnight fame was at first realized and her works were exhibited, lauded, and bought. In *The Waltz*—a masterpiece received with enthusiasm, a man and a woman quiver in passion to the point of collapse. Writer Octave Mirbeau praised the originality of these nervous, tormented works: "Here we have something unique, a revolt against nature: the woman of genius."

But Camille could not bear how, whenever people commented on her efforts, they almost always mentioned the name of Rodin in the same breath. Reclusive, aloof, she started suffering from persecution mania and, in a destructive rage, smashed many works to smithereens. Figuratively speaking it was this *Wave* (1897)—where three lovely bathers hold hands in a search for mutual comfort, tiny in comparison with the enormous wall of water about to toss them into the air—that drowned its creator. Betrayed by her family, her mother and brother interned her in the private hospital of Ville Evrad, before she was transferred to the psychiatric hospital in Mondevergues, a notorious death-trap in which she was to vegetate for some thirty years, in spite of her countless pleading letters: "The sufferings I'm undergoing here are terrible."

Camille died in total solitude: even her tomb disappeared. Her brother, the consul and much-celebrated poet and playwright, member of the Académie Française, Paul Claudel, concluded mercilessly: "All her superb gifts proved fruitless: after an extremely painful life, she ended up a total failure." And yet today she is world famous: major retrospectives of her oeuvre held at the Musée Rodin in 1951, 1984, and 2008 attracted visitors in droves, and her sculpture is displayed around the world.

Suzanne Valadon, Nude on a Red Couch, *1920.*

Suzanne Valadon

1865–1938, France

French painter and graphic artist, contributing member of the Salon d'Automne in 1920. Born out of wedlock, to a washerwoman and a builder's mate (she herself would become an unmarried mother, of Maurice, in 1883, who became the painter Utrillo), she started out as an acrobat, suffered a fall, and changed to modeling to earn a living, posing for the great painters of the time. She then took up drawing. In her paintings from 1908 on, Valadon concentrated on the female body; but, in *Neither White, Nor Black* (1907)—two colors that Valadon never in fact employed—she dared to paint naked men, as she did in her famous *Casting the Net* (1914): splendid, virile physiques, all grace and youthfulness, like that of her lover André Utter, a friend of her son's whom she married when forty-two. By 1932, Valadon was regarded as the foremost woman artist.

Sophia Hayden

1868–1953, United States

First American graduate of MIT (Massachusetts Institute of Technology), in architecture. Born in Chile to a South American mother, when six she was packed off to her paternal grandparents in Boston, by whom she was raised. She lost contact with her mother. Admitted to MIT in 1886, she proved a brilliant student. But men were far from keen on accepting a female colleague, and she found herself starved of work. Her career cut short, she built just one construction: in 1891, aged thirty-two, she was selected to build the Women's Building. After countless setbacks due to her sex, including being paid far less than a man, she managed to finish the project. Critics praised her artistic taste and the elegance of the hall, but she never obtained the professional recognition she craved. When she gave up architecture, the Press alleged she had fallen prey to her female emotions and had a nervous breakdown. In fact, Hayden paved the way for other women to take up architecture, and at the time of her death there were 308 women architects in the United States. By 1995, they numbered 10,000.

Emily Carr

1871–1945, Canada

Early twentieth-century Canadian painter, who became famous around 1930.

Captivated by the indigenous peoples of her native British Columbia, she painted the totem poles of the tribal villages along the Northwest coast and protested against the gradual extinction of those today termed First Nations, recognizing their right to their land. For a time close to Picasso, Matisse, and Signac, she forged a highly personal, spare, and rhythmical style in works crisscrossed by the massive tree-trunks of the endless Canadian forest. The curator of an exhibition devoted to her in 2007 described her as an angry woman, prey to a destructive fever that she channeled into action.

Paula Modersohn-Becker

1876–1907, Germany

Innovative German painter. After drawing lessons in London, studying painting at the Verein Berliner Künstler, and living in an artists' community near Bremen, in 1901 she settled in Paris where she discovered Gauguin. She inaugurated a new and deeply shocking genre for a woman: the nude self-portrait. In *Reclining Mother and Child*, Paula joins the two extremes of life and death. "Motherhood and death—these are the two great events on this earth." She herself died a few days after the birth of her daughter.

Although she sold few out of the 750 pictures she painted over fourteen years, and Nazi ideology had stigmatized her art as "degenerate," disposing of many of her paintings held in museums, Modersohn-Becker is a precursor of fauvism and expressionism. Her daughter set up the Paula Modersohn-Becker Foundation, and a museum bearing her name opened in the city of Bremen.

Gabriele Münter, The Fisherman's Cottage *(study), 1908.*

Gabriele Münter

1877–1962, Germany

German painter. She was one of the first artists to exhibit with the Blaue Reiter, an expressionist group led by Wassily Kandinsky, whose work has tended to overshadow that of a woman who was his companion for more than ten years. Even if she owed her artistic education to the Phalanx, another institution founded by Kandinsky (the official art academies in Düsseldorf and Munich did not admit women), her painting is completely original, imprinted with raw power, conveyed in clashing, unrestrained colors that arouse fierce emotions of joy tinged with deep angst. The Nazis, of course, lambasted her art as "degenerate."

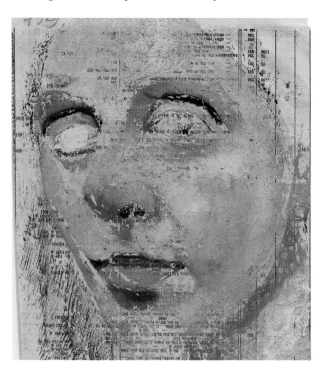

Paula Modersohn-Becker, Self-portrait *(detail), 1906.*

Georgia O'Keeffe

1887–1986, United States

One of the greatest American female painters of the century, she was responsible for the significant "realist" current in the United States during the interwar period. Studying in Virginia and New York, she became a teacher in Virginia and Texas.

Never satisfied with her art, when aged twenty-eight she destroyed all her work, deciding to "strip away what I had been taught—to accept as true my own thinking." This radical stance proved fruitful and her new pieces became sparser, more abstract, more musical. Her flowers are not ornamental as tradition has it for women artists, but vast corollas, petals the color of aching flesh, great swathes of black irises, and flaming blooms: O'Keeffe's paintings are meant to be "alive," betraying "desire to reveal the unknown." Her paintings can depict the first New York skyscrapers, Lake George landscapes, or the New Mexico desert, where she lived following the death of her husband, art dealer and photographer Alfred Stieglitz. Thus, in *New York with Moon* (1925), a building shoots through the night with a lamppost brighter than the moon, creating a vaguely surrealist image in the manner of Magritte. In *Black Cross, New Mexico*, meanwhile, the two planks plastered over the foreground have nothing religious about them; the background shows a landscape of mauve hills, feminine curves emblazoned by the rising sun. As in an enlarged, cropped photograph, the forms lose their naturalism, verge on the abstract. Caressing, erotic, other works are sensual evocations of female genitalia. She has received countless awards and her work has been the subject of numerous exhibitions. In 1997, an institution devoted to her opened in Santa Fe (the Georgia O'Keeffe Museum).

Tamara de Lempicka

1898–1980, Poland

French painter who emigrated from Poland in 1918. Born Maria Gorska, she was a diva of Paris high society between the wars. A liberated flapper, a tomboy, the harsh colors and clipped forms of *Self-portrait in a Green Bugatti* (below) show her at the wheel of a superb roadster flaunting bold lipstick, a silk scarf, and chic, sporty driving gloves. *The Portrait of the Duchesse de la Salle* (1925) shows the subject dressed as a man. The bellies of the *Two Friends* (1923) swell into mounds, ripple with muscular power; the handling is "neo-cubist," while the background is all futurist urban architecture. Close to the painter Romaine

Brooks, Lempicka and her scandals never went unnoticed.

Germaine Richier

1904–1959, France

French sculptress, winner of the art prize at the São Paulo Biennial in 1952. After studying at art school in Montpellier, she moved to Paris, where she worked with Antoine Bourdelle. The emaciated Christ, elongated to the point that his hands and feet have all but vanished, she carved for the chapel of Notre-Dame-de-Toutes-Grâces, was withdrawn by the religious authorities: a "carved stub," it was a travesty of "true art." In fact, the pathetic Christ d'Assy is a figure whose suffering and power are moving. Richier's works often combine strength and humanity: *The Man who Walks*, and the *Ouragane*, a thickset "hurricane woman" with strong, generous hips. The artist often added elements borrowed from the animal kingdom to her sculpture.

Frida Kahlo

1907–1954, Mexico

Mexican painter and veritable icon of Latin American art. A victim of polio when just seven, at eighteen she suffered a horrific accident in which an iron strut pierced her abdomen and emerged through her vagina; her right foot was crushed, her spinal column and pelvis broken. After months in hospital pinned to her bed, after countless operations and plaster corsets, it seems incredible that Kahlo ever gained the strength to paint 150 paintings and to enjoy a love-life worthy of the name. She even drew energy from her handicap, painting lying down, using a tester over her bed fixed with a mirror for painting self-portraits, as if in an attempt to repair her shattered image, to rebuild herself through art.

Frida Kahlo.

In 1929 in Mexico, she wed the famous Mexican painter, Diego Rivera, then divorced him, only to remarry him in San Francisco in 1940. Diego frequently betrayed her—including with her own sister; she too had lovers, Leon Trotsky being one, though there were women too. The surrealist André Breton was bewitched by her: "Frida is a bomb tied up with ribbon." Exploring the unconscious, offering it up to our gaze, in *My Nurse and Me*, she depicts a little girl with her own (adult) head suckling at a breast whose milky, flowering ducts belong to a towering black nurse, the mother goddess. "She paints at the same time the outside, the inside, and her depths and those of the world," as Diego succinctly observed. Her shows in Mexico, New York, and Paris met with great success. Her social life was intense and, joining the Mexican Communist Party (PCM) in 1928, in 1942 she was elected as member of the Seminario de Cultura Mexicana, whose mission is to encourage and promote cultural life in the country. She still had operations to undergo, however, seven in all, ending with her leg being amputated to the knee. *The Broken Column* testifies to her agony. In spite of everything, on her last picture she writes: "*Viva la Vida!*" Her funeral ceremony was presided over by the president of the Republic in person. Long eclipsed by Rivera, Kahlo is now a worldwide star. In June 2007, while several museums celebrated her centenary, a major retrospective was devoted to her work at the Palacio de Bellas Artes in Mexico City.

Leonor Fini

1908–1996, Italy/France

Italian painter. She specialized in witches, sphinxes, chimeras, hybrid beings, crosses between human and animal, plant and mineral. Riding roughshod over outworn definitions of sexual roles, in a 1947 painting she depicts a beautiful youth, his genitals half hidden and half revealed by a strip of pinkish silk, watched over by an infernal divinity, a magical, all-powerful, sexualized sphinx-woman.

In 1966, in *Sleeping Phoebus*, another wan and feminine youth displays himself in an innocent yet provocative pose to the contemplation of an unimpressed female. In her work, the feminine is imperious and electric, the men ambivalent and disconcerting. Leonor also created pearl- and feather-encrusted masks, as well as stage sets and costumes for the Paris Opera and La Scala, Milan, perfume bottles for Schiaparelli, wallpaper, and textiles.

Margaret Mee

1909–1988, Great Britain

British painter and botanist, the first woman to cross the Amazonian forest. This art-school graduate (she attended Saint Martins School of Art, in London), dressed in ironed blouse and wearing a hat with a veil, but waving a revolver, took part in fifteen expeditions through the depths of the Brazilian rainforest. One day she was abandoned and left for dead; the next, having escaped drowning, she pushed on, studying the sweet-smelling orchids and aggressive bromeliads that gave her a foretaste of paradise.

Her works combine the clarity and rigor of a scientist with the charm and refinement of an artist. It took her years to seek out the moonflower that blooms for just one night: on finding this extremely rare cactus, she spent the entire night in a dugout canoe to paint it. This was when she was seventy-nine years old, a few months before her death.

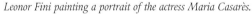

Leonor Fini painting a portrait of the actress Maria Casarès.

Louise Bourgeois

1911–2010, France/United States

American artist of French extraction. The first woman to be honored by a retrospective at MoMA (the Museum of Modern Art), New York. Winner of the Golden Lion at the Venice Biennial in 1999. Her original and multifarious oeuvre deploys bronze, metal, wood, fabric, plaster, and latex in sculptures, paintings, drawings, engravings, and installations. Her parents wanted her to leave the Lycée Fénélon and become a tapestry restorer, like them. Instead she studied painting with Fernand Léger and pondered her revenge: her enormous bronze *Spiders* evoke the maternal bond, a repulsive and aggressive if protective weaver. But the feeling is ambivalent, the arthropod monster being entitled *Maman* (Mummy). Her father was a tyrant who looked down on women ("I was supposed to beg forgiveness for only being a girl"). Hence *Destruction of the Father*, her first installation in 1974, a cave with remnants of a bloodthirsty feast, leftovers of a cannibalistic family meal at which the menu clearly included daddy.

Moving on, she settled definitively in the United States in 1938, with her husband, American art historian Robert Goldwater, who was also to be put in a cage—into *Cells*, "house-women," fitted with wire netting, domestic spaces clogged with clothing and

Louise Bourgeois, Nature Study, *1984–1994.*

dubious stains. The memory of the "primitive scene"—the horror of our parents' sex life that gave us life—still rankles, coming over particularly strong in the troubling *Red Room (Child)* and *Red Room (Parents),* awash with blood.

Struggle, ebb and flow, the oscillation between masculine and feminine are constants in the output of a radically innovative, strong yet angst-ridden mother of three boys. The artist expresses this sexual ambiguity in *Fragile Goddess* (1970), in which it is hard to tell penis from breast, testicles from a swelling belly. Freud assures us that women suffer cruelly from penis envy and spend their life wracked with desire. In a photograph by Robert Mapplethorpe (a companion of singer and photographer Patti Smith), however, beaming broadly, Louise Bourgeois holds a latex penis under her arm: this sculpture made in 1968 (the date of her engagement in the feminist movement) is entitled *Fillette* (Little Girl).

Louise Bourgeois, Mummy, *1999.*

beasts, somewhere between a horse and a rhinoceros, live in a pastoral idyll occasionally troubled by fear and sadness. From 1954, the Moomins appeared in comic strips for the English readers of London's *Evening News*. Tove published eight novels and four picture books. Her original illustrations for the Moomins are on show at the Tampere Art Museum.

Machiko Hasegawa

1920–1992, Japan

First woman to draw Japanese manga. Her serial Sazae-san tells of the adventures of a close-knit family, traditional except for the fact that the couple lives with their children in the house of the wife's—and not the husband's—parents. Apart from that, all is as it should be; at mealtimes, husband and father-in-law sit in the place of honor, the woman and her mother at the end of table, and the children between them. A typical, happy family of the postwar era. The manga appeared from 1946 to 1974—that is 6,477 times over twenty-eight years. A phenomenal success. Though Hazegawa laid down her pen in 1974, the serial now appears as an anime on TV, where it has lost none of its charm.

A "Moomin" (by Tove Jansson) surrounded by children.

Tove Jansson

1914–2001, Finland

Finnish writer, painter, and illustrator. Born into an artistic family, she spent her holidays on the islands of Porvoo, blissfully happy by the seaside where life was healthy and natural. After studying art in Stockholm and Helsinki, she went to Paris, devoting herself to painting and drawing for newspapers. In 1945, she created a group of characters that were to survive until 1970: the Moomins. Drawn freehand in a clear, lively line, these oversized but amiable

Niki de Saint-Phalle amidst some of her famous Nanas.

Niki de Saint-Phalle

born 1930, United States/France

Groundbreaking Franco-American sculptress. For Marie-Agnès (as she was born), raped by her father when eleven, art proved to be the only way out of her depression and mental distress. Marrying a poet, Harry Mathews, they had a daughter (1951) and a son (1955). These she left, however, to travel to Paris and devote herself to her art. From 1965 to 1970, she created the "*Nanas*" (Chicks), super-females bursting with joy and vitality, with more than generous forms, who cock a snook at the invariably skinny female images peddled in magazines. Saint-Phalle denounces female alienation—for example in *Crucifixion*, a sculpture showing a housewife in curlers, displaying her pubic hair, framed by an enormous garter belt and nailed on a cross: sacrificial hausfrau and sex object

in one. But in general, the Chicks, painted in playful, explosive colors with opulent buttocks and breasts, appear in jubilant spirits. Eschewing right-angles (because "nature is all undulation"), she brings the maternal to the fore.

Saint-Phalle is well aware that she is recreating the body of a mother who abandoned her when she was only three months old and is thus (re)inventing herself: "To live inside a sculpture was my dream, my need. A feminine sculpture that can invent a new mother, a mother goddess, a Supreme Mother, so as to be reborn within it, into a form without limits." She thus came up with *Hon* ("She"), a monumental sculpture of an enormous recumbent woman, the 100,000 visitors to the exhibition in Stockholm in 1966 entering it through the vaginal orifice. An inverted birth, a return to the "refuge for dreaming": "it's a cathedral, a factory, a whale, Noah's Ark, *Maman*. The biggest whore in the world."

Judy Chicago

born 1939, United States

Born Judy Cohen, American feminist and ceramist. A graduate of the University of Los Angeles and lecturer in visual art, her accomplice is the painter Miriam Schapiro, made famous by her *"femmages,"* collages made of lace, buttons, laces, and fabric oddments. In 1970, they set up the California Institute of Arts in Valencia that collects and distributes information concerning the history of women in art to publicize feminine creativity, too often sidelined. In 1972, assisted by their students, the two women renovated and decorated a kind of museum of female sculpture that challenges the traditional roles of masculine and feminine over and over again: *The Womanhouse.*

Initially in San Francisco, Chicago exhibited a monumental piece, *The Dinner Party* (1974–79): thirty-nine ceramic plates placed on an immense triangular table bearing 999 women's names inscribed on tiles. The work was designed to pay tribute to significant women in history, in fields such as politics, art, and religion, whether real (Queen Elizabeth I, the medieval writer Christine de Pisan, and birth control militant Margaret Sanger) or legendary (such as the goddess Astarte). The sacred is never far away, however, with the table evoking the Last Supper and the glasses reminiscent of chalices. Laid on embroidery or tapestry, these plate-sculptures symbolize their heroines. Thus, in an effect that raised some eyebrows, Virginia Woolf is represented by a diamond-shape evocative of a butterfly or vulva. The celebrated lesbian Nathalie Barney, partner of Romaine Brooks, is entitled to a star in relief with a crescent cut out of the middle (enamel on porcelain). Chicago has been reproached for signing the piece with her name alone, whereas—even if the idea and the designs are indeed hers—the realization of this collective piece required the cooperation of a team of

400 over five years. The same is true of *Birth*, a collection of embroidered pieces symbolizing childbirth, a theme rarely explored at that time. But isn't embroidery, a repetitive occupation traditionally undertaken solely by women, the very symbol of their incarceration in a noncreative role? The French psychoanalyst Luce Irigaray wrote: "If women stopped doing tapestry, the order would unravel." Judy Chicago, however, uses these "woman's" techniques to valorize feminine knowledge and subvert their codes. In France, other woman artists were employing materials such as textiles and fabrics creatively, exploiting their textures. Alma created garments she called "flexible sculpture"; Aline Gagnaire painted bolts of furnishing fabric with a *Horsewoman Dreaming of the Moon;* Elizabeth Baillon embroidered "woolen images," gaping knits that expose the innards of the body.

Annette Messager

born 1943, France

French visual artist, winner of the Golden Lion at the Venice Biennial in 2005. Positively received since 1960, her art uses (and abuses) all kinds of materials—oils, charcoal, watercolor on photographs, fabric sculpture, writing, drawing—and objects: stuffed birds wearing the sadistically tight cardies she knits for them; teddy bears and various cuddly animals piled up in heaps or eviscerated, mute witnesses to a dysfunctional, ambiguous childhood.

In 1974 she started exhibiting embroidery that ironically quotes the most misogynistic proverbs. In 2002, her *Ballad of the Hanged* shows a cortege of automata, of body parts that jump about, groaning in agonized tumult. Her terrifying *Casino*, awash with blood from a birth that floods over poor Pinocchio, was awarded a Golden Lion. Her *Gonflés-Dégonflés* (2006) inflate (and deflate) bodies made of parachute silk in slow erections, in titillating embrocations. The great 2007 retrospective at the Pompidou Center showed her mix of art brut influences and surrealist happenstance, with spectacular installations and dazzling phantasmagoria.

Orlan

born 1947, France

French artist whose provocative performances are prime examples of body art. In the 1960s, she was already gender-bending, claiming: "I am a man and a woman." She posed naked in photos with the title "Orlan gives birth to her herself." "I think the hardest thing to swallow is that I, a woman, am trying to get out of the straitjacket, away from the place the dominant ideology designates as being mine." The Foire Internationale d'Art Contemporain (FIAC) in 1977 saw the performance of *The Artist's Kiss*: she stood, hidden behind a full-size nude photograph of herself, selling kisses and candles at five francs a go. The coin, inserted into the neck, descends down to the gaping sex in what was a direct political attack: in particular the female body, supposed to conform to a narrow band of vital statistics, is *not* for sale. This scandalous work was front-page news that resulted in her dismissal from teaching.

Orlan ironically embraces the canons, by transforming her face with computer and scalpel or by showing close-ups of plastic surgery in her film *Omniprésence*.

Xiao Lu

born 1962, China

The most sought-after Chinese artist on the market today, who has torn up the traditional Chinese canon. Her father, mother, and sister are also artists, who express themselves through different genres in a personal style. An exhibition, initiated with cooperation from the Foundation of the Hassan Museum, Arte Communications, and the Italian Arts Centre, has been devoted to this original family, which has straddled the Chinese art scene for more than sixty years. In 2000, a sister, Xiao Ge (born Shanghai, 1971) showed a Chinese dress printed with copies of visas and French passports at the Paris Cité Internationale des Arts and the Salon de Printemps. Her installations present dressed men and women moving through a space encumbered by asymmetric bars. Xiao Ge's works show a playful world in which sexuality and identity fuse unashamedly. The elder, Xiao Lu, focuses research on installation art and human behavior. In 1988, the review *Meishu* (the Art School) published a photograph of the installation entitled *Dui Hua* (Dialog) on the rear cover. Two phone boxes are occupied by a young man and a girl, but the call seems to have been cut off. On February 5, 1989, two hours after the opening of an exhibition of Chinese avant-garde art featuring some 186 artists at the Museum of the Art Schools of China, Xiao Lu fired two shots into *Dialog*, at a mirror placed between the two telephones. Police flocked to the museum and the show was closed for four days, but the impact across the world was immense. Major news services (Associated Press, Agence France Presse, United Press International) all immediately reported on the event. *The New York Times*, *Time Magazine*, many European newspapers and of course the Chinese press commented on the act, concluding that the "gunshot incident" was one of the most creative, politically relevant, and subversive actions of recent decades.

Dorothea Lange

1895–1965, United States

American photographer. Born Margarette Nutzhorn, Lange (the name of her mother) learnt photography with Clarence H. White from New York, opening a portrait studio in 1918 in San Francisco.

When the Great Depression hit the nation she began taking emotionally charged photographs of the unemployed and the homeless. The Farm Security Administration commissioned her to work with immigrants and soon her photographs were being hailed as icons of the 1930s. Her famous *Migrant Mother*, a woman's face furrowed by poverty, appeared in 1936 in the magazine Life and sent shockwaves through public opinion. Dorothea's new husband (she had had two sons with the first, a painter), the economist Paul Schuster Taylor, professor at the University of California, specialized in social and political questions. Together, each in their own way, the couple dealt with rural poverty, composing *An American Exodus: A Record of Human Erosion*, published in 1939. In 1952, Lange launched the magazine *Aperture*. Some of her finest prints are held by the Museum of Modern Art, New York.

Lee Miller

1907–1977, United States

American photographer. In 1930 in Paris, she became
the muse-cum-collaborator of the famous surrealist
Man Ray. The inventor of solarization, a printing
technique that incorporates much of the pungency of
the negative, she was fashionable and attractive,
appearing in the company of Picasso, Dalí, Éluard,
Cocteau, a dazzling beauty and leading fashion
model for *Vogue*. In 1945, she became a war corre-
spondent for the fashion magazine. Crisscrossing the
ruins of immediate postwar Europe, she even took
photos of the mass graves and the skeletal bodies
gazing out vacantly in Dachau, entitling her devastating report: "Believe It."

Lee Miller.

Gisèle Freund

1908–2000, Germany/France

German-Jewish press photographer, naturalized
French: pioneer of the color portrait. In 1933, as a
student in sociology at the Frankfurt School, she
began resistance to Nazism, Xeroxing a clandestine
newspaper critical of the new regime. She just had
time to escape, "hiding about my person photographs
I'd taken of comrades beaten almost to death." Two of
her photographs appeared in the *Brown Book*, the first
anthology to denounce the terrors of the Third Reich.
Already photography was bearing witness, and
throughout her life Freund was to work as an
international reporter, her credo being that, to
become a decent photojournalist, "one has to love
human beings."

Her humanity pours out in photographs taken in
the north of England (*Distressed Areas*) or in Mexico of
peasants staggering under their burden. She had left

for Mexico intending to stay for a fortnight: she
remained two years in the company of the painters
Diego Rivera and Frida Kahlo. Fleeing anti-Semitic
persecution, in Argentina she was taken in by Victoria
Ocampo before being dispatched to Tierra del Fuego
by *Life* magazine. She was the first—and for a long
time only—woman on the books of the Magnum
agency founded by Robert Capa in 1947.

In 1938, she dared to try her hand at "the magic of
color," taking photographs of Colette, a portrait
published in *Arts et Métiers graphiques*, and for *Time*.
Her portraits, unretouched, went round the world:
Virginia Woolf, Gide, Marguerite Yourcenar, Simone
de Beauvoir, Sartre, Ionesco, Henri Michaux, André
Breton, André Malraux, and, in 1981, the official
photograph of French President François Mitterrand.
Paris-Match, *Art et décoration*, and *Images du monde*
fought for her photos. At the beginning of her career,
she had deplored how photographs were hung in rows
"like frankfurters." In 1965, however, she was the first
photographer to exhibit at the Musée d'Art Moderne
in Paris, also showing at the Centre Pompidou in 1991.
She was instrumental in elevating the status of
photography, turning it into an art in its own right.

Gerda Taro

1910–1937, Poland/France

Polish-Jewish photographer, who died in pursuit of her art. Possessing the "smile of eternal youth," she fled Nazi Germany (accused of belonging to the Communist Party), and called herself Gerta Pohorylle. The good-looking André Friedmann also had to flee Germany: down on their uppers, they frequented artistic and intellectual circles in Montparnasse, embarking on a passionate love affair.

Adopting the *noms de guerre* of Robert Capa and Gerda Taro (echoing Hollywood stars Frank Capra and Greta Garbo), they begun by sending illustrated reports, him with a Leica, she with a Rolleiflex, often signing their dispatches Capa & Taro. For both lovers, photography was a testimony, an engagement, and their cameras were (defensive) weapons. As Gerda edged ever closer to the Spanish front, she was mown down, aged only twenty-seven, crushed by a pro-Franco tank. Brought back to Paris, her young body was given "an extraordinary funeral at which flowers from all over the world congregated." Why then is only Capa's name known to posterity? In 2008, the International Center of Photography, New York, exhibited eighty prints by Gerda, many of which were formerly ascribed to Capa.

Diane Arbus

1923–1971, United States

Born Nemerov, a celebrated American photographer. When eighteen, she married Allan Arbus and they worked as fashion photographers for *Vogue*, *Glamour* and *Harper's Bazaar*, as well as in advertising. Divorcing, she decided to study photography with Lisette Model. Two Guggenheim grants enabled her to develop her original vein. She frequented circuses, encountering people on the margins of society, "deviant" beings, physical or social outcasts: transvestites, dwarves, contortionists, nudists, tattooed men, cripples. Though disturbing—or perhaps because of this—her photographs proved hugely popular. Her first reportage was snapped up in 1959 by *Esquire* magazine, which was preparing a special edition on Manhattan. She also sold to *Newsweek*, while in 1964 she showed at MoMA and at the Musée d'Art Moderne in Paris in 1967. Her singular idiom was rewarded by the Robert Levitt Award given by the American Society of Magazine Photographers in 1970. Committing suicide in 1971, the following year her work was shown at the Venice Biennial; the Musée d'Art Moderne has also dedicated a retrospective to her.

Diane Arbus at the Metropolitan Museum of Art, New York, 1969.

Index

The page featuring the main entry is marked in **bold**.

Bibliography

Adler, Laure, *Les Femmes politiques*, Paris: Seuil, 1993

Adler, Laure, *Marguerite Duras,* Paris: Fayard, 1998

Alessandrini, Marjorie, *Le Rock au féminin*, Paris: Albin-Michel, 1980

Amirpur Katajun, *L'Iran des réformes* (with Shirin Ebadi, Nobel Prize for Peace), Paris: Alvik, 2004 (*Gott ist mit den Furchtlosen*, Freiburg im Breisgau: Herder Verlag, 2003)

Antrobus, Peggy, *Le mouvement mondial des femmes*, Paris: éditions de l'Atelier, 2007

Antrobus, Peggy, The Global Women's Movement: Issues and Strategies for the New Century, London: Zed Books, 2004

Armand, Pierre and Thierry Terret, *Histoire du sport féminin*, Paris: L'Harmattan, 1996

Bair, Deirdre, *Simone de Beauvoir*, Paris: Fayard, 1990

Bair, Deirdre, *Simone de Beauvoir. A Biography,* New York: Touchstone, 2002

Baez, Joan, *Et une voix pour chanter, Paris:* Presses de la Renaissance, 1988

Baez, Joan, *And a Voice to Sing with*, New York: Simon & Schuster, 1987

Bard, Christine, *Les femmes dans la société française du 20ᵉ siècle*, Paris: Armand Colin, 2001

Barret-Ducroq, Françoise and Evelyne Pisier, *Femmes en tête, Femmes de tête*, Paris: Flammarion, 1997

Bascou-Bance, Paulette, *La Mémoire des femmes*, Paris: Elytis édition, 2002

Bécard, Carine, *Elles ont réussi!* Paris: Alvik, 2007

Bernhardt, Sarah, *Ma double vie*, Paris: Phoebus, 2000 (1907)

Bernhardt, Sarah, *My Double Life,* London: Suny Books, 2001

Bertin, Célia, *Louise Weiss*, Paris: Albin-Michel, 1999

Bhutto, Benazir, *Daugther of the East*, London: Hamish Hamilton, 1988

Billouin, Alain, Henri Charpentier, and Serge Laget, *Les Déesses du sport*, Paris: La Martinière, 2007

Bitoun, Carole, *La Révolte au féminin. Portraits de femmes exemplaires*, Paris: Ed. Hugo doc. 2007

Bonnet, Marie-Jo, *Les femmes dans l'art*, Paris: La Martinière, 2004

Bosio-Valici, Sabine, and Michelle Zancarini-Fournel, *Femmes et fières de l'être, un siècle d'émancipation féminine,* Paris: Larousse (collection 20/21), 2001

Bosworth, Patricia, *Diane Arbus, une biographie*, Paris: Seuil, 2007

Bosworth, Patricia, *Diane Arbus. A Biography,* New York: W. W. Norton & Co., 2001

Burgos, Elisabeth, *Moi, Rigoberta Menchù. Une vie et une voix, la révolution au Guatemala*, Paris: Gallimard, 1983

Burgos, Elisabeth, *I, Rigoberta Menchù. An Indian Woman in Guatamala,* London: Verso, 2010

Buet, Jackie (ed.): *Films de femmes. Six générations de réalisatrices*, Paris: Editions Alternatives, 1995

Burrus, Christina, *Frida Kahlo*, Paris: Gallimard (Découvertes), 2007

Burrus, Christina, *Frida Kahlo. Painting Her Own Reality,* New York: Abrams, 2008

Cadalin, Sophie, *Les Femmes de pouvoir. Des hommes comme les autres?* Paris: Seuil, 2008

Carbonnier, Annelise, Jean-Michel Lecat and Michel Toulet, *La longue marche des femmes,* Paris: Phébus, 2008

Chabaud Catherine, and Jean-Luc Garnier, *Femme libre, toujours tu chériras la mer*, Chasse-Marée, 2007

Chalon, Jean, *Le lumineux destin d'Alexandra David-Neel*, Perrin, 1985

Middleton, Ruth, *Alexandra David-Neel. Portrait of an Adventurer,* London: Shambala Books, 1998

Chantassier, Philippe de, *Les femmes dans l'Histoire de France*, De Vecchi S.A., 2005

Chavot, Pierre, *Ces femmes qui ont fait la France*, Paris: Marabout, 2006

Chazal, Gérard, *Les femmes et la science*, Paris: Ellipses, 2006

Child, Greg, *Climbing: the complete reference to Rock, Ice and Indoor Climbing*, New York: Facts on File, 1995.

Christie, Agatha, *Une autobiographie*, Agatha Christie Limited, 1977, éditions du Masque, 2006

Christie, Agatha, *An Autobiography,* New York: Dodd Mead & Co., 1977

Collin, Françoise (ed.), *Le sexe des sciences*, Paris: Autrement, 1992

Collomb-Boureau Colette and Claudette Fillard, *Les mouvements féministes américains*, Paris: Ellipses, 2003

Colombani Marie-France and Michèle Fitoussi, *ELLE. 1945/2005. Une histoire des femmes*, Costa Mesa Cal.: Filipacchi, 2005

Crémieu, Aurisse and Hélène Jullien, *Femmes libres. La résistance de 14 femmes dans le monde* (with Amnesty International), Paris: Le Cherche-Midi, 2005

Dall'Ava-Santucci, Josette, *Des Sorcières aux mandarines. Histoire des femmes médecins*, Paris: Calmann-Levy, 1989

Davis, Angela, *Autobiographie*, Paris: Albin-Michel, 1975

Davis, Angela, *An Autobiography,* New York: Random House, 1974

Davis, Angela, *Femmes, race et classe*, Paris: Des Femmes-Antoinette Fouque, 2007

Davis, Angela, *Women, Race and Class*, New York: Random House, 1982

Déon-Bessière, Danielle, *Premières...des pionnières?* Paris: Editions de l'Officine, 2006

De Stefano, Cristina, *Aventurières américaines*, Paris: Anatolia édition, 2008

Diamond Rosinsky, Thérèse, *Suzanne Valadon*, Paris: Flammarion, 2005

Diamond Rosinsky, Thérèse, *Suzanne Valadon*, New York: Universe Books, 1994

Dister, Alain, *L'âge du rock*, Paris: Gallimard (Découvertes), 1992

Dolto, Françoise, *Père et fille. Une correspondance,* Paris: Mercure de France, 2001

Ducrey, Guy, *L'adcdaire de Colette*, Paris: Flammarion, 2000

Duncan, Isadora, *La Danse de l'avenir* (texts selected and translated by Sonia Schoonejans), Paris: éditions Complexe, 2003

Duncan, Isadora, *My Life*, New York: Boni and Liveright, 1927

Ebadi, Shirin, *Iranienne et libre. Mon combat pour la justice*, Paris: La Découverte, 2006

Eisen Bergman, Arlene, *Femmes du Vietnam*, Paris: Des Femmes, 1975

Falise, Thierry (preface by Jane Birkin), *Aung San Suu Kyi. Le jasmin et la lune*, Florent Massot, 2007

Aung San Suu Kyi, *The Voice of Hope*, New York: Seven Stories Press, 2008

Febvre, Roselyne, *Le cœur des femmes. Les 50 femmes du XXe siècle*, Boulogne-Billancourt: Timée-Editions, 2004

Ferlder, Deborah G., *The 100 most Influential Women of all Time*, New York: Citadel Press, 1996

Ferrand, Michelle, *Féminin, masculin*, Paris: La Découverte, 2004

Fitoussi, Muriel, *Femmes au pouvoir, femmes de pouvoir*, Paris: Hugo doc, 2007

Freund, Gisèle, *Mémoires de l'oeil*, Paris: Seuil, 1977

Freund, Gisèle, *Gisèle Freund, Photographer*, New York: Abrams, 1898

Garrigue, Anne, *Japonaises, la révolution douce*, Arles: Philippe Piquier, 1998

Gaspard, Françoise, Claude Servan-Schreiber and Anne Le Gall, *Au pouvoir, citoyennes! Liberté, égalité, parité*, Paris: Seuil, 1992

Gattegno, Hervé, and Anne-Cécile Sarfati, *Femmes au pouvoir, Récits et confidences*, Paris: Stock, 2007

Gauthier, Xavière, *Leonor Fini*, Paris: Le Musée de Poche, 1973

Gauthier, Xavière, *Les Parleuses* (with Marguerite Duras) Paris: Minuit, 1974

Giroud, Françoise, *Marie Curie. Une femme honorable*, LGF, 1981

Giroud, Françoise, *Marie Curie. A Life,* Teaneck NJ: Holmes & Meier, 1987

Golemba, Beverly, *Lesser-known Women*, London: Lynne Rienner Publishers, 1992

Gonnard, Catherine and Elizabeth Lebovici, *Femmes artistes, artistes femmes. Paris, de 1880 à nos jours*, Paris: Hazan, 2007

Graham, Martha, *Blood Memory,* New York: Doubleday, 1991

Guéraiche, William, *Les Femmes et la République* (preface by Françoise Gaspard), Ivry-sur-Seine: L'Atelier, 1999

Haechler, Jean, *Les Insoumises. 18 portraits de femmes exceptionnelles*, Nouveau monde éditions, 2007

Haedrich, Marcel, *Coco Chanel, secrète*, Paris: Robert Laffont, 1971

Haedrich, Marcel, *Coco Chanel. Her Life*, London: Robert Hale, 1972

Heller, Nancy. G, *Femmes artistes*, Paris: Herscher, 1991

Heller, Nancy. G, *Women Artists. An Illustrated History,* New York: Abbeville Press, 1987

Héritier, Françoise (ed.), *Hommes, femmes, la construction de la différence*, Paris: éditions Le Pommier/Cité des Sciences et de l'Industrie, 2005

Hirsi, Ali Ayaan, *Insoumise*, Paris: Robert Laffont, 2005

Jackson, Buzzy, *A Bad Woman Feeling Good, Blues and the Women Who Sing Them*, New York/London: W. W. Norton & Co., 2005

Joly, Eva, *La force qui nous manque. Petit traité d'énergie et d'orgueil féminin*, Paris: Les Arènes, 2007

Kermer, Charlotte and Nicole Casanova, *Des femmes prix Nobel, de Marie Curie à Aung San Suu Kyi* (preface by Gidske Anderson, Member of the Committee for the Nobel Peace prize), Paris: Des femmes-Antoinette Fouque, 1992

Kristeva, Julia, *Le génie féminin. La vie, la folie, les mots*, Paris: Fayard (vol. 1, *Hannah Arendt,* 1999; vol. 2, *Mélanie Klein,* 2000; vol. 3, *Colette,* 2002)

Kristeva, Julia, *Hannah Arendt* (trans. R. Guberman), New York: Columbia University Press, 2003

Kristeva, Julia, *Melanie Klein* (trans. R. Guberman), New York: Columbia University Press, 2004

Kristeva, Julia, *Colette* (trans. J. M. Todd), New York: Columbia University Press, 2005

Lagier, Rosine, *Il y a un siècle...la femme*, Ed. Ouest-France, 2000

Lapierre, Alexandra and Christel Mouchard, *Elles ont conquis le monde. Les grandes aventurières (1850-1950)*, Paris: Arthaud, 2007

Lefébure, Nadine, *Femmes océanes, les grandes pionnières maritimes*, Grenoble: Glénat, 1995

Le Garrec, Evelyne, *Séverine, une rebelle,* Paris: Seuil, 1982

Le Joly, Edouard, *Mère Teresa* Paris: Seuil (vol. 1, *Les missionnaires de la charité,* 1979; vol. 2, *Messagère de l'amour de Dieu,* 1985; vol. 3, *La pauvreté et la gloire,* 1993)

Lever, Maurice, *Isadora*, Paris: Presses de la Renaissance, 1987

Liatard, Séverine, *Les femmes en politique, en France de 1945 à nos jours*, Paris: Complexe, 2000

Loriot, Noëlle, *Irène Joliot-Curie*, Paris: Presses de la Renaissance, 1991

McHenry, Robert, *Famous American Women*, New York: Dover Publications, 1983

Maathai, Wangari, *Celle qui plante les arbres*, Editions Eloïse d'Ormesson, 2007

Maquelle, Sylvie, and Catherine Rambert, *Des femmes d'influence. Pouvoirs et télévision*, Paris: Hachette/Carrère, 1991

Margerie, Diane de, *Edith Wharton*, Paris: Flammarion, 2000

— Lewis R. W. B., *Edith Wharton. A Biography,* New York: Fromm, 1993

Marck, Bernard, *Les Aviatrices*, Paris: L'Archipel, 1993

Marck, Bernard, *Elles ont conquis le ciel*, Paris: Arthaud, 2009

Marck, Bernard, *Women Aviators*, Paris/New York: Flammarion, 2009

Marry, Catherine, *Les femmes ingénieurs. Une révolution respectueuse*, Paris: Belin, 2004

Maruani, Margaret, *Femmes, genre et sociétés. L'état des savoirs*, Paris: La Découverte, 2005

Maspero, François, *L'ombre d'une photographe Gerda Taro*, Paris: Seuil, Fiction&Co, 2006

Mervin Sabrina, and Carol Prunhuber, *Women around the World and through the Ages*, Wilmington DE: Atomium Books, 1990

Mouvement Français pour le Planning Familial (gen. ed. Isabelle Friedman), *Liberté, sexualités, féminisme. 50 ans de combat du Planning pour les droits des femmes,* Paris: La Découverte, 2006

Muller, Martine Marie, *La belle camarade*, Paris: Robert Laffont, 2009

Nasreen, Taslima, *Femmes, manifestez-vous!* Paris: Éditions des femmes/Antoinette Fouque, 1994

Nazé, Yaël, *L'Astronomie au féminin*, Vuibert et Adapt, 2008

Oakley, Giles, *The Devil's Music. A History of the Blues*, London: British Broadcasting Corporation, 1976

Obligado, Clara, *Pionnières et scandaleuses. L'Histoire au feminine* (Fr. trans.), Paris: Jean-Claude Lattès, 2008 (2004)

Ockrent, Christine, *Madame la... Ces femmes qui nous gouvernent*, Paris: Plon, 2007

Pasteur, Claude, *Les pionnières de l'Histoire*, Paris: Albin-Michel, 1963

Perrot, Michelle, *Les femmes ou les silences de l'histoire*, Paris: Champs Flammarion, 1998

Pétillon, Pierre-Yves, *Histoire de la littérature américaine. Notre demi-siècle 1939-1989*, Paris: Fayard, 1992

Piaf, Edith (preface by Jean Cocteau), *Au bal de la chance*, Geneva: Jeheber, 1957

Piaf, Edith, *The Wheel of Fortune*, London: Peter Owen, 2005

Poirot-Delpech, Bertrand, *Bonjour Sagan*, Paris: Herscher, 1985

— Sagan, Françoise, *Scars on the Soul*, Harmondsworth: Penguin, 1958

Rennes, Juliette, *Le mérite et la nature. Une controverse républicaine, l'accès des femmes aux professions de prestige*, Paris: Fayard (l'Espace du politique), 2007

Reverzy, Catherine, *Femmes d'aventure. Du rêve à la réalisation de soi*, Paris: Odile Jacob, 2001

Riot-Sarcey, Michèle, *Histoire du féminisme*, Paris: La Découverte, 2002

Riva, Marie, *Dietrich par sa fille*, Paris: Flammarion, 1993

Riva, Maria, *Marlene Dietrich by her Daughter*, New York: Ballantine, 1994

Ripa, Yannick, *Les femmes, actrices de l'Histoire, France, 1789-1945*, Paris: Armand Colin, 1999

Sagan, Françoise, *Sarah Bernhardt. Le rire incassable*, Paris: Robert Laffont, 1987

Sagan, Françoise, *Dear Sarah Bernhardt*, New York: Henry Holt & Co., 1987

Sarazin, Michel, *Une femme, Simone Veil*, Paris: Robert Laffont, 1987

Sampat, Pal, *Moi, Sampat Pal, chef de gang en sari rose*, Oh éditions, 2008

Sampat, Pal, *Warrior in a Pink Sari*, New Dehli: Zubaan, 2009

Savigneau, Josyane, *Marguerite Yourcenar*, Paris: Gallimard, 1990

Schweitzer, Sylvie, *Les femmes ont toujours travaillé, Une histoire du travail des femmes aux XIXe et XXe siècle*, Paris: Odile Jacob, 2002

Sichtermann, Barbara, *Les Femmes les plus célèbres de l'histoire. 50 incontournables*, Paris: La Martinière, 2006

Smith, Jessie Carney, *Notable Black American Women*, Detroit/London: Gale Research,, 1992

Thiériot, Jean-Louis, *Margaret Thatcher. De l'épicerie à la chambre des Lords*, Paris: Fallois, 2007.

— Blundell, John, *Margaret Thatcher. A Portrait of the Iron Lady*, London: Algora, 2009

— Campbell, John, *Margaret Thatcher. From Grocer's Daughter to Iron Lady*, New York: Vintage, 2009

Trbuhovic-Gjunic, Desanka, *Milena Einstein, une vie*, Paris: Des Femmes-Antoinette Fouque, 1991

Veyssy, Jean-Luc, and Bernard Collignon, *Femmes en politique dans le monde. Angela, Michelle, Ségolène et les autres...* Le Bord de l'eau, 2007

Volode, Philippe, *Elles ont fait la France. De Sainte-Geneviève à Simone Veil*, L'Archipel, 2006

Witkovski, Nicolas, *Trop belles pour le Nobel*, Paris: Seuil, 2005

Zancarini-Fournel, Michelle, *Histoire des femmes en France, XIXᵉ-XXᵉ siècles*, Rennes: Presses Universitaires de Rennes, 2005

Dictionaries, Encyclopedias and Reference Works:

A Dictionary of 20th Century World Biography, Oxford: Oxford University Press, 1992

American Women: a Library of Congress Guide for the Study of Women's History and Culture in the United States, Washington D.C.: Library of Congress,, 2001

Ashby, Ruth and Deborah Gore Ohn, *Herstory. Women who changed the world* (introduction by Gloria Steinem), New York: Viking, 1995

Asimov, Isaac (ed.), *Biographical Encyclopaedia of Science and Technology*, New York: Doubleday and Company, 1982

Bard, Christine, Christian Baudelot, and Janine Mossuz-Lavau (eds.), *Quand les femmes s'en mêlent. Genre et pouvoir*, Paris: La Martinière, 2004

Bard, Christine, Annie Metz, and Valérie Neveu (eds.), *Guide des sources de l'histoire du féminisme*, Rennes: Presses Universitaires de Rennes, 2006

Benezit, E., *Dictionnaire des peintres, sculpteurs, dessinateurs et graveurs*, Paris: Gründ, 1999

The Cambridge Biographical Encyclopaedia, Cambridge: Cambridge University Press, 1994

Chronicle of the Olympics 1896-1996, New York: Dorling Kindersley, 1996

Collective, *Paris Aux noms des femmes*, Paris: Descartes et Cie, 2005

Commire, Anne, *Dictionary of Women Worldwide*, New York: Gale, 2007

Cornell Drucilla, Geneviève Fraisse, Niranjana Seemanthini, Slama Raja Ben, Linda Waldham, and Xiao-Jian Li, *Masculin-féminin* Paris: La Découverte (coll., Les Mots du monde), 2004

Cottenet-Hage, Madeleine and Christiane P. Makward, *Dictionnaire littéraire des femmes de langue française*, Paris: Karthala, 1996

Delaunay Jean-Marc and Yves Denéchère (gen. eds.), *Femmes et relations internationales au XXe siècle*, Paris: Presse Sorbonne Nouvelle, 2007.

Duby, Georges, and Michelle Perrot (gen. eds.), *Histoire des femmes. Le XXᵉ siècle*, (ed. Françoise Thébaud), Paris: Plon, 1992

Duby, Georges, and Michelle Perrot (gen. eds.), *History of Women in the West. The Twentieth Century*, (ed. Françoise Thébaud), Cambridge Mass.: Harvard University Press (Bollingen Series) 1992

Encyclopedia Universalis, Paris, 1992

Encyclopaedia of American Biography, New York: Harper & Row Publishers, 1974

Encyclopaedia of the 20th Century, Oxford/New York: Facts on File, 1991

Eurosport Guide 2002, l'Encyclopédie du sport, Paris: TV Sport, 2002

Femmes égalité de 1789 à nos jours (articles "Féminin passé," published in the journal *Antoinette* (foreword by Fanny Cottençon), Paris: Messidor, 1989

Fondation Ostal Elahi, *L'Universel au féminin*, Paris: L'Harmattan, 2007

Galerne, Daniel (et al.), *Femmes et société* (6 vols.), Romorantin: Martinsart, 1981

Henshaw, Richard, *The Encyclopaedia of World Soccer*, Washington D.C.: New Republic Books, 1979

Histoire (les collections de l') (Jan-March 2007, "Quand les femmes prennent le pouvoir")

Julliard, Jacques and Michel Winock, *Dictionnaire des intellectuels français*, Paris: Seuil, 1996

Kirsch, Harris, *Encyclopaedia of Ethnicity and Sports in the United States*, Westport: Greenwood Press, 2000

Mazenot, Lucienne, and Ghislaine Schoeller, *Dictionnaire des femmes célèbres de tous les temps et de tous les pays*, Paris: Robert Laffont (coll. Bouquins), 1992

Morineau, Camille, *elles@centrepompidou* (exh. cat.) Centre Pompidou, Paris, 2009 (from 27 May 2009).

Montreynaud, Florence, *L'Aventure des femmes, XXe-XXIe siècle*, Paris: Nathan, 2005

Porcu, Antoine, *Héroïques Femmes en Résistance*, Lille: Editions le Geai bleu, 2007

Salem, Dorothy, *African American Women: a Biographical Dictionary*, New York: Garland Publishing, 1993

Seager, Joni, *The State of Women in the World Atlas*, London: Myriad Editions Ltd., 1997

Thinkers of the Twentieth Century, London/Chicago: St. James Press, 1987

United Nations/Division for the Advancement of Women, *La place des femmes en politique dans le monde, 1945-2000* (Reports and documents), no. 37, 2000

Ware, Suzan (ed.), *Notable American Women. A Biographical Dictionary. Completing the Twentieth Century*, Cambridge Mass.: Harvard University Press, 2004

Photographic Credits

Rossi Xavier / Gamma 184 top
Schuk Erwin / Gamma 26 bottom
Scorcelletti Emanuelle / Gamma 33 top
Simon Daniel / Gamma 148
Simon Daniel / Gamma 201 left
Smith Brian / Gamma 95
Stills Catarina / Gamma 211 bottom
Ulf Andersen / Gamma 116, 231
Vandeville Eric / Gamma 134 top
Vereecken Nico / photo News / Gamma 189
Vogel Richard / Gamma 91 bottom
Wollenberg Roger L. / UPI / Gamma 78
Xihua / Gamma 94
Xinhua / Gamma 129, 159
Zeng Yi / Xinhua / Gamma 117

GAMMA / CAMERA PRESS
Beaton Cecil / Camera Press / Gamma front cover
Bown Jane / Camera Press / Gamma 113
Camera Press / SC / Man / Gamma 205
Casilli / Camera Press / Gamma 35 bottom
ILN / Camera Press / Gamma 123
Kawa Janusz / Camera Press / Gamma 5 right,190
Lucas Cesar / Camera Press / Gamma 216 bottom
Malhotra T.C. / Camera Press / Gamma 98
Norrington Nigel / Camera Press / Gamma 153
Paul Tina / Camera Press / Gamma 167 right, 208
Remo Castelle / Camera Press / Gamma 102
Stonehouse R. / Camerapress / Gamma 181, 240 top, 240 bottom
Summs Anthea / Camera Press / Gamma 152 bottom
SUS / Camera Press / Gamma 124
TSPL / Camera Press / Gamma 51 bottom
Turner / Gamma / M / Camera Press / Gamma 79
Yousuf Karsh / Camera Press / Gamma 80, 152 top, 225 left

GAMMA / UPI 62
Castey Gary C. / UPI / Gamma 31
Dietsch Kevin / UPI / Gamma 81 top
Don West / UPI / Gamma 96 top
Eco Clément / UPI / Gamma 92 top
Healey Matthieu / UPI / Gamma 61
Hill Debbie / UPI / Gamma 100 top
Starnes Arianne / UPI / Gamma 137 top
STR / UPI / Gamma 96 bottom

GETTY 38, 56 bottom, 130, 139, 147, 166 top, 166 bottom, 167 left, 179 bottom
Beaury-Saurel Armelle / Getty Images 40 top
Franklin Stuart / Getty Images Sport / APP 187
Gilardini Daisy / Getty Images 171 left
Johnson Cynthia / Time & Life / Getty Images 140
Macadams Cynthia / Time & Life / Getty Images 243
Michael Ochs Archives / Getty Images 198, 199

Popperfoto / Getty Images 30, 178, 179 top
Selkirk Neil / Time & Life / Getty Images 142
Time & Life Picture / Getty Images 69

HOAQUI
Dubocq Philippe / Hoaqui 60
Dunwell Steve / Age Fotostock / Hoaqui 110

KEYSTONE FRANCE 4 right, 5 left, 10, 12, 13, 14 top, 17, 20 top, 20 bottom, 22, 23, 25 bottom, 39, 40 bottom, 45, 54, 55 top, 58, 64, 65 top, 65 bottom, 66 top, 66 bottom, 67 top, 67 bottom, 68, 69 bottom, 84, 88, 89 top, 89 bottom, 99 top, 111, 115, 127, 132, 141, 144, 161 top, 161 bottom, 171 left, 172 left, 172 right, 173, 174, 175, 178, 180, 183, 186 top, 186 bottom, 194, 196, 200 top, 203 top, 204 bottom, 207 bottom, 209, 212 left, 212 right, 221, 222, 225 right, 246
L'Humanité / Keystone France 28

MARY EVANS
Nouvelle Image-Mary Evans 42
Mary Evans 43, 150 top, 150 bottom
Mary Evans / Keystone 134 bottom, 158 top, 158 bottom, 224 bottom

RAPHO 112 top, 171 right, 195
Ancellet François / Rapho 154
Bird Walter / Rapho 224 top
Box Patrick / Rapho 119
Brake Brian / Rapho 90
Charbonnier Jean-Philippe / Rapho 203 bottom, 239
Cogan Michel / Rapho 207 top
Dejardin Yves / Rapho 227
Doisneau Robert / Rapho 125, 156, 157, 192, 228, 242
Don Carl Steffen / Rapho 11
Ginet Pierre-Yves / Rapho 26 top, 27,49 top
Gubb Louise / Rapho 33 bottom
Hardy Elise / Rapho 4 left, 8, 193
Le Diascorn François / Rapho193
Niepce Jeanine / Rapho 56 top, 118, 197
Reyboz Lucille / Rapho 35 top
Silberstein Bernard G. / Rapho 238
Weiss Sabine / Rapho 232

STILLS
Alloca / DMI / Stills 24 top
Botti / Stills 55 bottom

TOP
Keystone Archives / Heritages-images / imagestate / TOP 201 bottom, 202 top
KPA / Heritages-images / imagestate / TOP 215
Library / Heritages-images / imagestate / TOP 37
Oxford Science Archives / Heritages-images / imagestate / TOP 4/5 middle,106
The Print Collector / Heritages-images / imagestate / TOP 122

Front cover: Maria Callas. © Cecil Beaton / CAMERAPRESS / GAMMA / Eyedea Presse.
Back cover: top, left: © KEYSTONE FRANCE; top, center: © Kawa Janusz / Camera Press / Gamma; top, right: Marguerite Duras and Xavière Gauthier in 1974. © Jean Meunier; bottom, left: © Hardy Elise / Rapho; bottom, center: © KEYSTONE FRANCE; bottom, right: © Oxford Science Archives / Heritages-images / imagestate / TOP.

Acknowledgments

I have worked at the Bibliothèque Nationale, the Médiathèque Simone de Beauvoir at Athis-Mons and above all at the Bibliothèque Marguerite Durand–the rich fund of information and the competent staff there were of great help to me. My thanks to James Elliot for his invaluable research in English language encyclopedias. My thanks to Asli Davaz (from the Women's Library and Information Center, Istanbul) who provided me with information on Turkish pioneering women. My thanks to Daniel for his patient and constant support; and to Jacquie, Simone, Alexis, and Danielle as well.